BEST *of the* BEST
from
Ohio
COOKBOOK

Selected Recipes from Ohio's
FAVORITE COOKBOOKS

May 23, 2008

Enjoy Grace!

Thank you

Love

Shirley

Hale Farm, located in historic Wheatfield Village near Bath, offers a unique look at life in the Western Reserve during the time shortly after the War Between the States. Once the home of settler Jonathan Hale, the museum features livestock, 19th-century working artisans, and the original red brick farmhouse.

BEST *of the* BEST
from
Ohio
COOKBOOK

Selected Recipes from Ohio's
FAVORITE COOKBOOKS

Edited by
Gwen McKee
and
Barbara Moseley

Illustrated by Tupper England

QUAIL RIDGE PRESS
Preserving America's Food Heritage

Library of Congress Cataloging-in-Publication Data

Best of the best from Ohio cookbook : selected recipes from Ohio's favorite cookbooks / edited by
Gwen McKee and Barbara Moseley ; illustrated by Tupper England. – New ed.
   p. cm. – (Best of the best state cookbook series)
Includes index.
ISBN-13: 978-1-893062-90-0
ISBN-10: 1-893062-90-2
   1. Cookery, American. 2. Cookery–Ohio. I. McKee, Gwen. II. Moseley, Barbara.
   TX715.B48564175 2007
   641.5973–dc22   2007030643

ISBN-13: 978-1-893062-90-0 • ISBN-10: 1-893062-90-2

First edition
Printed in Canada

Cover photo: Fall at Dawes Arboretum by Dianne Johnson,
USDA Natural Resources Conservation Service

Back cover photo by Greg Campbell

QUAIL RIDGE PRESS • 1-800-343-1583
email: info@quailridge.com • www.quailridge.com

Contents

The U.S. Department of Agriculture's Natural Resources Conservation Service puts seventy years of experience to work in assisting owners of Ohio's private land with conserving their soil, water, and other natural resources. Shown here: Clardale Farm, Stark County.

The Quest for the Best

by Gwen McKee

I am frequently asked how the idea for the BEST OF THE BEST STATE COOKBOOK SERIES came about, and how it got started.

It all began with my love for cooking and entertaining, which I have been doing all of my married life. Having collected a variety of cookbooks, most of which have splatters or turned-down pages or notations on the recipes, one day it occurred to me that if I could compile all these favorite recipes, it would be an incredible cookbook! And wouldn't it be even more special if I could get favorite recipes from the best cookbooks from all over each state—the Best of the Best! Wow! The idea consumed me and became a passion. I knew I had to pursue this quest.

In the days before Internet, faxes, cell phones, or even inexpensive long-distance calling, the only way to gather everything I needed was to strike out and do my research in person. I started in my home state, and that is how *Best of the Best from Mississippi* became the first BEST OF THE BEST cookbook in 1982.

Completing the first cookbook was a lot of work, and I knew if I wanted to tackle Louisiana next, with all its cookbooks, I would need help.

My golfing buddy Barbara Moseley and I were always talking about food and recipes on the golf course, and I knew she was an excellent cook. Besides being my sounding board for all the decisions I faced with *Best of the Best from Mississippi,* she had a lot of office savvy and experience, and was not working at the time. So I asked her if she would be interested in helping me with the *Best of the Best from Louisiana.* Without a moment's hesitation, she replied, "When do we leave?" We left the next day, and we have been hitting the road ever since.

In 2005, we were finally able to say, "We did it!" The BEST OF THE BEST STATE COOKBOOK SERIES now covers all fifty states. The result is more than 19,000 recipes gathered from every corner of our country. With more than two million copies sold, we are very proud that the series is known as the definitive source for state and regional cooking. (A free booklet entitled *We Did It!* that tells the story of how the series was developed is available upon request.)

Gwen McKee and Barbara Moseley

Because it has become so much a part of our lives, and to further continue our motto of "Preserving America's Food Heritage," we have begun to revisit states, finding outstanding new cookbooks with more wonderful recipes to showcase and share. Journey with us to Ohio through the pages of this book, and catch the flavor and excitement of the Buckeye State as Barbara and I did.

Gwen McKee

Contributing Cookbooks

America Celebrates Columbus

Asthma Walk Cook Book

Aunt Paula's American Hungarian Cookbook

Beginnings

Busy People's Diabetic Cookbook

Busy People's Down-Home Cooking Without the Down-Home Fat

Busy People's Fun, Fast, Festive Christmas Cookbook

Busy People's Low-Carb Cookbook

Busy People's Low-Fat Cookbook

Busy People's Slow Cooker Cookbook

Camp Whitewood Camp Cookbook

Carroll County Humane Society Members & Friends Cookbook
Volume I

Carroll County Humane Society Members & Friends Cookbook
Volume II

Causing a Stir

Cincinnati Recipe Treasury

Columbus Colony Creations

Cookies & Tea

Cooking Along the Lincoln Highway in Ohio

Cooking Up a Cure

Country Collections Cookbook II

Crowd Pleasers

Dawn to Dusk

Discover Dayton

Don't Forget the INNgredients!

Entertaining Made Easy

Favorite Recipes

Favorite Recipes from the Delaware Police Department

Favorite Recipes Home-Style

Contributing Cookbooks

Feeding the Flock—First Church of God
Feeding the Flock—Trinity United Methodist Women
A Festival of Recipes
50 Years and Still Cookin'!
Food, Glorious Food
Food for Thought
Franklin County 4-H Favorites
The "Friends" Cookbook
I'll Cook When Pigs Fly
Love, Mom: Stories and Recipes from Kingston, Ohio
More Nutritious Still Delicious
Mt. Zion Lutheran Church Cookbook
Ohio Cook Book
Ohio State Grange Cookbook (Gold)
Ohio State Grange Cookbook (Blue)
Ohio Traditions with P. Buckley Moss
Recipes and Remembrances: Around St. George's Tables
Rose Hill Recipes
Sharing Our Best
Sharing Recipes Cookbook
Sharing the Best from Our Kitchen
A Taste of Faith
A Taste of the Murphin Ridge Inn
Tasteful Treasures Cookbook
A Treasury of Recipes for Mind, Body & Soul
With Great Gusto

Beverages *and* Appetizers

The Scioto River (pronounced sigh-OH-tuh), located in central and southern Ohio, is more than 231 miles long. Too small for modern commercial shipping, its primary economic importance is for recreation and drinking water. Here, the river offers a beautiful view of the Columbus skyline.

Cincinnati Red

This famous beer recipe from the Hudepohl Brewing Company is suggested as a "pick up" for breakfast or brunch. Some residents claim it is a good hangover cure.

12 ounces Hudepohl beer,
  chilled
12 ounces tomato juice, chilled

Dash of cayenne
Dash of Worcestershire

Combine ingredients in large pitcher. Stir well and serve chilled or over ice. Makes 6 servings.

Cincinnati Recipe Treasury

Tasty V-8 Juice

16 tomatoes, chopped
½ cup chopped carrots
½ cup chopped onion
½ cup chopped celery

2 tablespoons salt
2 tablespoons lemon juice
1 teaspoon Worcestershire
Red pepper sauce to taste

Put all ingredients in large pot and cook about 25 minutes or until veggies are tender. Press through a sieve or put in blender until puréed. Ladle hot juice into hot jars, leaving ¼ inch head space. Seal with hot rings. Makes 6 quarts.

Camp Whitewood Camp Cookbook

 Ohio produces the most tomato juice in the country, so much that the state adopted it as its official beverage in 1965. Ohio is the second largest producer of tomatoes used for processing. (California is first.)

Cheesecake Kahlúa Milkshake

2 scoops vanilla ice cream
1 slice cheesecake
1 cup milk

2 shots Kahlúa
Whipped cream
1 maraschino cherry

Combine ice cream, cheesecake, milk, and Kahlúa in blender or food processor. Process until smooth. Pour into chilled stemmed glasses and garnish with whipped cream and a maraschino cherry. Serves 2.

Note: I keep a frozen cheesecake in the freezer just for this purpose. You'll be glad you did, too! People will kill for this recipe.

50 Years and Still Cookin'!

Sherbet Punch

2 (48-ounce) cans pineapple
  juice, chilled

2 quarts ginger ale, chilled
½ gallon orange sherbet

Combine juice and ginger ale in punch bowl. Stir in scoops of sherbet. Serve.

Franklin County 4-H Favorites

Ruby Punch

4 packages cherry Kool-Aid
4 cups sugar
24 cups water

2 (48-ounce) cans pineapple juice
2 (2-liter) bottles 7-UP
½ gallon strawberry ice cream

Mix Kool-Aid, sugar, and water together until sugar is dissolved. Add pineapple juice and 7-UP. Stir together. Add ice cream in scoops on top. Serve in punch bowl. Makes 50 servings.

Favorite Recipes–First Church of God

Tequila Sunrise Punch

1 (6-ounce) can frozen orange
  juice
1 (6-ounce) can frozen lemonade
1 (6-ounce) can frozen limeade

9 cups water
⅔ cup (or more) light tequila
1 (12-ounce) bottle ginger ale
Grenadine for color

Mix all together except grenadine; gradually add grenadine to make sunrise (this should be done just before serving). Makes 12 cups.

Don't Forget the INNgredients!

Peach Bellini

4 large peaches, skinned
  and cut
4½ tablespoons powdered
  sugar, or to taste

Crushed ice
1 bottle champagne

Process peaches in blender until frothy. Blend in powdered sugar. Add crushed ice (about 2 cups); blend just until mixed. Pour into pitcher and add champagne. Stir slowly until combined thoroughly. Yields 16–18 servings.

With Great Gusto

Hot Spiced Cider

2 quarts cider
½ cup packed brown sugar
1 teaspoon whole cloves
1 teaspoon allspice

1 teaspoon ground cinnamon
3 (3-inch) sticks cinnamon
⅛ teaspoon nutmeg

Place cider in a 2-quart capacity electric percolator. Place all remaining ingredients in percolator basket. Perk for 7 minutes. Serve hot in mugs—with doughnuts of course! Yields 2 quarts.

Discover Dayton

Eggnog

This is not as thick as regular eggnog, but is every bit as delicious and has the smooth consistency of the high-fat version. With this new low-fat recipe, I can't see why anyone would even want to waste calories on the old high-fat, high-sugar eggnog.

2¼ cups pasteurized liquid
  egg substitute
1 cup Splenda granular
1½ teaspoons vanilla extract

10 cups fat-free, low-carb milk
1½ teaspoons rum extract
Ground nutmeg

In a large bowl, combine egg substitute, Splenda, vanilla, milk, and rum extract, and beat with an electric mixer on medium speed until well blended. The eggnog is ready to drink; or pour it into a pitcher, cover, and keep chilled until ready to serve. Sprinkle each serving with a dash of nutmeg just before serving. Yields 16 (¾-cup) servings.

Nutritional analysis: Cal 69 (9% fat); Fat 0gm; Choles 3mg; Carbo 4gm; Dietary Fiber 0gm; Prot 11gm; Sod 202mg; Diabetic Exchanges 1 very lean meat, ½ skim milk.

Busy People's Fun, Fast, Festive Christmas Cookbook

Baked Cheese in a Sourdough Bread Bowl

1 (10-inch) round sourdough
  bread, unsliced
1 (14-ounce) can artichoke
  hearts, drained, chopped
1 cup shredded Cheddar
  cheese
1 cup shredded Monterey
  Jack cheese

1 cup grated Parmesan cheese
1 clove garlic, minced
1 cup mayonnaise
1 small onion, finely chopped

Preheat oven to 350°. Slice top off bread and hollow out inside, reserving top slice. Combine chopped artichoke hearts, cheeses, garlic, mayonnaise, and onion in a bowl. Spoon mixture into bread shell. Replace top slice of bread and place bread loaf on a baking sheet. Bake at 350° for 1 hour and 15 minutes. Serve with crudités or crackers.

Editor's Extra: Crudités are raw seasonal vegetables frequently served with a dipping sauce.

Crowd Pleasers

Nacho Cheese Pinwheels

4 (8- to 10-inch) spinach or plain
  flour tortillas
½ cup bean dip

½ cup nacho cheese dip
3–4 tablespoons chopped green
  onions

Spread each tortilla with about 2 tablespoons bean dip and 2 tablespoons cheese dip. Sprinkle with onions. Tightly roll up tortillas; wrap individually in plastic wrap. Refrigerate at least 1 hour, but no longer than 24.

To serve, cut off ends from each roll and discard. Cut rolls into ½- to ¾-inch slices. Secure with toothpicks, if desired.

Food for Thought

Baked Caramel Cinnamon Brie

½ cup (1 stick) butter
½ cup packed brown sugar
⅓ cup sugar
½ cup heavy cream
¼ teaspoon nutmeg
¼ teaspoon cinnamon

1 (12-ounce) round Brie cheese
2 tablespoons sliced almonds,
   toasted
1 baguette French bread, thinly
   sliced

Combine butter, brown sugar, and sugar in a saucepan. Cook over low heat until butter melts and sugars dissolve, stirring frequently. Add heavy cream gradually, stirring constantly. Stir in nutmeg and cinnamon. Cook until thickened, stirring constantly.

Place Brie in a round baking pan. Drizzle brown sugar mixture over top of Brie. Bake at 225° in a preheated oven for 10 minutes or until Brie is heated through. Remove from oven. Sprinkle with almonds. Let stand 5–10 minutes before serving. Garnish with fresh strawberries and/or Golden Delicious or Granny Smith apple slices. Serve with sliced bread. Yields 8–10 servings.

Beginnings

California Sun Cheese Ball

1 (8-ounce) package cream
cheese, softened
1 teaspoon Dijon mustard
1/2 teaspoon garlic powder
2 tablespoons white wine
1 cup chopped pitted black
olives

2 cups shredded mild Cheddar
cheese
2 tablespoons minced fresh
parsley
1/2 cup shelled sunflower seeds

Beat cream cheese, mustard, garlic powder, and wine until smooth. Stir in olives, cheese, and parsley. Form mixture into a ball and wrap in wax paper or plastic wrap. Refrigerate until chilled. When ready to serve, roll ball in sunflower seeds. Serve with crackers and sliced salami.

Crowd Pleasers

Thomas Alva Edison was born in Milan on February 11, 1847. Edison developed many devices that greatly influenced life around the world, including the phonograph and a long-lasting light bulb. Edison did not invent the first electric light bulb, but instead invented the first commercially practical incandescent light. He was one of the first inventors to apply the principles of mass production to the process of invention, and is credited with the creation of the first industrial research laboratory. Edison is considered one of the most prolific inventors in history, holding 1,093 U.S. patents in his name, as well as many patents in the United Kingdom, France, and Germany.

Pimento Cheese Spread

1 (2-pound) loaf Velveeta
cheese, grated
1 (8-ounce) package sharp
Cracker Barrel cheese, grated
1 (4-ounce) jar chopped
pimentos

8 eggs, well beaten
¾ cup vinegar
1 cup sugar
2 tablespoons butter

Combine cheeses and pimentos and set aside. In a saucepan, combine eggs, vinegar, and sugar. Cook over low heat until thick, stirring constantly. Add butter. Cool slightly. Fold egg mixture into cheese. Refrigerate. Share with friends!

Feeding the Flock—Trinity United Methodist Women

Crab and Shrimp Spread

¼ cup packed, chopped fresh
parsley leaves (no stems)
½ cup chopped onion
2 scallions, chopped
½ (8-ounce) package cream
cheese, softened
⅓ cup sour cream
¼ cup mayonnaise
1½ tablespoons bottled
cocktail sauce
1 tablespoon lemon juice
1½ teaspoons horseradish,
drained

1 teaspoon Worcestershire
1 clove garlic, minced
¾ teaspoon lemon pepper
seasoning
2 dashes Tabasco
1 teaspoon salt
¾ pound medium-size shrimp,
cleaned, cooked
1 (6-ounce) can crabmeat,
drained

Combine all ingredients except seafood, and stir until mixture is well blended. Add seafood. Cover and chill. Make this at least 6 hours before serving so that the flavors blend. Serve with thin, crunchy bread, Melba toast, or pita chips.

A Festival of Recipes

Mushroom Tarts

4 tablespoons butter
3 tablespoons finely chopped
  shallots
8 ounces mushrooms, finely
  chopped
2 tablespoons flour
1 cup heavy cream
1 tablespoon finely chopped
  chives

½ teaspoon salt
⅛ teaspoon cayenne pepper
½ teaspoon lemon juice
45 purchased frozen mini phyllo
  tart shells
Parsley sprigs for garnish

Preheat oven to 350°. Melt butter in a heavy skillet. Add shallots and sauté 4 minutes, or until softened but not browned. Add mushrooms; cook 10–15 minutes, or until all moisture evaporates. Sprinkle flour over top; mix well.

Stirring constantly, add cream to mixture and bring to a boil. When thickened, reduce heat and simmer 1–2 minutes. Remove from heat. Stir in chives, salt, cayenne pepper, and lemon juice. Cool. Fill each tart shell with mushroom mixture. Bake 10 minutes. Garnish with parsley sprigs and serve immediately. Yields 45 tarts.

Causing a Stir

Mini Cheese Tarts

1 (8-ounce) package cream
cheese, softened
1 stick (½ cup) margarine,
softened
1 cup plus 1–2 tablespoons
all-purpose flour, divided

2 eggs
6 ounces grated Swiss cheese
½ pint whipping cream

Mix cream cheese, margarine, and flour. Pinch off enough dough to line muffin cups in miniature muffin pans. Beat eggs; add grated cheese and flour mixture. Whip cream until stiff peaks form and fold into cheese mixture. Fill each tart full. Bake at 350° for 25–30 minutes.

Entertaining Made Easy

Festive Chicken and Spinach Cups

48 slices white bread
1 pound cooked boneless
chicken, shredded
1 (10-ounce) package frozen
chopped spinach, thawed,
pressed dry
2 cups shredded Gruyére
cheese

6 green onions, chopped
⅔ cup sun-dried tomatoes in
oil, drained, chopped
½ teaspoon salt
¼ teaspoon ground red pepper

Using 2½- to 3-inch biscuit cutter, cut bread slices into circles. Roll each to flatten. Press bread circles firmly in lightly buttered cups of muffin pans. Bake at 400° about 6 minutes or until lightly browned. Remove from pans, cool on wire rack, and place on baking sheet.

Combine chicken, spinach, cheese, onions, tomatoes, salt, and red pepper, mixing well. Spoon mixture into bread cups. Bake at 350° for 10 minutes. Makes 48.

I'll Cook When Pigs Fly

Won Ton Quiche

1–3 packages won ton wrappers
1 dozen eggs
1 quart heavy whipping cream
2 cups milk
Salt to taste

White pepper to taste (optional)
4 ounces or more smoked ham, chopped
4–6 cups grated Swiss cheese

Spray muffin tins with nonstick cooking spray. Place 2 won ton wrappers over each muffin tin at opposing angles. Push down into tin to form crust for quiche.

Whisk together eggs, heavy cream, milk, salt, and pepper. Pour mixture into each crust until they are about ¾ full. Add ham and cheese to taste. Bake at 350° for 20 minutes, or until crusts are browned and center is set. Makes about 5 dozen.

Cooking Up a Cure

Lale's Crab Appetizer

1 (8-ounce) package cream cheese, softened
1–2 tablespoons plus 1–2 teaspoons horseradish, divided

1 (7-ounce) can crabmeat
1 cup ketchup
1 teaspoon lemon juice

Blend cream cheese and 1–2 tablespoons horseradish. Check crabmeat for shells, then add to cheese mixture. Form into a ball and chill, wrapped in plastic wrap. Make cocktail sauce by mixing well the ketchup, remaining 1–2 teaspoons horseradish, and lemon juice. To serve, place on platter and cover with cocktail sauce. Serve with crackers.

Favorite Recipes–First Church of God

Sauerkraut Balls

1 pound bulk sausage
¼ pound ground beef
½ cup chopped onion
3 tablespoons snipped fresh
  parsley
1 teaspoon each: garlic powder,
  salt, and sugar
½ teaspoon dry mustard

⅛ teaspoon pepper
1–2 pounds drained sauerkraut,
  chopped
½ cup bread crumbs
3 eggs, beaten, divided
¼ cup milk
Seasoned bread crumbs

Brown sausage and ground beef with onion, parsley, garlic powder, salt, sugar, dry mustard, and pepper in a skillet, stirring until sausage and ground beef are crumbly; drain. Stir in sauerkraut. Add ½ cup bread crumbs and 1 egg and mix well. Chill, covered, in refrigerator.

Shape sausage mixture into 1-inch balls. Dip balls in a mixture of milk and remaining 2 eggs. Coat with seasoned bread crumbs. Arrange balls on a broiler pan. Broil in a preheated oven until golden brown; drain. May freeze sauerkraut balls before broiling for future use.

Note: May be served with hot sweet mustard sauce.

Beginnings

Ohio is steeped in German heritage. The German Heritage Museum in Cincinnati serves as the focal point in presenting and displaying German-American culture. This museum is the first of its kind in the region, and a testament to the many contributions German immigrants and their descendants have made toward the building of the Ohio Valley and America.

Quick Appetizer Pizza

6 English muffins, split, toasted
1 (8-ounce) jar pizza sauce
1 (4-ounce) package sliced
  pepperoni
1 cup shredded mozzarella
  cheese

Spread each toasted muffin half with pizza sauce. Top with 3 slices pepperoni, then cheese. Place 4 halves on microwave serving plate in a circle. Cook on 70% power for 3–4 minutes, or until cheese is melted. Let stand 3 minutes before serving. Repeat with remaining muffins.

Ohio State Grange Cookbook (Blue)

Roasted Vegetable Tart

3 or 4 portobello mushrooms
½ red bell pepper, cut into
  strips
½ yellow bell pepper, cut into
  strips
¾ cup sliced zucchini
2 tablespoons olive oil
1 tablespoon onion and chive
  cream cheese
2 tablespoons feta cheese
1 egg
1 tablespoon grated Parmesan
  cheese
1 prepared pie crust
1–2 tablespoons chopped green
  onion for garnish
2 or 3 slices fresh tomatoes for
  garnish

Roast mushrooms, peppers, and zucchini in olive oil in foil on a cookie sheet in 450° oven for 12–14 minutes. Blend cream cheese, feta cheese, egg, and Parmesan cheese. Place prepared pie crust on foil on a separate cookie sheet and spread cheese-egg mixture in pie crust 2 inches from edge of crust. Place roasted vegetables on top of cheese-egg mixture. Fold over 2 inches of pie crust toward center. Garnish with green onion and tomatoes. Bake 15–20 minutes at 450°. Cool 10 minutes. Slice tart into wedges while warm.

Rose Hill Recipes

Gorgonzola Biscuits

Quick and extraordinarily good.

1 stick butter
1 (6-ounce) tub crumbled
  Gorgonzola cheese

1 tube grand-size flaky biscuits,
  each torn into 4 pieces

Melt butter in pie plate or serving dish that can go into oven. Sprinkle Gorgonzola cheese and top with torn-up biscuits. Bake at 350° for 15–20 minutes.

Food, Glorious Food

Hidden Valley Ranch
Oyster Crackers

1 (1-ounce) package Hidden
  Valley Ranch Salad Dressing
  Mix
½ teaspoon dill weed

¾ cup oil
¼ teaspoon lemon pepper
¼ teaspoon garlic powder
5 cups plain oyster crackers

Preheat oven to 250°. Combine salad dressing mix with dill weed and oil. Pour over crackers; stir to coat. Sprinkle with lemon pepper and garlic powder; toss to coat. Place in oven for 15–20 minutes. Stir gently halfway through baking.

Carroll County Humane Society Members & Friends
Cookbook Volume II

Eggrolls

Easy and delicious.

2 tablespoons vegetable oil
2 cloves garlic, minced
1 medium onion, thinly sliced
½ pound lean ground pork
Soy sauce to taste

2 packages cole slaw blend
  (prepackaged)
Salt and pepper to taste
15 eggroll wrappers

Heat vegetable oil in skillet and sauté garlic and onion until tender. Add pork and soy sauce and sauté until browned. Remove and drain in strainer. Stir in cole slaw mix and salt and pepper; let cool 10–15 minutes.

Carefully separate eggroll wrappers. Lay one wrapper on clean surface with corner of roll pointing toward you. Place about 2 tablespoons of filling near corner facing you, and roll edge toward middle. Fold in both sides and continue rolling. Moisten opposite edge with water to seal. Repeat with other wrappers.

Fill basket of small fryer with 3–4 rolls at a time; fry in 375° oil until golden brown, about 3 minutes on each side. Drain on paper towels.

Note: May use ground turkey, chicken, or shrimp for the pork. Easy to freeze for future use.

Asthma Walk Cook Book

On February 20, 1962, Ohio native John Glenn was the first American to orbit the Earth, aboard *Friendship 7*. He was also the oldest living person to have flown in space when, at the age of 77 in 1998, he flew aboard the Space Shuttle *Discovery* mission STS-95. Glenn served as a United States Senator (D-Ohio, 1974–1999), and received the Congressional Space Medal of Honor.

Sam's Frito Plate

1 pound ground beef
½ can water
1 (16-ounce) can refried beans
1 (10.5-ounce) bag Fritos Scoops
Shredded lettuce

Chopped onion
Chopped tomatoes
Sliced black olives
Sour cream
Grated Cheddar cheese

Brown ground beef and drain off grease. Add water to refried beans and heat in a saucepan. Layer ingredients on a serving plate starting with Fritos, then ground beef, refried beans, lettuce, onion, tomatoes, black olives, sour cream, and cheese. Serve with Fritos Scoops.

Ohio Traditions with P. Buckley Moss

Taco Dip

2 (16-ounce) cans refried beans
1 (8-ounce) container sour cream
1 (8-ounce) package cream cheese, softened
½ package taco seasoning mix
1 small to medium onion, chopped

½ head lettuce, shredded
1 (8-ounce) package shredded Cheddar cheese
1 medium tomato, chopped
Black olives (optional)
Tortilla chips

Spread refried beans on serving tray (or pizza pan). Mix together sour cream, cream cheese, and taco seasoning mix. Spread on top of beans. Sprinkle onions on top of mixture. Spread lettuce on top of onion. Layer cheese over lettuce and top with tomato and black olives. Serve with tortilla chips.

Tasteful Treasures Cookbook

Hot Reuben Dip

1 (14-ounce) can sauerkraut,
   drained
4 ounces cooked corned beef
1 small onion, finely chopped
1 cup mayonnaise
1 cup sour cream

1 cup shredded Swiss cheese
2 tablespoons prepared
   horseradish
1 teaspoon Dijon mustard
   (optional)
Party rye bread

Squeeze excess moisture from sauerkraut. Process sauerkraut, corned beef, and onion in a blender or food processor fitted with a steel blade until finely chopped. Combine corned beef mixture, mayonnaise, sour cream, cheese, horseradish, and Dijon mustard in a bowl and mix well.

Spoon corned beef mixture into a 1-quart baking dish sprayed with nonstick cooking spray. Bake at 350° in a preheated oven for 30–40 minutes or until bubbly. Serve with party rye bread. May use reduced-fat mayonnaise and sour cream. Yields 5 cups.

Beginnings

Beef Dip

1 small onion, chopped
1 (2½-ounce) jar dried beef,
   chopped
1 (8-ounce) package cream
   cheese, softened
1 (16-ounce) carton sour cream

1 tablespoon Worcestershire
1½ teaspoons seasoning salt
½ teaspoon horseradish
   (optional)
Corn chips

Combine onion and dried beef; set aside. Mix other ingredients well with mixer. Manually mix in beef and onion; chill in refrigerator at least 20 minutes. Serve with corn chips.

A Taste of Faith

Marshmallow Fruit Dip

1 (7-ounce) jar marshmallow
crème
1 (8-ounce) package cream
cheese, softened

Seedless grapes, cherries,
strawberries, or fruit of your
choice

In bowl, blend marshmallow crème and cream cheese well. Place fruits on plate around bowl of dip to serve.

Carroll County Humane Society Members & Friends
Cookbook Volume II

That Dip

2 (8-ounce) packages cream
cheese, softened
½ cup mayonnaise
¼ cup lemon juice
1 teaspoon basil
1 teaspoon chili powder
1 clove garlic, mashed
1 (8-ounce) bottle cocktail sauce
1 onion, chopped
½ cup finely chopped celery
1 green bell pepper, chopped

1 package frozen salad shrimp
1 package frozen crab delights,
chopped
1 package frozen lobster delights,
chopped
1 (4-ounce) package pepperoni,
chopped
2 cups shredded mozzarella
cheese
2 cups shredded Cheddar cheese

Combine cream cheese, mayonnaise, lemon juice, basil, chili powder, and garlic and place on a pizza pan or quiche dish. Layer with remaining ingredients, in order given. Serve with nacho or tortilla chips.

Asthma Walk Cook Book

On October 10, 1920, Jim Bagby of the Cleveland Indians became the first pitcher to hit a home run in a modern World Series game.

Savory Artichoke and Spinach Dip

1 (10-ounce) package frozen
   chopped spinach, thawed,
   drained
1¼ cups coarsely grated
   Parmesan cheese
1 cup mayonnaise

1 garlic clove, crushed
8–10 artichoke hearts, coarsely
   chopped
Chopped green onions (optional)
Butter crackers

Squeeze excess moisture from spinach. Combine it with cheese, then mayonnaise, garlic, and artichokes in a bowl, mixing well after each addition. Spoon into an ungreased quiche dish or baking dish and press lightly. Bake at 325° in a preheated oven for 25–30 minutes, or until brown and bubbly. Sprinkle with chopped green onions. Serve warm with butter crackers. Yields 8–12.

Beginnings

Artichoke Dip

1 cup mayonnaise
1 cup grated Parmesan cheese
1 (4-ounce) can chopped green
   chiles
1 (14-ounce) can artichokes,
   drained, chopped

1 garlic clove, minced
2 tablespoons sliced green onion
2 tablespoons chopped tomato

Mix all ingredients except onion and tomato and place in a 9-inch pie plate. Microwave on MEDIUM setting 6–8 minutes. (If using an oven, set at 350° and bake 20–25 minutes.) Sprinkle with onion and tomato. Serve with crackers.

Carroll County Humane Society Members & Friends
Cookbook Volume II

Gazpacho Salsa with Creole Spiced Tortilla Chips

2½–3 pounds tomatoes,
  chopped
1 hothouse or English cucumber,
  chopped
1 medium red onion, chopped
1 yellow bell pepper, chopped
½ bunch cilantro
2 jalapeño peppers

2 garlic cloves
2–3 tablespoons olive oil
1–2 tablespoons red wine
  vinegar
½–1 teaspoon sugar
Salt and freshly ground pepper to
  taste

Combine tomatoes, cucumber, red onion, and yellow pepper in a bowl and toss to mix well. Remove leaves from cilantro and discard stems. Process cilantro leaves, jalapeños, garlic, olive oil, red wine vinegar, sugar, salt and pepper in a blender until smooth. Add vegetable mixture and mix well. Chill, tightly covered, in refrigerator. Drain slightly before serving. Serve with Creole Spiced Tortilla Chips. Yields 3½–4 cups.

CREOLE SPICED TORTILLA CHIPS:

2 (10-count) packages 7-inch
  tortillas

1–2 tablespoons Creole seasoning
  or chili powder

Cut each package of tortillas into halves. Cut each half into 4 wedges. Arrange in single layers on baking sheets. Spray wedges lightly with nonstick cooking spray. Sprinkle with seasoning. Bake at 350° for 5 minutes. Cool and store in an airtight container.

America Celebrates Columbus

Ohio became the 17th state on March 1, 1803. With an area of 116,103 square miles, it ranks 34th in size and 7th in population. The state's capital and largest city is Columbus.

Fresh Salsa

4 cups chopped, peeled fresh
  tomatoes
¼ cup finely chopped onion
1–4 jalapeño peppers or mild
  yellow banana peppers,
  seeded, finely chopped

1 tablespoon olive oil or
  vegetable oil
1 tablespoon vinegar
1 teaspoon ground cumin
1 teaspoon salt (optional)
1 garlic clove, minced

Combine ingredients; mix well. Let stand 1 hour. Serve at room temperature.

Carroll County Humane Society Members & Friends
Cookbook Volume II

Black Bean Salsa

2 cups canned black beans,
  drained
½ cup canned corn
1 avocado, chopped
½ cup chopped red bell
  pepper
½ cup chopped red onion
1 or 2 jalapeño chiles, seeded,
  chopped

2–3 tablespoons extra virgin
  olive oil
½ cup finely chopped fresh
  cilantro
3–4 tablespoons lime juice, or to
  taste
Salt and pepper to taste
Blue tortilla chips or toasted pita
  wedges

Combine beans, corn, avocado, red bell pepper, onion, jalapeños, olive oil, and cilantro in a bowl and mix well. Stir in lime juice. Season with salt and pepper. Serve with tortilla chips or pita wedges. Yields 6–8 servings.

Beginnings

Portage Trail Mix

1 (12-ounce) package Crispix
cereal
1 (16-ounce) jar dry-roasted
peanuts
1 (16-ounce) package small
pretzels

2 cups packed brown sugar
1 cup (2 sticks) margarine
½ cup light corn syrup

Combine cereal, peanuts, and pretzels in a roasting pan and toss to mix well. Combine brown sugar, margarine, and corn syrup in saucepan. Bring to a boil, stirring occasionally. Boil for 1½ minutes, stirring occasionally. Pour over cereal mixture, stirring until coated.

Bake at 350° in a preheated oven for 15 minutes, stirring 3 or 4 times. Spread cereal mixture in a thin layer on a sheet of wax paper. Let stand until cool. Yields 20–25 servings.

Beginnings

Granola

6–7 cups oatmeal
1–1½ cups Grape-Nuts
¾ cup nuts
¾ cup seeds (optional)*
1 cup shredded coconut
 (optional)
½ cup oil
½ cup honey

⅓ cup water
¼ cup brown sugar
1½ teaspoons salt
1½ teaspoons vanilla extract
2 cups chopped dried fruits,
 such as raisins, cranberries,
 apricots, etc. (optional)

Mix together oatmeal, Grape-Nuts, nuts, seeds, and coconut. Mix together well the oil, honey, water, brown sugar, salt, and vanilla extract. Pour over dry ingredients and mix thoroughly. Bake, stirring every 10 minutes, for 30–45 minutes at 325° or until it is dry but not too brown. Remove from oven and cool. Stir in fruit, if desired. Store in airtight container. Stays fresh for several weeks.

*Shelled sunflower or pumpkin seeds work well. Use larger amount of oatmeal and/or Grape-Nuts if you omit seeds and/or coconut.

Sharing Our Best

One of Ohio's nicknames is "The Heart of It All," purportedly because of its shape (kind of like a heart), its central location to the densely populated areas of the United States, its mosaic of big commercial cities, small towns, industry, and farmland, and its critical role in "America's Heartland."

Bread *and* Breakfast

Rotaynah, sculpted by Peter Toth in 1985 out of a huge Red Oak, weighs seventeen tons and stands thirty-six feet tall. Located in front of Akron's Fairlawn Elementary School, Rotaynah commemorates Akron's native American heritage.

Sweet Potato Biscuits

Autumn on the ridge brings out all the city folks looking for pumpkins, gourds, and Indian corn. In the last few years, these biscuits have been a big fall attraction as well. Try them with a slice of ham and honey mustard, or make mini biscuits and serve them as part of an appetizer table.

2 cups self-rising flour	⅓ cup butter
1 cup sugar	1¾ cups cooked mashed sweet
⅓ cup plus 1 tablespoon	potatoes
shortening	⅛–¼ cup milk

Preheat oven to 400°. Combine flour and sugar; cut in shortening and butter. Add sweet potatoes and enough milk to make a dough you can work. This is a delicate dough, though, so be careful. Knead dough, then roll it out until it is ¼ inch thick. Cut dough with a 2-inch biscuit cutter. Place biscuits on a lightly greased baking sheet and bake for 10–15 minutes. Watch carefully so as not to burn them. Yields 8–10 biscuits.

BROWN SUGAR AND CINNAMON BUTTER:

½ cup butter, softened	2 teaspoons cinnamon
⅓ cup brown sugar	

While biscuits are baking, mix together all ingredients for sugar and cinnamon butter, and serve it with the hot biscuits.

A Taste of the Murphin Ridge Inn

With fifteen Swiss cheese factories in and around Sugarcreek, Ohio ranks first in the United States in Swiss cheese production, producing more than ten million pounds annually.

Ham & Swiss Cheese Biscuits

2 cups all-purpose flour
2 teaspoons baking powder
½ teaspoon baking soda
½ cup butter or margarine,
   chilled, cut into pieces
½ cup shredded Swiss cheese
¼ cup minced ham
About ⅔ cup buttermilk

Preheat oven to 450°. Grease baking sheet. Sift flour, baking powder, and baking soda into medium bowl. Using pastry blender or 2 knives, cut in butter until mixture resembles coarse crumbs. Stir in cheese, ham, and enough buttermilk to make a soft dough. Turn out dough onto lightly floured surface; knead lightly. Roll out dough ½ inch thick. Cut biscuit rounds with 2-inch cutter. Place on greased baking sheet. Bake about 10 minutes or until browned. Makes 18 biscuits.

Dawn to Dusk

Old-Fashioned Cornbread

¾ cup yellow cornmeal
1 cup all-purpose flour
⅔ cup sugar
¾ teaspoon salt
3½ teaspoons baking powder
1 cup milk
1 egg, beaten
¼ cup oil

Stir together dry ingredients; make a well in center. Blend milk, egg, and oil together; pour into well of dry ingredients. Beat thoroughly. Pour into greased 8x8-inch square pan. Bake at 400° for 22–25 minutes. Center will be set and edges golden brown when done.

Favorite Recipes from the Delaware Police Department

Buttery Pan Rolls

They're called buttery pan rolls for a good reason—don't skimp on the butter.

4½ teaspoons dry yeast	1 teaspoon salt
½ cup warm water	9 ounces butter, melted, cooled,
4½ cups all-purpose flour,	divided
divided	1 egg
¼ cup sugar	1 cup milk, scalded, cooled

Dissolve yeast in water. Mix ½ the flour with sugar and salt in bowl with yeast, 3 ounces butter, egg, and milk. Knead until blended. Add remaining flour as needed and knead until smooth (dough will be soft and sticky). Cover and proof until dough is doubled in volume.

Punch down and drop by small spoonfuls into a 9x13-inch baking dish evenly coated with 2 ounces butter. Drizzle rolls with 2 ounces of melted butter. Proof rolls again until double in size.

Bake at 400° for 8–12 minutes or until golden brown. Brush rolls with remaining 2 ounces of butter when they come out of oven. Yields 2 dozen rolls.

Editor's Extra: 9 ounces of butter = 2¼ sticks.

Food, Glorious Food

In 1892, the Wright Brothers opened a bicycle repair shop in addition to their established printing business. From 1895 until 1897, both businesses were located at 22 South Williams Street, "known as the Wright Cycle Company." Explore the times and trials of the Wright brothers through a glimpse of their family history at the Wright Cycle Company Complex in Dayton, which includes the Aviation Trail Visitor Center and Museum.

Barbara's Rolls

1 cup shortening
1 cup sugar
1 teaspoon salt
1 cup boiling water

2 eggs, beaten
2 packages dry yeast
1 cup warm water
6 cups all-purpose flour

Put shortening, sugar, and salt in a large bowl. Over this mixture pour boiling water. Add eggs and stir together well. Add yeast that has been dissolved in warm water. Stir in flour. Mix all together and refrigerate overnight.

Roll out ½ inch thick and cut with 2-inch cutter. Put in greased muffin tins and let rise until double (about 3–4 hours). Bake at 425° for 7–8 minutes. Makes 4 dozen rolls.

Note: This dough will keep several days in refrigerator; so bake only as many rolls as you will need for a meal.

Camp Whitewood Camp Cookbook

Scottish Oat Scones

1 ½ cups all-purpose flour
1 cup quick or old-fashioned
  oats, uncooked
¼ cup sugar
1 tablespoon baking powder
¼ teaspoon salt
1 stick butter, chilled, cut in
  pieces

½ cup craisins
⅓ cup milk
1 egg, lightly beaten
1 tablespoon sugar
⅛ teaspoon cinnamon

Heat oven to 400°. Spray cookie sheet with nonstick spray. In large bowl, combine flour, oats, sugar, baking powder, and salt. Mix well. Cut in butter with pastry blender until like coarse crumbs. Stir in craisins.

In small bowl, mix milk and egg. Add to dry mix all at once. Stir with fork just until all ingredients are moistened. Do not overmix. Turn dough out onto lightly floured surface. Knead gently 8–10 times. Roll or pat dough into 8-inch circle, about ½ inch thick. Combine sugar and cinnamon and sprinkle over dough. Cut into 10 wedges. Bake on cookie sheet 12–15 minutes until light golden brown. Serve with honey, jam, apple butter, or favorite spread.

Rose Hill Recipes

Jerry Ayers of Baltimore is the world's fastest pumpkin carver. He set the world record in 1999 by carving a very detailed jack-o'-latern in 1 minute 37 seconds. He beat his own record the following year with a time of 1 minute 18 seconds. Jerry now sells his knives and pumpkin-face designs nationwide under the name of "Designer Pumpkins."

Cream Scones

2 cups all-purpose flour
1 tablespoon baking powder
¼ teaspoon salt
¼ cup sugar
⅓ cup butter
1 cup whipping cream

Combine first 4 ingredients. Cut in butter. Add cream and stir just till moist. Turn out and knead 5–6 times. Roll out to ½ inch thick and cut with biscuit cutter. Bake at 375° for 15 minutes on greased cookie sheet.

Dawn to Dusk

Pumpkin Spice Muffins

2 cups whole-wheat flour
2 teaspoons baking powder
1 teaspoon baking soda
2 teaspoons ground cinnamon
2 teaspoons ground nutmeg
2 eggs, beaten
1 cup pumpkin purée
¼ cup white sugar
2 cups unsweetened applesauce
2 tablespoons vegetable oil
1 teaspoon almond extract

Preheat oven to 350°. In medium bowl, mix together flour, baking powder, baking soda, cinnamon, and nutmeg; set aside. In a large bowl, combine eggs, pumpkin, sugar, applesauce, vegetable oil, and almond extract. Slowly add flour mixture to large bowl until just blended. Do not overbeat.

Pour batter into 18 nonstick muffin cups. Bake 25–30 minutes. Remove muffins from oven; let cool slightly. Remove muffins from pan and let cool completely.

Food for Thought

Cranberry Pumpkin Bread

2 eggs, beaten
2 cups sugar
½ cup oil
1 cup pumpkin
2¼ cups all-purpose flour

1 tablespoon pumpkin pie spice
1 teaspoon baking soda
½ teaspoon salt
1 cup whole cranberries, fresh or
 frozen

Combine eggs, sugar, oil, and pumpkin. Mix well. Combine flour, pie spice, soda, and salt. Stir into other ingredients until moistened. Stir in cranberries. Spoon into 2 greased and floured 8x3¾-inch loaf pans. Bake at 350° for 1 hour, until toothpick inserted in center comes out clean. Cool in pans 5 minutes, then remove from pans to finish cooling.

Cooking Up a Cure

Sweet Potato Cranberry Bread

2 large eggs
1⅓ cups granulated sugar
⅓ cup canola oil
1 teaspoon vanilla extract
1 cup mashed sweet potatoes,
 canned or cooked fresh

1½ cups all-purpose flour
1 teaspoon ground cinnamon
¼ teaspoon ground allspice
1 teaspoon baking soda
1 cup chopped fresh cranberries

Preheat oven to 350°. Spray a 9-inch loaf pan with cooking spray; dust with flour. In a large bowl, combine eggs, sugar, oil, vanilla, and sweet potatoes. In a separate bowl, combine flour, cinnamon, allspice, and baking soda. Make a well in center. Pour sweet potato mixture into well. Mix just until moistened. Stir in cranberries. Spoon batter into prepared loaf pan. Bake in 350° oven for 1 hour or until a toothpick in center comes out clean. Slice loaf into 15 slices to serve. Makes 1 loaf.

Nutritional analysis: Cal 189; Prot 2gm; Carbo 32gm; Dietary Fiber 1 gm; Fat 6gm; Sat. Fat .5gm; Choles 28mg; Sod 100mg.

More Nutritious Still Delicious

Peanut Butter Bread
with Strawberry Butter

2 cups all-purpose flour
2 teaspoons baking powder
½ cup peanut butter
1 cup sugar
1 egg
1 teaspoon salt

1 cup milk
½ cup unsalted butter, softened
⅓ cup strawberry jam
Fresh lemon juice to taste
½ teaspoon sugar, or to taste

Mix flour and baking powder together. Beat peanut butter, 1 cup sugar, egg, and salt in a mixer bowl until smooth. Add flour mixture and milk alternately, mixing well after each addition. Spoon into a greased 9x5-inch loaf pan. Bake at 350° for 60–70 minutes or until loaf tests done. Beat butter, jam, lemon juice, and ½ teaspoon sugar in a mixer bowl until smooth and creamy. Serve with sliced bread. Yields 12 servings.

America Celebrates Columbus

Strawberry Nut Bread
with Strawberry Butter

3 cups all-purpose flour
2 cups sugar
1 teaspoon baking soda
1 teaspoon salt
1 teaspoon cinnamon
4 eggs, beaten
¼ cup vegetable oil

2 (10-ounce) packages frozen
   strawberries, thawed, juice
   reserved
1 cup chopped nuts of choice
½ cup butter, softened
¾ cup powdered sugar

In large mixing bowl, combine flour, sugar, baking soda, salt, and cinnamon. Make a well in center of dry ingredients. Pour eggs, oil, and strawberries into well. Mix thoroughly. Stir in nuts. Butter 2 (9x5x3-inch) loaf pans or 5 miniature loaf pans.

Bake at 350° for 50–60 minutes for large loaves, or 20–25 minutes for small loaves. Cool in pans for 10 minutes, then remove and cool on wire rack.

Combine ½ cup strawberry juice, butter, and powdered sugar. Mix by hand on in food processor until smooth. Offer with sliced bread, or pour over loaves.

I'll Cook When Pigs Fly

Cranberry Sour Cream Coffeecake

1 stick margarine or butter, softened
1 cup sugar
2 eggs
1 teaspoon baking powder
½ teaspoon baking soda
2 cups all-purpose flour
½ pint sour cream
1 teaspoon almond extract
1 (8-ounce) can whole cranberry sauce, divided
½ cup chopped walnuts

Cream margarine and sugar gradually. Add unbeaten eggs one at a time. Add dry ingredients alternately with sour cream, ending with dry ingredients. Add extract. Grease and flour tube pan.

Put ½ batter in bottom of pan. Add ½ the cranberry sauce and spread evenly. Add remaining batter. Place remaining cranberry sauce on top. Sprinkle with walnuts. Bake in 350° oven for 55–60 minutes. Remove from pan after cooling for 10 minutes.

GLAZE:

¾ cup powdered sugar
1–2 tablespoons warm water
½ teaspoon almond extract

Mix ingredients and drizzle on top of coffeecake after it cools.

Franklin County 4-H Favorites

The Cincinnati Red Stockings, so-named for the color of their game hosiery, were the first professional baseball team in U.S. history. The Red Stockings began playing in 1869. Long stockings were then a novelty in team uniforms. The first African-American to play professional baseball, Moses Fleetwood Walker from Mount Pleasant, signed with the Toledo Blue Stockings in 1883. Jackie Robinson (from Cairo, Georgia) was the first African-American to play at the Major League level when he joined the Brooklyn Dodgers in 1947. Larry Doby (from Camden, South Carolina) became the first black player in the American League with the Cleveland Indians in 1948.

Yummy-to-Your-Tummy Jelly Rolls

My daughters, Whitney and Ashley, created this yummy recipe.

10 teaspoons jelly (any flavor)   **2 tablespoons sugar**
1 (7½-ounce) can biscuits

Preheat oven to 450°. Spray a 10-inch square pan with nonfat cooking spray. With you hands, flatten each biscuit into a 3-inch circle. Spoon 1 teaspoon jelly in center of each biscuit. Fold each in half and stick a toothpick through center. Arrange jelly rolls in prepared pan. Lightly sprinkle sugar over jelly rolls. Bake 5–7 minutes, or until golden brown. Yields 10 servings.

Nutritional analysis (per roll): Cal 78 (9% fat); Fat 1gm; Choles 0mg; Carbo 17gm; Dietary Fiber 0gm; Prot 1gm; Sod 168mg.

***Busy People's Down-Home Cooking
Without the Down-Home Fat***

Mrs. Harding's Waffles

This recipe, multiplied, is the Trinity Waffle Day recipe.

2 cups all-purpose flour   **2 eggs, separated**
1 teaspoon salt   **2 cups milk**
4 teaspoons baking powder   **4 tablespoons shortening, melted**
2 tablespoons sugar   **(may substitute oil)**

Sift dry ingredients together. Separate eggs and beat whites. Stir milk into yolks and beat. Add shortening to yolk mixture and continue beating. Add dry ingredients gradually. Beat well. Fold in egg whites. Bake 3 minutes on hot waffle iron.

Feeding the Flock—Trinity United Methodist Women

German Apple Pancake

PANCAKE:

3 large eggs
¾ cup milk
¾ cup all-purpose flour
½ teaspoon salt
½ teaspoon vanilla
1½ tablespoons butter

Preheat oven to 450°. Beat eggs, milk, flour, salt, and vanilla until smooth. In a heavy 12-inch skillet, melt butter; pour batter into skillet. Bake 15 minutes; lower temperature to 350°; bake 10 minutes more.

FILLING:

1 pound tart apples (and/or peaches and pears), peeled, cored, sliced
¼ cup butter, melted
¼ cup brown sugar
Ground cinnamon and nutmeg

Sauté apples in butter and sugar; season to taste with cinnamon and nutmeg. Place pancake on serving dish, then with slotted spoon, add apples to half of pancake; fold over. Pour remaining apple syrup in pan over folded pancake. Serve with additional maple syrup if desired, although not necessary.

Dawn to Dusk

Oatmeal Pancakes

½ cup whole-wheat or
  all-purpose flour
½ cup old-fashioned oats
1 tablespoon sunflower seeds
1 tablespoon sugar

1½ teaspoons baking powder
¼ teaspoon salt
1 egg, beaten
¾ cup milk
1 tablespoon butter, melted

Set a heavy 10-inch skillet or sauté pan over low heat and preheat 5 minutes. In mixing bowl, stir flour, oats, sunflower seeds, sugar, baking powder, and salt. Mix egg, milk, and oil, and blend with dry ingredients. (Mix only to blend.) Pour butter into hot greased skillet, then batter. Flip when bubbles appear. Makes 9 pancakes.

Sharing Our Best

Grandma Mac's Cinnamon Toast

½ cup butter, softened
1 cup firmly packed light
  brown sugar
2 teaspoons half-and-half or
  milk

½ teaspoon cinnamon, or
  to taste
Dash of salt (optional)
4 slices lightly toasted bread

In a small mixing bowl, cream together butter and brown sugar until light and fluffy. Beat in half-and-half, cinnamon, and salt. Lightly toast 4 slices of bread, and spread entire top with cinnamon-sugar mixture. Place on a cookie sheet, and broil briefly until mixture bubbles. (Watch carefully as these will burn quickly.) Cool slightly on a rack; cut into triangles, and serve warm for breakfast toast. Cover and refrigerate remaining mixture for future use. Yields about 1 loaf.

Note: Add brown sugar, cinnamon, and salt to the end of a bowl of whipped or soft-type margarine. Butter taste is better, margarine easier—no bowl or beaters to clean.

Discover Dayton

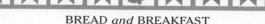
French Toast Sticks

This is yummy and fun to eat, but a whole lot healthier version of the popular fast-food variety.

12 slices Texas toast (or any thick-sliced white bread)
2 (4-ounce) containers Egg Beaters (or 8 egg whites with 2 drops yellow food coloring)

⅔ cup skim milk

Preheat nonstick griddle to 400°, or a nonstick skillet over high heat. Spray with nonfat cooking spray. Cut each slice of bread into 3 strips; set aside. Combine Egg Beaters and skim milk in a mixing bowl and beat until well blended. Dip bread slices one at a time into egg mixture. Cook on griddle until bottoms are toasty brown. Turn a quarter turn until all 4 sides of bread slices are cooked. Yields 12 (3-piece) servings.

Note: For Cinnamon French Toast Sticks, add 1 teaspoon cinnamon to egg mixture. Stir until well mixed.

Nutritional analysis: Cal 134 (11% fat); Fat 2gm; Choles 1mg; Carbo 23gm; Dietary Fiber 1 gm; Prot 6gm; Sod 280mg.

***Busy People's Down-Home Cooking
Without the Down-Home Fat***

Located in Akron, the Goodyear Tire and Rubber Company began production on November 21, 1898, making bicycle and carriage tires, horseshoe pads, and even poker chips. Since the first bicycle tire in 1898, Goodyear became the world's largest tire company in 1916. *More people ride on Goodyear tires than on any other kind.®* Goodyear became the world's largest rubber company in 1926.

Blueberry Cream Cheese-Stuffed Baked French Toast

1½ loaves French bread or sourdough bread, presliced (no crust), divided
1 (12-ounce) bag frozen blueberries, rinsed
1 (8-ounce) package cream cheese
½ cup sugar
½ cup sour cream
1 teaspoon vanilla
8 eggs
½ cup milk
1 pint half-and-half
1 teaspoon cinnamon
1 teaspoon nutmeg
½ cup powdered sugar

Cut 1 loaf bread into cubes and place into bottom of a greased 9x13-inch baking dish. Dish should be ¾ full. Sprinkle blueberries evenly over bread. Microwave cream cheese in bowl for 2 minutes. Stir carefully and add sugar, sour cream, and vanilla. Spread over blueberries. Place remaining 6–8 large slices of bread over cream cheese. (Judge by how many guests you are serving.) Beat eggs, milk, half-and-half, cinnamon, and nutmeg, and pour over bread. Make holes with knife so liquid goes throughout. Cover and refrigerate overnight.

Bake at 350°, covered, 1 hour, then uncovered, 25–30 minutes, until top is golden brown. Let sit 10 minutes before slicing. Sift powdered sugar over before serving.

Don't Forget the INNgredients!

Apple French Toast

1 cup brown sugar
½ cup butter, melted
3 teaspoons ground cinnamon
3 Granny Smith apples, peeled,
   cored, sliced thinly

1 loaf French bread, cut in 1-inch
   slices
6 large eggs
1½ cups half-and-half
1 tablespoon vanilla

Combine brown sugar, butter, and cinnamon in a 10x15-inch glass baking dish. Add apples and coat well. Spread apple mixture evenly on bottom of dish. Arrange slices of bread on top. Mix eggs, half-and-half, and vanilla. Pour mixture over bread, soaking tops. Cover and refrigerate 4–24 hours.

Bake, covered, with aluminum foil in preheated 375° oven for 40 minutes, and uncovered for 5 minutes.

Sharing the Best from Our Kitchen

Ham and Swiss Soufflés

8 slices day-old bakery bread,
   preferably sourdough*
1 (8-ounce) package cooked ham,
   chopped
2 cups shredded Swiss cheese
6 eggs

1½ cups milk
1 teaspoon dry mustard
¼ teaspoon salt
Dash of freshly ground black
   pepper

Coat 4 (8-ounce) ramekins with cooking spray. Remove crusts from bread and cut slices into ½-inch cubes. Place a layer of cubes in each ramekin. Top with a layer of chopped ham and a layer of cheese. Whisk together eggs, milk, and seasonings. Pour over bread. Cover ramekins and refrigerate overnight.

In the morning, remove from refrigerator and allow to warm slightly while you preheat oven to 400°. Bake for 25–30 minutes. (Cooking time will depend on the temperature of the soufflés when you put them in the oven.) Soufflés will puff up. Serve immediately. Serves 4.

*Do not use soft grocery store-type bread; bakery bread works better.

Sharing the Best from Our Kitchen

Zesty Cheese Egg Bake

1 loaf French bread
1 (8-ounce) package cream
  cheese
1 (4-ounce) can green chiles,
  drained
2 cups grated Monterey Jack
  cheese

2 cups grated Cheddar cheese
8 eggs
1½ cups milk
1½ cups half-and-half
1½ teaspoons dried mustard
Paprika or red cayenne pepper

Grease a 9x13-inch baking dish. Cut enough bread into 1-inch cubes to fill baking dish half full. Set aside 8 whole slices to use for topping. Cut cream cheese into small cubes and place evenly over cubes. Combine grated cheeses and sprinkle over bread. Cover with remaining 8 slices of bread evenly over top.

In medium bowl, beat eggs well, then add milk, half-and-half, and dry mustard; blend well. Slowly pour egg mixture evenly over top giving it time to soak in. Spray tin foil with Pam and cover dish with it; let sit overnight.

Preheat oven to 350°. Leave foil on dish and place in oven. Bake for 45–50 minutes; remove foil (hopefully it did not stick to top of bread since you sprayed it with Pam) and bake another 15 minutes. Check often to make sure top does not get too brown. Knife inserted should come out clean. Let stand 10–15 minutes before serving. Sprinkle with paprika before serving. Serves 8.

Variation: One pound sausage, cooked and drained, may be added before covering with cheeses and bread slices.

Don't Forget the INNgredients!

Egg and Sausage Casserole

Our family enjoys this recipe for Christmas brunch. I am able to prepare it the day before; therefore, I can enjoy Christmas morning under the tree.

8 slices bread, without crusts,
   cubed
1 pound pork sausage, cooked,
   crumbled, drained
1½ cups fresh mushrooms,
   sautéed, drained
2 cups grated Cheddar cheese

4 eggs
2½ cups milk
¼ teaspoon dry mustard
1 (10¾-ounce) can cream of
   mushroom soup
½ soup can milk
Buttered bread crumbs

Place bread cubes in bottom of a greased 8x12-inch dish. Add sausage, mushrooms, and cheese to the bread cubes. In a separate bowl, mix together eggs, milk, and dry mustard. Pour liquid ingredients over ingredients in casserole. Cover and refrigerate overnight.

The next day, bring casserole to room temperature. Mix mushroom soup with ½ can milk. Pour over casserole. Cover with buttered, seasoned bread crumbs. Bake in a preheated 325° oven for 75 minutes. Yields 10–12 servings.

Discover Dayton

Did you know that Play-Doh was originally designed as a wallpaper cleaner? It's true. In 1956, Joseph McVicker of Kutol Products in Cincinnati added a pleasant scent to his company's clay wallpaper cleaner, and soon discovered that the similarity to regular modeling clay without the toxicity or mess made Play-Doh a great toy. McVicker became a millionaire before his 27th birthday after re-releasing the product as a toy. More than 700 million pounds of Play-Doh have been sold. National Play-Doh Day is September 16th.

Brunch Strata

3 cups sliced fresh mushrooms
3 cups chopped zucchini
2 cups cubed fully cooked ham
1½ cups chopped onions
1½ cups chopped green bell
  peppers
2 garlic cloves, minced
⅛ cup vegetable oil

2 (8-ounce) packages cream
  cheese, softened
½ cup half-and-half
12 eggs
4 cups cubed day-old bread
3 cups shredded Cheddar cheese
1 teaspoon salt
½ teaspoon pepper

In a large skillet, sauté first 7 ingredients until vegetables are tender. Drain and pat dry; set aside. In a large mixing bowl, beat cream cheese and half-and-half until smooth. Beat in eggs. Stir in bread, cheese, salt, pepper, and vegetable mixture. Pour into 2 greased 7x11-inch baking dishes. Bake uncovered at 350° for 35–40 minutes or until a kinfe inserted near center comes out clean. Let stand 10 minutes before serving. Makes 16 servings.

Asthma Walk Cook Book

Eggs Benedict Casserole

2½ cups cut-up cooked ham
10 eggs, poached
¼ teaspoon black pepper

1 cup crushed cornflakes or
  fine bread crumbs
¼ cup margarine, melted

Put ham in a 9x13-inch baking pan; place poached eggs on ham. Sprinkle with pepper. Prepare Mornay Sauce and pour over eggs. Toss butter and cornflakes, sprinkle over sauce in rectangle around each egg. Refrigerate no longer than 24 hours. Heat in 350° oven until sauce is bubbly.

MORNAY SAUCE:

¼ cup butter
¼ cup flour
½ teaspoon salt
⅛ teaspoon nutmeg

2½ cups milk
1½ cups shredded Gruyére
  or Swiss cheese
½ cup grated Parmesan

Heat butter over low heat till melted. Stir in flour, salt, and nutmeg. Cook, stirring constantly, till bubbly. Remove from heat, then stir in milk. Heat to boiling, stirring constantly. Boil 1 minute. Add cheese and stir till smooth.

Dawn to Dusk

The Bicycle Museum of America in New Bermen has more than 300 bicycles on display, with a rotation of more than 1,000. One bicycle on display is a Boneshaker, circa 1870, which is thought to be the only surviving example of this type bicycle to exist. The wheels are wooden with iron rims, and the main frame is made from solid iron. The iron section supporting the leather seat provided minimal comfort for the "bone shaking" shocks coming from the rough 19th-century roads.

Breakfast Pizza

1 (8-ounce) tube refrigerated
crescent rolls
1 pound bulk pork sausage,
hot or mild
1 cup frozen shredded hash
brown potatoes, thawed

1 (4-ounce) package shredded
Cheddar cheese
3 eggs
¼ cup milk
¼ teaspoon pepper
¼ cup grated Parmesan cheese

Unroll crescent dough and place on a greased 12-inch pizza pan; press seams together and press up sides of pan to form a crust. In a skillet, brown sausage over medium heat; drain and cool slightly. Sprinkle sausage, hash browns, and Cheddar cheese over crust.

In a bowl, beat eggs, milk, and pepper; pour over pizza. Sprinkle with Parmesan cheese. Bake at 375° for 28–30 minutes or until golden brown. Let stand 10 minutes before cutting. Yields 6–8 servings.

Favorite Recipes–First Church of God

Vanilla Cream Sauce

A rich topping for French toast, waffles, and pancakes.

1 cup white corn syrup
1 cup brown sugar

1 cup whipping cream
1 teaspoon vanilla

Heat corn syrup, sugar, and cream in saucepan over medium heat. Heat until boiling, then remove from heat and add vanilla. Serve warm.

Note: For peach sauce, add 1 finely chopped peach with vanilla.

Dawn to Dusk

Easy Apple Butter

2 (20-ounce) jars applesauce
5 cups sugar
¼ teaspoon salt
¼ cup cinnamon red hots

1 teaspoon cinnamon
2 tablespoons cider vinegar
¼ teaspoon cloves

Mix all ingredients in crockpot. Start on HIGH. Don't use lid. Simmer all day. Put a little apple butter in a small container in the freezer a few minutes just to see if it's thick enough. Cook until desired thickness. Double recipe to fill crockpot.

Feeding the Flock—Trinity United Methodist Women

Jerome M. Smucker got his start pressing apple cider at a mill he opened in Orrville in 1897. Later, he also prepared apple butter, which he sold in crocks bearing a hand-signed seal, his personal guarantee of quality. Today, the J. M. Smucker Company is still headquartered in Orrville, and is known nationwide for its jams and jellies. *With a name like Smucker's, it has to be good.*®

Savory Stuffing

My assistants, friends, and family went nuts over this stuffing recipe. With great enthusiasm one friend said, "Next year you'll have to taste my homemade dressing, Dawn. It's going to taste very familiar." Really?" I asked, puzzled that my original recipe tasted like hers. "How can that be?" "Yeah, it's going to be this recipe," she said with a grin from ear to ear as she licked her spoon.

¾ cup chopped celery
1 cup frozen chopped onion
1 (14½-ounce) can chicken
  broth
¾ teaspoon rubbed sage, or ½
  teaspoon ground sage
¼ cup imitation butter-flavored
  sprinkles*

1 (12-ounce) bag vegetarian
  sausage-flavored crumbles*, or
  1 pound low-fat Italian turkey
  sausage, cooked, drained, and
  crumbled
14 slices seedless rye bread,
  toasted and cubed into ½-inch
  pieces

In a large saucepan, bring celery, onion, chicken broth, sage, butter-flavored sprinkles, and sausage-flavored crumbles to a boil. Once to a full boil, stir in toasted bread cubes. Turn off heat. Cover and let stuffing sit 5–10 minutes. Keep stuffing warm until ready to serve. Fluff with a fork before serving. Yields 14 (½-cup) servings.

*Veggie crumbles are vegetarian meat substitutes made by Morning Star Farms. They are found in the frozen food section.

Nutritional analysis (with vegetarian sausage crumbles): Cal 132 (16% fat); Fat 2gm; Choles 0mg; Carbo 20gm; Dietary Fiber 3gm; Prot 8gm; Sod 530mg; Diabetic Exchanges ½ very lean meat, 1½ starch.

Nutritional analysis (with turkey sausage): Cal 134 (15% fat); Fat 2gm; Choles 15mg: Carbo 18gm; Dietary Fiber 2gm; Prot 8gm; Sod 554mg; Diabetic Exchanges ½ very lean meat, 1 starch.

Busy People's Fun, Fast, Festive Christmas Cookbook

Soups, Stews, *and* Chilis

Whether it be racing, catching some air, or cruising down a great trail, a snow-mobile ride through miles of untracked snow in Ohio is quite an adventure!

Chinese Vegetable Soup

3 quarts chicken broth
2 leeks, thinly sliced
2 cloves garlic, minced or
  pressed
Black pepper, cayenne pepper,
  basil to taste
3 medium carrots, peeled,
  chopped
4 large cauliflower buds (small
  florets trimmed from stem)
1 (8-ounce) can sliced water
  chestnuts

1 medium zucchini, chopped
1 (6-ounce) jar baby corn,
  drained, halved lengthwise
1 (8-ounce) can bamboo shoots,
  drained
6 ounces straw mushrooms
4 ounces enoki mushrooms
¼ pound shiitake mushrooms,
  trimmed, sliced
16 ounces frozen salad shrimp,
  rinsed, drained

In large saucepan, combine broth, leeks, and garlic. Simmer 30 minutes. Add peppers and basil to taste. Simmer an additional 30 minutes to allow flavors to blend. Add remaining vegetables, mushrooms, and shrimp. Cook over medium-high heat approximately 10 minutes, or until shrimp are cooked and vegetables are crisp, yet tender. Serves 10.

A Treasury of Recipes for Mind, Body & Soul

Professor William Holmes McGuffey, known as the "Schoolmaster of the Nation," is the author of the classic *McGuffey's Readers*. While McGuffey was teaching in Oxford, he established a reputation as a lecturer. In 1835, the small Cincinnati publishing firm of Truman and Smith asked McGuffey to create a series of readers for primary level students. McGuffey was recommended for the job by Harriet Beecher Stowe, a longtime friend. He completed the first two readers within a year of signing his contract, receiving a fee of $1,000. While McGuffey compiled the first four readers (1836–1837 edition), the fifth and sixth were created by his brother Alexander during the 1840s. The series consisted of stories, poems, essays, and speeches. It is estimated that at least 120 million copies of *McGuffey's Readers* were sold between 1836 and 1960. Since 1961, they have continued to sell at a rate of some 30,000 copies a year. *McGuffey's Readers* are still in use today in some school systems, and by parents for home-schooling purposes.

Mrs. Mozelle Morris'
Corned Beef and Vegetable Soup

2 (14-ounce) cans chicken broth
1 can water
3 potatoes, peeled, diced
1 large onion, diced
3 carrots, diced
1 (12-ounce) can corned beef

1 small head cabbage, chopped
    fine
1 (28-ounce) can tomatoes
Additional vegetables, diced
    (optional)
Salt, pepper, and sugar to taste

In a large soup kettle, combine chicken broth and water with potatoes, onion, and carrots. Break the corned beef into small pieces; add to mixture. Simmer 15–20 minutes, then add cabbage, tomatoes, and other vegetables, if desired. Add seasonings to taste. Simmer until vegetables are tender, 15–20 minutes.

Carroll County Humane Society Members & Friends
Cookbook Volume I

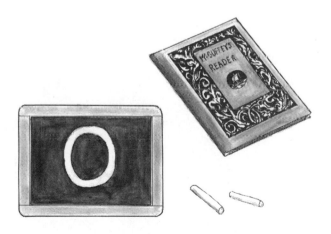

Italian Wedding Soup

MEATBALLS:

2 pounds lean ground chuck
Salt and pepper to taste
2 cloves garlic, chopped
2 cups bread crumbs

4 eggs
¼ cup parsley
¼ cup grated Parmesan

Mix meatball ingredients well. Roll into balls the size of a dime. Place on cookie sheet and bake 10 minutes.

3 pounds chicken breasts
  (3 double breasts)
1 large whole onion, peeled
6 large carrots, peeled
3 large celery ribs, cut in half
  (leaves included)

2 tablespoons salt
2 gallons water
2 pounds escarole, cleaned,
  cooked, squeezed, chopped

In a large pot, place chicken breasts, onion, carrots, celery, and salt. Cover with water and bring to a boil. Cook until chicken is tender, approximately 1½ hours. Strain soup through colander into another large pot. Let chicken and vegetables cool. Cut into small pieces; set aside. Put soup back into original pot on stove and bring to a boil. Add chicken, vegetables, escarole, and Meatballs. Simmer ½–¾ hour. Serve with croutons.

Favorite Recipes Home-Style

Kelton House Gazpacho

1 large sweet onion
2 green bell peppers
10–12 Roma tomatoes
1 English cucumber
5–6 garlic cloves, minced
½ cup olive oil
1 tablespoon Worcestershire

1–2 teaspoons dried ground
   coriander, or to taste
1 tablespoon kosher salt, or to
   taste
2 cups tomato juice or vegetable
   juice cocktail, divided
Hot pepper sauce to taste

Chop onion, green peppers, tomatoes, and cucumber separately in a food processor, removing to a large bowl; do not purée. Combine garlic, olive oil, Worcestershire, coriander, kosher salt, and 1 cup tomato juice in food processor container and process until smooth. Add to vegetables and mix well. Add enough of the remaining tomato juice to achieve desired consistency. Season with hot pepper sauce. Chill 2 hours or longer to blend flavors. Yields 4 servings.

America Celebrates Columbus

Shaker Tomato Soup

1 small onion, chopped
½ cup finely chopped celery
2 tablespoons butter
1 (10¾-ounce) can tomato soup
1 soup can water
1 teaspoon finely chopped
   parsley

1 tablespoon lemon juice
1 teaspoon sugar
Salt and pepper to taste
Whipped cream, unsweetened, for
   garnish
Parsley

Sauté onion and celery in butter until onion looks transparent. Add tomato soup, water, parsley, lemon juice, sugar, salt and pepper. Simmer 5 minutes. Celery will remain crisp. Top with unsweetened whipped cream and chopped parsley. Yields 6 servings.

Cincinnati Recipe Treasury

Southwestern Tortilla Soup

1 (24-ounce) jar Randall's Mixed Beans
1 (16-ounce) can Bush's Black Beans
1 (15-ounce) can corn
1 (14-ounce) can Swanson Chicken Broth
1 (10¾-ounce) can cream of chicken soup
1 (10-ounce) can Swanson Chicken Breast
1 (12-ounce) package shredded Cheddar cheese
1 tablespoon Ac'cent
1 tablespoon chili powder
½ tablespoon crushed red pepper
4 tablespoons onion flakes
1 package tortillas, sliced
1 (8-ounce) carton sour cream
½ jar real bacon bits

Combine in saucepan mixed beans, black beans, corn, chicken broth, chicken soup, chicken breast, Cheddar cheese, Ac'cent, chili powder, red pepper, and onion flakes. Heat. Slice tortillas into strips and brown them. Set aside. Place tortilla strips into soup bowls and add the soup. Top with sour cream and bacon bits.

Favorite Recipes–First Church of God

Taco Soup

1 pound ground chuck
1 large onion, chopped
2 (15-ounce) cans Mexican-style
 chili beans, undrained
1 (15-ounce) can whole-kernel
 corn, undrained
1 (15-ounce) can tomato sauce
1 (14½-ounce) can diced
 tomatoes, undrained

1 (4-ounce) can chopped green
 chiles
1 envelope taco seasoning mix
1 envelope ranch-style dressing
 mix
1½ cups water
Toppings: corn chips, shredded
 lettuce, chopped onion,
 shredded Cheddar cheese

Cook beef and onions in a Dutch oven or skillet over medium-high heat until meat is browned and onions are tender, stirring until meat crumbles; drain. Stir beans, meat mixture, and remaining ingredients, except toppings, into a large soup pot; bring to a boil. Reduce heat; simmer uncovered 15 minutes, stirring occasionally. Spoon soup into bowls; top with desired toppings. Serves 6.

Recipes and Remembrances: Around St. George's Tables

Born April 18, 1857, in Kinsman, Clarence Darrow is one of America's most famous lawyers. Darrow volunteered his services and represented teacher John Thomas Scopes in the Scopes "Monkey Trial" in Tennessee. Scopes was a high school teacher arrested for teaching evolution as set out in Charles Darwin's book, *The Origin of Species.* At that time (1925), the theory of evolution was considered controversial in public opinion, and a law had been passed that forbade its teaching in any state-funded educational establishment. The trial was covered by journalists from around the world, including H. L. Mencken for *The Baltimore Sun.* It was Mencken who labeled it as the "Monkey Trial." It was the first U.S. trial to be broadcast on national radio. The famous trial was made infamous by the fictionalized accounts given in the 1955 play *Inherit the Wind,* the 1960 Hollywood motion picture, and the 1965, 1988, and 1999 television films of the same name.

Too Good Tortellini Soup

A hearty soup for fall or winter.

1 pound bulk Italian sausage
1 cup chopped onion
2 cloves garlic, sliced
5 cups beef broth
½ cup water
½ cup red wine
2 cups canned diced tomatoes
1 cup sliced carrots
½ teaspoon basil

½ teaspoon oregano
1 (8-ounce) can tomato sauce
8 ounces fresh tortellini
1½ cups sliced zucchini
3 tablespoons chopped fresh
   parsley
1 medium green bell pepper, cut
   into ½-inch pieces
Parmesan cheese

Brown sausage in a soup pot. Remove sausage from pot. Discard all but 1 teaspoon of fat from pot. Add onion and garlic to pot; sauté until tender. Add cooked sausage, broth, water, wine, tomatoes, carrots, basil, oregano, and tomato sauce. Bring to a boil. Reduce heat and simmer, uncovered, for 30 minutes.

Skim fat from soup. Stir in tortellini, zucchini, parsley, and bell pepper. Simmer, covered, for 20 minutes. Sprinkle individual servings with Parmesan cheese. Yields 6 servings.

Note: Onions, carrots, zucchini, and bell pepper may be chopped and refrigerated separately the day before. Sausage may be browned and refrigerated up to 2 days ahead.

Causing a Stir

At nearly a quarter of a mile long, five feet high, and twenty feet wide, Serpent Mound is the largest and finest effigy mound in the United States. Atop a plateau overlooking the Brush Creek Valley near Peebles, Serpent Mound represents an uncoiling serpent, but archaeologists and scientists are still uncertain as to why or when it was built. A recent excavation revealed that the serpent effigy was likely created by the Fort Ancient Indians, however, this is still widely debated.

Spaetzle

SOUP:

1½ cups finely diced celery
1½ cups grated carrots

¾ cup finely chopped onion
3 quarts rich chicken broth

Cook vegetables in chicken broth until tender, 15–20 minutes. Keep Soup simmering while adding Batter.

BATTER:

2 eggs, beaten
½ teaspoon salt

1 cup all-purpose flour
⅓–½ cup milk

Beat eggs; add salt and flour; add milk gradually. Batter should be about the consistency of pancake batter. Pour Batter into Soup from pitcher onto a wire whisk (keep turning the whisk). This will break up the spaetzle into small pieces. Simmer until pieces are tender. Serve with sprinkles of chopped parsley. This is a good hearty soup. Serves 10–15.

Feeding the Flock—Trinity United Methodist Women

Serpent Mound near Brush Creek Valley

Potato Soup

4 or 5 large potatoes
1 teaspoon diced onion
2½ teaspoons salt, divided
2 cups all-purpose flour (scant)

2 eggs, beaten
2 tablespoons butter
1 pint half-and-half

Peel and cube potatoes. Put potatoes, onion, and 1½ teaspoons salt in large pot. Add enough water to cover potatoes and cook over medium-high heat.

Meanwhile, mix flour with eggs and remaining 1 teaspoon salt to make rivels. Drop rivels, about the size of a quarter, into potato mixture. Bring to a boil, stirring frequently so the rivels don't stick. When rivels and potatoes are done, spoon off all the liquid that you can. (DO NOT POUR the liquid off because you will also pour off the tiny pieces of potatoes and rivels that are now in the bottom of your pot.)

Add butter and enough half-and-half to cover potatoes. Taste, and season as needed. Cook over low heat approximately 15–20 minutes or until soup is hot.

Love, Mom: Stories and Recipes from Kingston, Ohio

Onion Bisque

Our most requested soup, Murphin Ridge's Onion Bisque was awarded "Best Soup" by Cincinnati *magazine. On top of that, it's easy to make. Feel free to substitute vegetable stock or even water for the unsalted chicken stock.*

6 onions, or 1 sweet or Vidalia onion per person, sliced
½ cup butter
2 tablespoons sugar
Unsalted chicken stock to cover (at least 4 cups)

½ cup heavy cream
1½ cups grated Parmesan cheese
Bowl-sized croutons, toasted with butter and sprinkled with Parmesan cheese

In a large saucepan, sauté onions in butter until they become limp; sprinkle onions with sugar while they sauté. Cover onions with stock and cook slowly, 30–45 minutes, watching to see that the stock does not boil away. Turn off heat, and taste soup for seasoning. Purée soup in batches in food processor, or blend soup in saucepan with an immersion blender. Leave some small bits of onion for texture. Return soup to saucepan, if necessary. Add cream and cheese and heat soup through slowly. Serve with croutons on side. Yields 8–10 servings.

A Taste of the Murphin Ridge Inn

The Dublin Irish Festival has quickly become one of the nation's premiere Irish festivals, drawing more than 90,000 visitors annually. Musicians from Ireland and the United States are the highlight of every Dublin Irish Festival, featuring nonstop live performances on seven stages. The festival brings in an estimated 4.5 million dollars to the local economy.

Fresh Mushroom Soup

8 cups chicken broth
¼ cup soy sauce
¼ cup red wine vinegar
1 bay leaf
1 teaspoon minced fresh
  parsley
¼ teaspoon crumbled dried
  thyme

¼ cup butter
4 medium onions, minced
2 pounds mushrooms, sliced
¼ cup all-purpose flour
Salt and freshly ground
  black pepper
Snipped fresh chives

Simmer chicken broth, soy sauce, vinegar, bay leaf, parsley, and thyme in a large saucepan for 30 minutes. Meanwhile, melt butter in large heavy saucepan over low heat. Add onions and cook until translucent, about 10 minutes, stirring occasionally. Add mushrooms and stir until liquid is released. Add flour and stir for 3 minutes. Strain broth and then slowly stir into mushroom mixture. Season with salt and pepper. Bring soup to a boil, reduce heat, and simmer 25 minutes. Garnish with chives. Yields 6–8 servings.

With Great Gusto

Broccoli-Mushroom Chowder

1 pound fresh broccoli
½ cup water
2 sticks butter
1 cup all-purpose flour
1 quart chicken stock
1 (8-ounce) carton fresh
  mushrooms, sliced

1 quart half-and-half
1 teaspoon salt
¼ teaspoon white pepper
¼ teaspoon crushed tarragon
  leaves

Cut broccoli into ½-inch pieces. Steam in water until tender. Do not drain. Melt butter in saucepan over medium heat. Add flour. Cook 2–4 minutes. Add chicken stock and stir until it comes to a boil. Turn heat to low. Add broccoli, mushrooms, half-and-half, salt, pepper, and tarragon. Heat, but do not boil. Serves 8.

Note: For chicken stock, use homemade, canned, or 4 bouillon cubes dissolved in 1 quart water. Milk may be substituted for half-and-half.

A Taste of Faith

Smoky Cheese Chowder

1 (10-ounce) package frozen
 whole-kernel corn
½ cup chopped onion
½ cup water
1 teaspoon instant chicken
 bouillon granules
¼ teaspoon pepper

2½ cups milk
3 tablespoons all-purpose flour
1 cup shredded smoked Cheddar
 cheese
1 tablespoon diced pimiento,
 drained

In a saucepan, combine corn, onion, water, bouillon, and pepper. Bring to a boil; reduce heat. Cover and simmer about 4 minutes or till corn is tender. Do not drain. Stir together milk and flour; stir into corn mixture. Cook and stir till thickened and bubbly, about 30 minutes. Cook and stir 1 minute more. Add cheese and pimento; heat and stir till melted.

To serve, spoon into 4 soup bowls. If desired, garnish each serving with baby corn, chives, and red pepper. Makes 4 side-dish servings.

Note: To make ahead, prepare chowder as directed, except do not add cheese and pimiento; cool. Transfer to covered container. Chill up to 2 days. Reheat in saucepan over low heat till heated through, stirring. Add cheese and pimiento. Serve as above.

Dawn to Dusk

Seven U.S. presidents were born in Ohio, second only to Virginia's eight. Ulysses S. Grant (1869–1877); Rutherford B. Hayes (1877–1881); James A. Garfield (1881); Benjamin Harrison (1889–1893); William McKinley (1897–1901); William Howard Taft (1909–1913); Warren G. Harding (1921–1923).

Grant   *Hayes*   *Garfield*   *Harrison*   *McKinley*   *Taft*   *Harding*

White Chili

1 pound Great Northern beans, rinsed, picked over
2 pounds boneless, skinless chicken breasts
1 tablespoon oil
2 medium onions, chopped
4 garlic cloves, minced
2 (4-ounce) cans chopped green chiles
2 teaspoons ground cumin
1½ teaspoons crumbled dried oregano
¼ teaspoon ground cloves
¼ teaspoon cayenne pepper
6 cups reserved chicken broth
3 cups shredded Monterey Jack cheese, divided
Salt and pepper to taste
Sour cream
Salsa

Place beans in large heavy pot. Add enough cold water to cover; soak overnight.

Place chicken in large heavy saucepan. Add cold water to cover, and bring to a simmer. Cook until tender. Drain and reserve broth; cool. Cut chicken into cubes. Drain beans.

Heat oil in same pot over medium-high heat. Add onions and sauté until translucent, about 10 minutes. Stir in garlic, chiles, cumin, oregano, cloves, and cayenne; sauté 2 minutes.

Add beans and reserved broth; bring to a boil. Reduce heat and simmer until beans are very tender, about 2 hours, stirring occasionally. Add chicken and 1 cup cheese to chili and stir until cheese melts. Season to taste with salt and pepper. Ladle chili into bowls. Serve with remaining cheese, sour cream, and salsa.

Food for Thought

Cathy, a comic strip about a single career woman, debuted in 1976. Its creator, Cathy Guisewite, was born in Dayton in 1950. In 1993, Guisewite received the Reuben Award for Outstanding Cartoonist of the Year from the National Cartoonists Society.

Cincinnati Chili

The first chili parlor opened its doors next to the Empress Burlesque (later named the Gaiety) in downtown Cincinnati in 1922, naming itself The Empress Chili Parlor. This establishment was owned by Greek Tom Kiradjieff who banked on the city sharing his taste for the unusual blend of spices. The rest is history. The original recipe, which has always been mixed secretly at home, was never revealed. Yet chili restaurants sprang up all over town, including Skyline and Gold Star. Local chili aficionados developed preferences for their favorites. Al Heitz, a Camp Washington devotee, liked the old recipe best because it left his lips numb; old timers say that the chilies have indeed "cooled off" through the years. (There should be a piece of pepper for every serving for absolute authenticity.) Inevitably, various chili recipes were published in homemade cookbooks. Recently, a packaged Cincinnati Chili Mix has appeared on supermarket shelves. Whether the chili is hot or not, Cincinnati prides itself on being a true chili capital.

2–3 pounds ground beef
1 quart cold water
1 (6-ounce) can tomato paste
2 large onions, chopped (about 1 ½ cups)
1 ½ tablespoons vinegar
1 teaspoon Worcestershire
1 garlic clove, chopped fine
2 tablespoons chili powder
5 bay leaves
2 teaspoons cinnamon

1 teaspoon allspice
2 cayenne peppers (more to taste)
1 ½ tablespoons unsweetened cocoa
Salt and pepper to taste
1 ½ pounds cooked spaghetti
1 pound grated Cheddar cheese
1 (16-ounce) can kidney beans
1 onion, chopped fine (optional)
1 box oyster crackers

Crumble raw ground beef into water. Add all ingredients except spaghetti, cheese, crackers, beans, and onions, and bring to a boil. Stir well, breaking all the meat up before it cooks. Cover and simmer 2 or more hours, stirring occasionally. Serve chili over spaghetti in an oval dish—this is called a "2-Way." For a "3-Way," top it off with a pile of grated cheese with a dish of crackers on the side. To make a "4-Way," add a spoonful of onions before the cheese is placed on top. For a "5-Way," add beans in addition to onions and cheese. Serve with crackers, if desired. Yields 8–10 servings.

Note: May use whole spices tied in a bag: 5 bay leaves, 6 whole allspice, 4 red peppers.

Cincinnati Recipe Treasury

Lentil Chili Cincinnati Style

1 tablespoon olive oil
1½ cups chopped onions, fresh
  or frozen
2 stalks celery, chopped
2 cloves garlic, minced
¼ teaspoon ground cinnamon
¼ teaspoon ground cloves
1 teaspoon ground cumin

4 cups reduced-sodium vegetable
  broth
1 cup lentils, rinsed
1 cup chopped carrots
¼ teaspoon black pepper
1 (14½-ounce) can diced
  tomatoes with juice

In a large saucepan, heat oil for 1–2 minutes. Add onions and celery; sauté until onions are tender, about 5 minutes. Reduce heat; add garlic, cinnamon, cloves, and cumin. Cook for 1 minute. Add broth, lentils, carrots, and black pepper; bring to a boil. Reduce heat, cover, and simmer for 40–50 minutes or until lentils and carrots are soft. Add tomatoes with juice; cook another 10 minutes, until soup is hot throughout. Adjust seasonings to taste. Makes 6 (1-cup) servings.

Nutritional analysis: Cal 204; Prot 12gm; Carbo 35gm; Dietary Fiber 8gm; Fat 3gm; Sat. Fat 0gm; Choles 0mg; Sod 427mg.

More Nutritious Still Delicious

Salads

PHOTO COURTESY OF THE OHIO DIVISION OF TRAVEL AND TOURISM

The only natural population of the Lakeside Daisy in the United States grows on the Marblehead Peninsula in Ottawa County. In 1988, the Lakeside Daisy was listed as a federally threatened species. In early to mid-May, its bright yellow flowers adorn the otherwise bleak landscape of the Marblehead quarry.

75

Greek Roasted Potato Salad

6 medium white potatoes
½ cup lemon juice plus 2
  tablespoons, divided
¼ cup water
5 tablespoons olive oil, divided
2 medium garlic cloves, minced
1 teaspoon oregano
½ teaspoon salt
Pepper to taste

3 medium plum tomatoes, cut in
  small cubes
4 green onions, finely chopped
1 small cucumber, peeled, cut
  into cubes
2 teaspoons Dijon mustard
½ cup chopped fresh parsley
½ cup feta cheese

Cut potatoes into cubes in large bowl with ½ cup lemon juice, water, and 1 tablespoon olive oil, garlic, oregano, salt, and pepper. Transfer to greased baking dish and bake at 400° for 35–40 minutes or until potatoes are tender. Stir twice while baking, then cool. Combine cooled potatoes with tomatoes, green onions, and cucumber. Mix together the mustard, remaining 2 tablespoons lemon juice, and remaining 4 tablespoons olive oil. Toss into salad. Add parsley and feta cheese. Serve at room temperature.

A Festival of Recipes

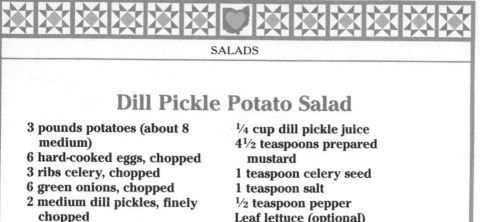

Dill Pickle Potato Salad

3 pounds potatoes (about 8
  medium)
6 hard-cooked eggs, chopped
3 ribs celery, chopped
6 green onions, chopped
2 medium dill pickles, finely
  chopped
1½ cups mayonnaise

¼ cup dill pickle juice
4½ teaspoons prepared
  mustard
1 teaspoon celery seed
1 teaspoon salt
½ teaspoon pepper
Leaf lettuce (optional)

Place potatoes in a Dutch oven or large kettle and cover with water. Bring to a boil. Reduce heat, cover, and simmer for 20–30 minutes or until tender; drain and cool. Peel and cube potatoes. Place in a large bowl; add eggs, celery, onions, and pickles.

In a small bowl, combine mayonnaise, pickle juice, mustard, celery seed, salt, and pepper. Pour over potato mixture; mix well. Cover and refrigerate for at least 4 hours. Serve in a lettuce-lined bowl, if desired. Yields 8–10 servings.

Columbus Colony Creations

Copper Penny Carrots

2 packages carrots (about 2
  quarts), cleaned, sliced
1 small onion, chopped
1 small green bell pepper,
  chopped (optional)
Salt and pepper to taste

1 (10¾-ounce) can tomato soup
½ cup oil
1 teaspoon mustard
1 cup sugar
¼ cup white vinegar

Cook carrots until partially done; drain. Add onion and green pepper. Add salt and pepper to taste. Mix remaining ingredients and pour over carrots; mix well. Chill 24 hours before serving.

Country Collections Cookbook II

Asparagus, Spinach, Pasta, and Cashew Salad

A one-dish salad perfect for summer guests.

DRESSING:

½ cup olive oil
1 cup sliced green onions
6 tablespoons rice wine vinegar

2 tablespoons soy sauce
1 teaspoon sesame oil

Combine all ingredients in a blender or food processor until smooth. Chill.

SALAD:

1 pound dry bow-tie pasta
1 tablespoon olive oil
1 pound asparagus
1 cup cherry or grape tomatoes, halved
6 ounces baby spinach, cleaned, stemmed
Salt and freshly ground black pepper to taste

Dried red pepper flakes to taste
1 cup cashew pieces, roasted, salted
1½ pounds boneless, skinless chicken breasts, grilled, sliced on the diagonal

Cook pasta according to package directions; drain and rinse. Add olive oil and stir with a wooden spoon. Cool. Blanch asparagus for about 3 minutes, or until crisp-tender. Diagonally slice into 1-inch pieces. Reserve some asparagus tops for garnish.

Pour Dressing over pasta and toss lightly. Add asparagus, tomatoes, and spinach. Toss; season with salt, pepper, and pepper flakes. Place Salad on individual dinner plates and sprinkle with cashews. Arrange chicken on top of salad. Garnish with reserved asparagus tops. Serve at room temperature. Yields 6–8 servings.

Note: Chicken may be grilled and refrigerated 1 day ahead. Dressing may also be prepared and refrigerated 1 day ahead. Buying grilled chicken breasts from the deli saves time.

Causing a Stir

Spinach Salad

SALAD DRESSING:

½ cup vegetable oil
¼ cup sugar
¼ cup chili sauce
1 small onion, minced
2 tablespoons red wine vinegar

½ teaspoon salt
½ teaspoon dry mustard
½ teaspoon Worcestershire
¼ teaspoon red pepper

Combine ingredients and mix well in jar; refrigerate for 24 hours.

SALAD:

1 pound fresh spinach, torn
⅔ cup torn lettuce

4 hard-cooked eggs
¾ cup cooked crumbled bacon

Combine ingredients in individual salad plates; pour Dressing on top.

Entertaining Made Easy

Deviled Eggs

6 hard-cooked eggs
¼ teaspoon salt
1 teaspoon mustard
1 teaspoon vinegar

Dash of pepper
Lettuce leaves
Paprika

Peel and split eggs lengthwise; remove yolks and mash. Add remaining ingredients and mix well. If not moist enough, add a little cream. Place in hole in egg whites. Place egg halves on lettuce leaves and sprinkle with paprika.

Ohio State Grange Cookbook (Gold)

Taco Salad

1 pound ground beef
1 package taco seasoning mix
½ cup water
1 head lettuce, chopped
2 tomatoes, diced
1 small onion, diced
1 pound Colby cheese, grated
1 small bag Doritos, crushed

1 (15-ounce) can kidney beans
  (optional)
1 cup oil
½ cup ketchup
¼ cup vinegar
¾ cup sugar
1 tablespoon Worcestershire

Brown and drain ground beef. Add taco mix and water to ground beef; simmer until thick. Cool. In large bowl, layer lettuce, tomatoes, onion, cheese, crushed Doritos, and ground beef. Drain and rinse kidney beans; add to salad. Mix remaining ingredients and pour over salad just before serving.

Tasteful Treasures Cookbook

Taco Dip Salad

1 (8-ounce) package cream
  cheese, softened
1 (16-ounce) container cottage
  cheese
1 (10-ounce) bottle salsa
  (medium)
1 (8-ounce) bottle taco sauce

1 green bell pepper, chopped
1 onion, chopped
½ head lettuce, chopped
1 (8-ounce) package shredded
  Cheddar cheese
2 tomatoes, chopped
Doritos

Mix cream cheese and cottage cheese together. Spread on platter. Mix together salsa and taco sauce and spread over cheese mixture. Sprinkle chopped pepper and onion over salsa mixture. Scatter lettuce on next. Sprinkle shredded cheese, then top with chopped tomatoes. Serve with Doritos.

Carroll County Humane Society Members & Friends
Cookbook Volume I

Taco Salad and Dressing

1 pound hamburger
1 package taco seasoning
1 head lettuce, chopped
1 (8-ounce) package shredded
   Cheddar cheese

1 (14-ounce) can kidney beans
1 large onion, chopped
4 medium tomatoes, diced
1 package taco chips, smashed

Brown meat and drain fat. Add taco seasoning to meat. In a large salad bowl, layer ingredients, except for the taco chips. Refrigerate one hour.

DRESSING:

1 (16-ounce) bottle Thousand
   Island Dressing
2 tablespoons taco seasoning

⅔ cup sugar
2 tablespoons taco sauce

Combine ingredients. Pour over taco salad, add taco chips, mix, and serve.

Feeding the Flock—First Church of God

The first vacuum cleaner was invented by a Canton department store janitor named James Murray Spangler, who devised a vacuum cleaner using a soap box, electric motor, broom handle, and pillow case in 1907. Spangler suffered from asthma attacks, and he suspected the carpet sweeper he was using at work was the cause of his ailment. Spangler then gave one of the vacuums to a friend, Susan Hoover, who used it at her home. Impressed with the machine, she told her husband W. H. Hoover about it. Hoover bought the patent from Spangler in 1908 and retained Spangler as a partner in the new vacuum cleaner business. Hoover's business flourished, and in 1926, Hoover invented the "beater bar," a rotating brush and metal bar mechanism at the bottom of the vacuum to loosen dirt trapped in carpets. Ten years later, in 1936, Hoover got another patent—this time for a new self-propelling mechanism for vacuum cleaners. In the UK, the term "hoover" has long been colloquially synonymous with vacuum cleaner, owing to the Hoover Company's dominance there in the first half of the 20th century. Over the years, Hoover diversified into other product lines, including kitchen appliances, hair dryers, and industrial equipment.

Wild Rice & Turkey Salad

5 cups water
⅓ cup tamari
1 cup wild rice, cleaned
¾ cup brown rice
4 tablespoons butter or oil
1 pound turkey breast slices

4 scallions, thinly sliced
½ medium red bell pepper,
 julienned
¼ cup slivered almonds
Leaf lettuce

Combine water and tamari in medium saucepan. Bring to a boil. Add wild rice. Reduce heat, cover, and simmer 10–15 minutes. Add brown rice. Cook an additional 30 minutes or until rice is tender.

Meanwhile, cook turkey in butter or oil until no longer pink. Cut into ½-inch cubes. Combine prepared scallions, pepper, turkey, and rice in large bowl. Stir to combine.

DRESSING:
6 tablespoons balsamic vinegar
4 tablespoons safflower oil

2 cloves garlic, minced
2 thin slices gingerroot, minced

In small container with tight-fitting lid, combine vinegar, oil, garlic, and gingerroot. Shake to blend. Pour over rice mixture. Sprinkle sliced almonds over salad; stir to combine. Serve over leaf lettuce at room temperature. Serves 6–8.

A Treasury of Recipes for Mind, Body & Soul

Asparagus, Spinach & Turkey Salad

1 pound turkey breast, thick
  sliced
Olive oil
1–1½ pounds fresh asparagus

2 bunches spinach
4 hard-cooked eggs, chopped
2 green onions, chopped

Saute* turkey slices in oil and cut into cubes. Steam asparagus, then cut diagonally into 1-inch pieces. Wash and stem spinach and coarsely chop. When ready to serve, toss all salad ingredients together in a bowl. Pour Mustard Dressing over salad and serve immediately. Serves 8.

MUSTARD DRESSING:

½ cup Dijon mustard
6 tablespoons water

¾ cup oil
¼ cup red wine vinegar

Place mustard in a bowl, gradually whisking in the water until it is thoroughly blended. Slowly beat in oil. Add vinegar and whisk until well combined.

A Treasury of Recipes for Mind, Body & Soul

Mary's Hot Chicken Salad

SALAD:

2 cups bite-size cooked chicken
½ cup toasted almonds
1 (8-ounce) can sliced water
  chestnuts
1 (2-ounce) jar pimientos
1 cup chopped celery

1 tablespoon chopped onion
1 teaspoon salt
⅛ teaspoon pepper
3 tablespoons lemon juice
1 cup mayonnaise
½ cup sour cream

Combine all ingredients well; place in casserole dish. Add Topping. Cover and bake at 350° for 30 minutes. Uncover and bake another 10 minutes.

TOPPING:

¾ cup grated Cheddar cheese

½ cup French fried onion rings

Rose Hill Recipes

Berried Treasure Chicken Salad

½ (16-ounce) package torn
mixed greens (6 cups)
8 ounces sliced, fully cooked
chicken breast
2 cups mixed fresh berries
(sliced strawberries,
blueberries, raspberries,
or blackberries)
2 oranges, peeled, sliced, cut
into quarters

1 (8-ounce) container mixed berry
or strawberry yogurt
½ cup mayonnaise or salad
dressing
Dash of ground cinnamon
Orange juice (optional)
½ cup broken walnuts or pecans
(optional)

Place mixed greens in a large bowl. Stack chicken slices; halve the stack lengthwise. Cut crosswise into ¼-inch strips; add chicken strips to lettuce in bowl. Add fresh berries and orange pieces.

Stir together yogurt, mayonnaise or salad dressing, and cinnamon in a small bowl. If necessary, add orange juice, 1 teaspoon at a time, to make a drizzling consistency. Spoon salad onto 4 dinner plates; drizzle with dressing. If desired, sprinkle with walnuts or pecans.

Franklin County 4-H Favorites

Born in Wapakoneta on August 5, 1930, Neil Alden Armstrong is best known as the first human to set foot on the moon. He was mission commander of the *Apollo 11* moon landing mission on July 20, 1969. Armstrong and Buzz Aldrin descended to the moon's surface in the lunar module *Eagle* ("The *Eagle* has landed."), while Collins orbited above in the command module *Columbia*. Armstrong's first words after touching the moon's surface were, "That's one small step for man, one giant leap for mankind." The Neil Armstrong Air & Space Museum in Wapakoneta tells the entire thrilling saga through models, real aircraft, photos, film footage, and eerie radio transmissions.

Famous Ohioans

A Sampling of Famous People from Ohio

SPORTS / ENTERTAINMENT

Halle Berry (Cleveland)

Erma Bombeck (Dayton)

Drew Carey (Cleveland)

Dorothy Dandridge (Cleveland)

Doris Day (Cincinnati)

Phyllis Diller (Lima)

Phil Donahue (Clevland)

Hugh Downs (Akron)

Bob Evans (Gallipolis)

Jamie Farr (Toledo)

Clark Gable (Cadiz)

Lillian Gish (Springfield)

Woody Hayes (Clifton)

John Heisman (Cleveland)

Hal Holbrook (Cleveland)

Paul Lynde (Mount Vernon)

Dean Martin (Steubenville)

Burgess Meredith (Cleveland)

Paul Newman (Cleveland)

Jack Nicklaus (Columbus)

Annie Oakley (Darke County)

Sarah Jessica Parker (Nelsonville)

Johnny Paycheck (Greenfield)

Tyrone Power (Cincinnati)

Roy Rogers (Cincinnati)

Pete Rose (Cincinnati)

Steven Spielberg (Cincinnati)

Ted Turner (Cincinnati)

Nancy Wilson (Chillicothe)

Cy Young (Gilmore)

POLITICAL / HISTORICAL / LITERARY

Neil Armstrong (Wapakoneta)

Louis Bromfield (Mansfield)

George Armstrong Custer
(New Rumley)

Clarence Darrow (Kingsman)

Thomas Edison (Milan)

James A. Garfield
(Cuyahoga County)

John Glenn (Cambridge)

Ulysses S. Grant (Point Pleasant)

Zane Grey (Zanesville)

Warren G. Harding (Morrow County)

Gregory Harbaugh (Cleveland)

Benjamin Harrison (North Bend)

Rutherford B. Hayes (Delaware)

Charles Kettering (Loudonville)

Lowell Thomas (Woodington)

William McKinley (Niles)

Toni Morrison (Lorain)

Norman Vincent Peale (Bowersville)

Judith Resnick (Akron)

Eddie Rickenbacker (Columbus)

Arthur Schlesinger (Columbus)

William Sherman (Lancaster)

Gloria Steinem (Toledo)

William H. Taft (Cincinnati)

James Thurber (Columbus)

Orville and Wilbur Wright (Dayton)

Cilantro Cole Slaw

The most beautiful cole slaw you've ever seen.

DRESSING:

½ cup canola oil
4 cloves garlic, minced
¼ bunch fresh cilantro,
    finely chopped

Juice of 3 limes
Salt to taste

Mix oil, garlic, cilantro, lime juice, and salt. Blend thoroughly; set aside.

SALAD:

2 large Granny Smith apples,
    julienned
1 large red bell pepper,
    julienned
1 large green bell pepper,
    julienned
1 large yellow bell pepper,
    julienned

1 small head green cabbage,
    julienned
1 small head red cabbage,
    julienned
1 cup fresh cilantro leaves
1 cup lightly crushed blue
    or yellow corn tortilla chips
    for garnish

Combine apples, bell peppers, cabbage, and cilantro leaves in a salad bowl. Mix well. Pour Dressing over Salad; toss well. Garnish with tortilla chips and serve immediately. Yields 18 servings.

Note: This recipe makes lots of slaw; you may want to halve the recipe.

Causing a Stir

 The card game UNO was invented by Merle Robbins in 1971 and sold at his barbershop in Reading.

Oriental Salad

1 package slaw mix
3–4 green onions, chopped
1 package chicken-flavored
  ramen noodles

¼ cup sunflower seeds
½ cup slivered (blanched)
  almonds

Combine slaw, onions, and noodles in large bowl. Broil sunflower seeds and almonds until lightly toasted. Add to slaw.

DRESSING:
¼ cup cider vinegar
½ cup oil
½ cup sugar

Seasoning packet from ramen
  noodles
Salt and pepper to taste

Combine vinegar, oil, sugar, seasoning, and salt and pepper; mix well. Pour over slaw mixture and stir to coat.

Columbus Colony Creations

Cabbage and Carrot Salad

1 (3-ounce) package lemon
  gelatin
1 pint hot water
2 tablespoons vinegar
1 teaspoon salt

1 cup grated carrots
1 cup shredded cabbage
1 cup chopped celery (optional)
Lettuce leaves
Mayonnaise for garnish

Dissolve gelatin in hot water; add vinegar and salt. Chill. Fold in carrots, cabbage, and celery, if desired. Turn into individual molds. Chill until firm. Unmold onto crisp lettuce leaves; garnish with mayonnaise. Serves 8.

Ohio State Grange Cookbook (Gold)

Roasted Beet Salad

Roasting beets takes advantage of their naturally high sugar content and creates a rich, caramelized flavor that makes this salad special. Even people who think they don't like beets, love roasted beets.

4 large raw beets
2 tablespoons olive oil, divided
¾ teaspoon salt, divided
1 tablespoon balsamic vinegar
¼ cup chopped fresh basil

¼ cup chopped fresh parsley
⅛ teaspoon black pepper
2 ounces feta or goat cheese,
  crumbled

Peheat oven to 400°. Cut leaves off the top of beets. Scrub beets with vegetable brush. Place beets on a piece of aluminum foil; drizzle with 1 tablespoon olive oil and ½ teaspoon salt. Roll beets around to be sure beets have a light coating of oil and salt. Wrap with foil; bake in 400° oven for 30 minutes. Allow beets to cool, then remove skin.

Cut beets into ½- to 1-inch chunks. Place in large bowl. Add remaining 1 tablespoon oil, baslamic vinegar, basil, parsley, remaining ¼ teaspoon salt, and black pepper; mix. Add crumbled cheese; stir gently. Chill at least 30 minutes before serving. Makes 6 (¾-cup) servings.

Nutritional analysis: Cal 117; Prot 4gm; Carbo 7gm; Dietary Fiber 2gm; Fat 8gm; Sat. Fat 3gm; Choles 10mg; Sod 283mg.

More Nutritious Still Delicious

Cauliflower Relish Salad

1 (15-ounce) can white kernel
corn, drained
1 (10-ounce) package frozen
Italian beans, cooked
1 (10-ounce) package frozen
lima beans, cooked
½ cup chopped green pepper

½ cup diced onion (optional)
1 cup diced celery
½ cup chopped pimentos
3 cups bite-size cauliflower
1 (10-ounce) package frozen peas,
cooked

Blend in large bowl all ingredients except peas.

DRESSING:
¾ cup sugar
¾ cup salad vinegar

Dash of pepper
½ cup oil

Bring to a boil. Pour over vegetables, except peas. Marinate several hours, stirring occasionally. Add peas 1 hour before serving.

The "Friends" Cookbook

Cranberry Salad

1 (12-ounce) package
cranberries
1 apple, peeled
1 orange, peeled
¾ cup sugar
1 (8-ounce) can crushed
pineapple, with juice

½ cup chopped pecans
2 (3-ounce) packages raspberry
Jell-O
1½ cups hot water

Coarsely grind cranberries, apple, and orange. Add sugar and mix well. Add pineapple and nuts. Dissolve Jell-O in hot water. Add to cranberry mixture. Refrigerate.

Don't Forget the INNgredients!

Golden Fruit Salad

2 large Golden Delicious apples, cored, diced
2 large Red Delicious apples, cored, diced
4 large bananas, sliced
2 (20-ounce) cans pineapple chunks, drained (reserve juice)
2 (16-ounce) cans Mandarin oranges, drained
2 cups whole green grapes
1 cup sugar
4 tablespoons cornstarch
2 tablespoons lemon juice
⅔ cup orange juice

Mix all fruit in a large bowl. Mix together sugar, cornstarch, reserved pineapple juice, lemon juice, and orange juice in a saucepan. Bring to a boil and boil for 1 minute. Pour hot mixture over fruit and leave uncovered until cool.

Cooking Up a Cure

Grape Salad

1 (8-ounce) package cream cheese, softened
1 (8-ounce) carton sour cream
½ cup white sugar
1 tablespoon vanilla
1½–2 pounds each: red and white seedless grapes
½ cup brown sugar
½ cup chopped pecans or walnuts

Mix softened cream cheese, sour cream, white sugar, and vanilla; fold in grapes. Sprinkle with brown sugar and chopped pecans or walnuts. Refrigerate for several hours.

Asthma Walk Cook Book

James J. Ritty of Dayton invented the cash register in 1879. Ritty was a barkeeper who opened his first saloon in 1871. He came up with the idea to prevent employees from stealing.

Apple Salad

DRESSING:

1 cup sugar
4 tablespoons flour
2 tablespoons butter

⅛ teaspoon salt
2 eggs, beaten
Juice from pineapple

In a saucepan, combine sugar, flour, butter, salt, eggs, and pineapple juice; cook until thick; cool.

SALAD:

4–6 apples, peeled, diced
Juice from 1 lemon
1 (15-ounce) can pineapple
  tidbits, reserve juice for
  Dressing

1 cup white or red grapes
1 cup chopped celery
1 cup mini marshmallows
1 cup Cool Whip
1 cup chopped nuts

In large bowl, combine fruits and marshmallows. Pour Dressing over mixture. When ready to serve, add Cool Whip and nuts.

Ohio State Grange Cookbook (Blue)

Caramel Apple Salad

1 (8-ounce) can crushed
  pineapple
1 tablespoon flour
1 cup sugar
1 tablespoon cider vinegar
3 large Granny Smith apples,
  cored, cut into bite-size pieces

2 large Snickers bars, cut in
  bite-size pieces
1 (16-ounce) container Cool
  Whip
1 cup chopped dry roasted
  peanuts

In saucepan, combine pineapple, flour, sugar, and vinegar. Boil for 5 minutes; cool completely. Mix cooled mixture with apples, Snickers, Cool Whip, and peanuts. Serves 6–8.

Tasteful Treasures Cookbook

"Stick 'Em Up" Salad

1 cup regular 7-UP
2½ cups mini marshmallows
1 (3-ounce) package lime Jell-O
2 (3-ounce) packages cream
   cheese, softened

1 (20-ounce) can crushed
   pineapple, undrained
¾ cup chopped walnuts
2 cups Cool Whip

Combine 7-UP and marshmallows in double boiler. Heat on low until melted. Add Jell-O (dry). Add this hot mixture to cream cheese. Beat until smooth. Add pineapple and walnuts. Chill until partially set. Fold in Cool Whip. Pour into oiled 9x13-inch glass pan. Refrigerate until firm.

Favorite Recipes from the Delaware Police Department

Spinach Chutney

Very different and tasty.

¼ cup white wine vinegar
¼ cup vegetable oil
2 heaping tablespoons chutney
2 teaspoons sugar
½ teaspoon salt
2 teaspoons curry powder
1 teaspoon dry mustard
1 pound fresh spinach, torn into
   bite-size pieces

1½ cups chopped unpared apples
½ cup light raisins
¾ cup almondized peanuts, such
   as Jump's
3 tablespoons sliced green
   onions

In a blender or food processor, combine vinegar, oil, chutney, sugar, salt, curry powder, and mustard; blend well. Cover and chill well before serving. Combine remaining ingredients in a large salad bowl; shake dressing well and toss with salad. Yields 6–8 servings.

Discover Dayton

Spiced Cranberry Sauce

The cranberry plant is an evergreen that is native to North America. The color of this cranberry sauce is gorgeous. This would be great served warm over ice cream.

2 cups sugar
2 teaspoons ground allspice
2 cups water

2 (12-ounce) bags fresh or frozen
cranberries

Heat sugar, allspice, water, and cranberries in a nonstick medium-size saucepan over medium heat until mixture comes to a low boil. Reduce heat, cover, and cook at a low boil 10 minutes, stirring occasionally. Cool completely before refrigerating. Serve chilled. Yields 20 (¼-cup) servings.

Nutritional analysis: Cal 94 (0% fat); Fat 0gm; Choles 0mg; Carbo 24gm; Dietary Fiber 2gm; Prot 0gm; Sod 1mg; Diabetic Exchanges 1½ other carbo.

Busy People's Fun, Fast, Festive Christmas Cookbook

Poppyseed Salad Dressing

Once sold at Findlay Market, bulk poppyseeds, a staple of European cooking, are now available at the Cincinnati Food Co-op on Hamilton Avenue in Northside. The diversified storefront has every intention of reserving a place for itself in this city's history.

½ cup vinegar
½ cup honey
1 cup oil
1 tablespoon chopped onion

1 teaspoon lemon juice
1 teaspoon dry mustard
2 tablespoons poppyseeds
Salt to taste

Place in the blender in the order given and process about one minute. Yields 2 cups.

Note: This dressing is exquisite on spinach salad.

Cincinnati Recipe Treasury

Celery Seed Dressing

This dressing always ties with French as our most popular dressing. It is also by far the easiest to make, and is one of the best all-purpose dressings—great on BLTs, chicken salad, seven-layer salad, and others.

This is our original version, an all-purpose dressing from Darryl's grandmother, Nettie. You must make it ahead of time so that the sugar dissolves in the dressing.

1⅓ cups mayonnaise	**⅓ cup cider vinegar**
1 cup sugar	**1 teaspoon celery seeds**

Blend all ingredients well.

VERSION 2:
The version below has more depth of flavor due to the honey, and you don't have to wait for the sugar to dissolve.

1⅓ cups mayonnaise	**1 teaspoon celery seeds**
⅔ cup honey	**1 teaspoon celery salt**
⅓ cup cider vinegar	**1 teaspoon kosher salt**

Blend all ingredients well. For best flavor, put the dressing on salad right before serving. Yields 6–8 servings.

A Taste of the Murphin Ridge Inn

Vegetables

The Circleville Pumpkin Show is America's sixth largest festival with an annual attendance of over 300,000. Begun in 1903, it has been dubbed the "greatest free show on earth." Each year approximately 23,000 pumpkin pies and over 100,000 pumkins are sold during the show.

Terry's Beans

1 pound fresh pork sausage, or
  1 pound lean hamburger, or
  ½ of each
1 large white onion, diced
2 (15-ounce) cans baked beans
2 (15-ounce) cans lima beans

2 (15-ounce) cans butter beans
1 tablespoon dry mustard
2 cups ketchup
2 cups dark brown sugar
4 ounces sherry
4 ounces liquid hickory smoke

Brown meat with diced onion in skillet. Mix meat with remaining ingredients in crockpot. Cook on LOW for 8 hours.

Country Collections Cookbook II

"Code 8" Crazy Beans

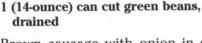

1 pound Bob Evans or Jimmy
  Dean spicy sausage
1 small onion, chopped
1 (31-ounce) can baked beans
1 (14-ounce) can lima beans,
  drained
1 (14-ounce) can cut green beans,
  drained

1 (14-ounce) can cut waxed beans,
  drained
1 (10-ounce) can tomato soup
1 (6-ounce) can tomato paste
1 cup brown sugar

Brown sausage with onion in skillet. Place in greased 3-quart casserole dish, then add remaining ingredients; mix well. Bake in 375° oven for 1 hour.

Note: You may cook in slow cooker for 4 hours on HIGH. May substitute ground beef for sausage.

Favorite Recipes from the Delaware Police Department

One of America's funniest-named intersections is located in West Chester— the intersection of Grinn and Barrett.

Baked Beans with Garlic

1 (29-ounce) can Bush's
  Homestyle Baked Beans
2 (15-ounce) cans pork and
  beans
1 medium onion, chopped
½ heaping teaspoon minced
  garlic
½ cup ketchup
½ cup brown sugar

Use a 3-quart crockpot. Open beans and drain as much liquid off as possible. Put beans, onion, garlic, ketchup, and brown sugar in crockpot and cook on HIGH for about 3 hours. Turn down to LOW for an additional hour. Caution: keep an eye on the liquid; don't let it go dry. Add a little water only if they look dry. Yields 15–20 servings.

Favorite Recipes–First Church of God

Calico Beans

1–1½ pounds ground beef
1 medium onion, diced
½ pound bacon slices, cut in
  pieces
½ cup ketchup
2 tablespoons vinegar
½ cup packed brown sugar
½ teaspoon dry minced garlic
1 (28-ounce) can Bush's Original
  Baked Beans
1 (15.5-ounce) can pinto beans
1 (15.5-ounce) can Great Northern
  beans
1 (15-ounce) can butter beans
1 (15-ounce) can kidney beans
1 (15-ounce) can navy beans
1 (15-ounce) can black-eyed peas
  (optional)
1 (7-ounce) can diced green chiles
  (optional)

Brown ground beef, onion, and bacon; drain fat. In a small bowl, mix ketchup, vinegar, and brown sugar until smooth. Add to meat and onion mixture. Stir in garlic; mix well. Stir in all beans, peas, and chiles. Pour into large, deep, greased baking dish. Bake at 350° for 1 hour.

A Taste of Faith

Trucker Beans

1 pound ground beef
½ cup water
1 envelope onion soup mix
2 (16-ounce) cans pork and
  beans, undrained
1 (15-ounce) can butter or lima
  beans, drained

1 (15-ounce) can kidney beans,
  undrained
1 pound kielbasa sausage, cut up
1 tablespoon brown sugar
1 teaspoon dry mustard
1 (8-ounce) can tomato sauce

Brown meat in water until no longer pink. Do not drain. Pour into large greased casserole dish. Swirl to cover dish. Combine remaining ingredients and pour into casserole dish. Bake at 350° for 1½ hours.

Carroll County Humane Society Members & Friends
Cookbook Volume II

Green Beans Italiano

I got this idea from Kenny Roger's Restaurant. I'm not sure what he has in his recipe, but this is a pretty close match and just as good. And I can almost bet that mine is a lot less fattening. These beans are popular primarily with adults.

2 medium onions, thinly sliced
  (about 1½ cups)
¾ cup fat-free Italian dressing
1 (14½-ounce) can diced
  tomatoes, drained

2 (16-ounce) bags frozen green
  beans
½ tablespoon lite salt (optional)

In a large nonstick skillet, approximately 12 inches in diameter, sauté onions in salad dressing over medium heat until tender, about 2–3 minutes. Add tomatoes and green beans. Increase heat to medium high. Stir until well coated. Salt, if desired. Cover and cook 5–7 minutes until beans are tender. Serve hot. Yields 12 (⅔-cup) servings.

Nutritional analysis: Cal 44 (0% fat); Fat 9gm; Choles 0mg; Carbo 10gm; Dietary Fiber 3gm; Prot 3gm; Sod 256mg.

Busy People's Low-Fat Cookbook

Vegetable Tourlou

1 eggplant, sliced
½ pound green beans
3 zucchini squash, sliced in
   rounds
7 stalks celery, sliced
6 carrots, sliced
3 onions, sliced

1 (16-ounce) can tomato sauce
¾ cup vegetable oil
1 teaspoon salt
1 clove garlic, chopped
Fresh parsley
Pepper to taste

Slice eggplant; let sit in a little salted water for 20 minutes. Pat dry and place in baking pan; broil each slice slightly on both sides. Combine all ingredients and place in 9x13x2-inch baking pan. Bake, covered, at 400° for 45 minutes. Uncover pan and bake an additional 45 minutes at 375°. Serves 8–10.

A Festival of Recipes

Mushroom Casserole

1½ pounds sliced mushrooms
4 tablespoons butter
½ cup diced celery
½ cup diced green bell pepper
½ cup diced onion
½ cup mayonnaise
6 slices Pepperidge Farm bread,
   cubed

1 (10¾-ounce) can cream of
   mushroom soup
3 eggs
¾ teaspoon salt
¾ teaspoon pepper
½ cup fine bread crumbs for
   topping
1 cup grated Cheddar cheese

Sauté mushrooms in butter; add diced veggies and sauté. Drain well. Mix mayonnaise, bread cubes (must be Pepperidge Farm), and soup. Mix with veggies and pour into buttered 2-quart casserole.

Combine eggs, salt, and pepper; pour over top of mixture in casserole. Refrigerate overnight. Yes! Overnight with the egg mixture on it.

Before putting into oven, top with bread crumbs. Bake at 350° for 1 hour. The last 10 minutes, top with cheese.

A Taste of Faith

Hungarian Stuffed Cabbage

1 large firm head cabbage
Boiling water to cover
1½ pounds sauerkraut
Bacon slices
1 cup tomato purée, or 2 cups
   tomato juice
Water

Salt to taste
1 large onion, sliced
½ green bell pepper, cut up
8–10 peppercorns
2 bay leaves
2 tablespoons shortening
2 tablespoons flour

Cut out core from cabbage. Place in a deep pan and pour enough boiling water to cover completely. Let it stand for 10 minutes or until leaves soften a little, so cabbage rolling will be made easier. Then carefully loosen and remove leaves one by one. Cut out middle stem without cutting leaves through, and place leaves on top of each other. Remove only larger leaves that are big enough for stuffing. Cut the rest of cabbage into fine long thin shreds with a sharp knife; mix with sauerkraut and set aside.

STUFFING:

1½ pounds mixed ground
   beef and pork
¾ cup rice, well washed
1 onion, finely chopped

1 whole egg
Salt and pepper to taste
½ cup cold water

Mix ingredients thoroughly to a smooth consistency. Then place about 1 tablespoonful meat mixture on cabbage leaf; roll up snugly, shaping into a small 3- to 4-inch long, thin round roll. Tuck in edges securely to prevent rolls from falling apart during cooking.

Spread ½ of sauerkraut on bottom of a large deep kettle; place all stuffed cabbage neatly side by side, and top each with a slice of bacon. Then cover with the remaining half of sauerkraut. Add tomato purée or juice and enough water to cover stuffed cabbage completely. Season with salt to taste. Add sliced onion, green pepper, peppercorns, bay leaves, and more slices of bacon, if desired. Bring to a boil, then cover pan tightly and simmer very gently for about 1½ hours. Do not stir; just shake pan occasionally to mix. Keep adding hot water as needed during cooking to keep stuffed cabbage fully covered with liquid to the finish.

(continued)

(Hungarian Stuffed Cabbage continued)

Stuffed cabbage is so delicious with its own fine flavor that no extra thickening should be added to better its flavor. But if thickening is required, please, not too much. Make a roux in skillet with equal amounts of shortening and flour; when light yellow in color, dilute with liquid from stuffed cabbage, boil and stir until smooth. Blend gently into sauerkraut and just shake pan to mix thoroughly. Cook 5 more minutes and serve.

Aunt Paula's American Hungarian Cookbook

Beer Batter Onion Rings

1 cup all-purpose flour
1 cup beer, room temperature
2 teaspoons Old Bay Seasoning

2 Vidalia onions, sliced to form
   rings
Oil for deep-frying

Mix first 3 ingredients and let rest for 30 minutes. Soak sliced onions in ice water for 30 minutes. Drain onions and dry with paper towels. Heat oil to 365°. Dip onions in batter, letting excess drain off, and fry in batches without crowding for 3–4 minutes. Drain and salt.

Don't Forget the INNgredients!

Ermal C. Fraze of Kettering invented the pop-top can after a family picnic in 1959 when he found himself with a can of beer and no opener. In 1963, Fraze, founder of the Dayton Reliable Tool Co., obtained the patent for a removable pull-tab opener for cans.

Vegetarian Casserole

½ cup finely chopped celery
¼ cup finely chopped onion
3 tablespoons butter
½ pound mushrooms, sliced
2 cups chopped broccoli
1 cup chopped spinach
3 cups day-old whole-wheat
  bread, cubed into 1½-inch
  squares

1½ cups white Cheddar cheese
2 eggs
1½ cups milk
1 teaspoon dry mustard
Salt and pepper to taste
Basil or oregano (optional)

Sauté celery and onion in butter until tender. Add sliced mushrooms and sauté over medium heat until tender. Fill a buttered casserole dish with alternate layers of broccoli, spinach, bread squares, mushroom mixture, and grated cheese, beginning and ending with bread.

In another bowl, mix eggs, milk, mustard, salt, pepper, and seasoning to taste. Pour this mixture over top layer of bread. Bake in moderate 350° oven for 45 minutes, uncovered, until top is browned. Let stand 5 minutes before serving. Serves 4.

A Treasury of Recipes for Mind, Body & Soul

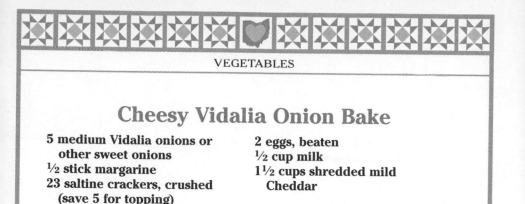

Cheesy Vidalia Onion Bake

5 medium Vidalia onions or
  other sweet onions
½ stick margarine
23 saltine crackers, crushed
  (save 5 for topping)
1 (10¾-ounce) can cream of
  mushroom soup, undiluted

2 eggs, beaten
½ cup milk
1½ cups shredded mild
  Cheddar

Grease a 2-quart casserole. Slice onions ¼ inch thick. In skillet, melt margarine over medium heat and sauté onions until clear and tender. Line dish with cracker crumbs, reserving 5 (about 3 tablespoons crumbs) for topping. Add onions and soup alternately until dish is full. Pour beaten eggs over, then milk over all. Cover top with shredded Cheddar and reserved cracker crumbs. Bake at 350° about 30 minutes until brown and bubbly. Serves 6.

Rose Hill Recipes

Caramelized Onions

2 tablespoons butter
1½ pounds onions, thinly
  sliced

1 teaspoon sugar

In large skillet, melt butter over medium heat. Add onions and sugar. Cook, stirring occasionally, until onions turn dark golden brown, about 30 minutes. Serve over grilled hamburgers, steak, or add to mashed potatoes.

Ohio Traditions with P. Buckley Moss

My Version of McDonald's Fries

2 large russet potatoes   Salt to taste
1 (48-ounce) can shortening

Peel potatoes, dry them, and slice using a mandoline or other slicer with a setting as close to ¼-inch square strips as you've got. If your fries are a little thicker than ¼ inch, the recipe will still work, but it won't be an exact clone, and you definitely don't want super thick steak fries here.

Rinse fries in a large bowl filled with around 8 cups cold water. The water should become milky. Dump water out and add another 8 cups cold water plus some ice and let fries sit for an hour. Spoon shortening into deep fryer and set it to 375°. On many fryers, this is the highest setting. Remove fries from water and spread them out to dry for 10–15 minutes. Don't let them sit much longer than this, or they will begin to turn brown. The oil should now be hot enough for blanching stage. Split up fries and add them in batches to oil for 1½ minutes at a time. Watch them carefully to be sure they don't begin to brown. If they start to brown on edges, take them out.

Remove fries to paper towels to drain and cool. When fries have cooled, put them into a resealable bag or covered container and freeze for 4–5 hours or until potatoes are completely frozen. As fries freeze, turn off fryer, but turn it back on and give it plenty of time to heat up before the final frying stage for your fries. Split up frozen fries and add one-half at a time to hot oil. Fry for 4½–6 minutes or until fries have become a golden brown color and are crispy on outside when cool. The second batch may take a tad longer than the first, since the oil may have cooled. Drain fries on paper towels and salt generously. Makes 4 servings.

Sharing the Best from Our Kitchen

Stone City Hash Browns

1 (2-pound) package frozen hash browns
¼ cup margarine, melted
¼ teaspoon pepper
½ cup chopped onion, or 1 teaspoon onion powder
1 (10¾-ounce) can cream of chicken soup
1 (16-ounce) carton sour cream
4 cups grated sharp Cheddar cheese

Mix all ingredients and put in 9x13-inch baking dish. Sprinkle Topping over and bake at 350° for 45–50 minutes.

TOPPING:

1½ cups crushed cornflakes, or 2 stacks Ritz Crackers
¼–½ cup margarine, melted

Combine ingredients; sprinkle over casserole.

Sharing Our Best

Lucy's Scalloped Potatoes

10 pounds potatoes
2 tablespoons flour
1 pound Velveeta cheese, divided
1 stick butter, divided
1 small onion, chopped, divided
3 cups milk
Salt and pepper to taste

Peel and slice potatoes. Create first layer using ⅓ of potatoes. Sprinkle flour over top. Add ⅓ of cheese, butter, onion, and milk. Season with salt and pepper. Add second layer of potatoes and ⅓ of cheese, butter, onion, and milk. Salt and pepper again. Add third layer of potatoes and remaining ingredients. Salt and pepper again. Bake, with lid on, 1½ hours at 350°. Yields 30–40 servings.

Mt. Zion Lutheran Church Cookbook

Patrician Potatoes

4 large potatoes
⅓ cup sour cream
1⅓ cups cottage cheese
1 tablespoon minced onion

1½ teaspoons salt
Pepper to taste
2 tablespoons butter, melted
¼ cup slivered almonds

Cook and mash potatoes, but do not add milk or cream. Mix first 6 ingredients together. Bake in greased glass baking dish at 350° for 30 minutes. Put melted butter and almonds on top and bake 10 more minutes. Serves 6.

Food, Glorious Food

Dan's Potatoes

Yukon Gold potatoes
Sliced onions
2 (16-ounce) cans chicken
broth, or more

Morton's Nature's Seasoning
Blend
Grated Parmesan cheese
1 stick butter

Peel as many potatoes as you wish, and slice only ¾ way through (do not cut all the way through) so they appear to fan out. Place potatoes in a Dutch oven that has been covered with a generous layer of sliced onions. Pour in several cans of chicken broth so that liquid covers ¾ the way up the potatoes. (Have extra cans of chicken broth handy in case broth cooks down and potatoes appear to be drying out.) Sprinkle potatoes with Morton's Seasoning Blend. Then sprinkle generously with freshly grated Parmesan cheese. Slice butter over potatoes and cook uncovered in oven for about 1½ hours at 400° until most of the broth evaporates. Be careful not to allow it to burn.

50 Years and Still Cookin'!

Whipped Mashed Potatoes

These are too light and creamy to be called mashed. There are small pieces of potato in each bite. No one will ever know you didn't have to peel potatoes. It seems like too many servings of potatoes, but they are so good you will want to have extra for second helpings.

2 (30-ounce) bags frozen fat-free shredded hash browns
2 (14.5-ounce) cans fat-free chicken broth
¼ cup imitation butter-flavored sprinkles
1 cup fat-free evaporated milk

In a large saucepan or Dutch oven, place hash browns and chicken broth. Cover and heat on high until it comes to a full boil. Remove pan from heat and let sit, covered, for 5 minutes. Drain potatoes and discard chicken broth. Place potatoes back into pan and stir in butter-flavored sprinkles and milk until well mixed.

In food processor, whip half of potato mixture at a time for 3–4 minutes and place into a large serving bowl. These may seem too runny, but they will thicken as they sit for a minute. Cover bowl with plastic wrap and wrap bowl in a large bath towel to keep warm until dinner is served. Yields 22 (½-cup) servings.

Nutritional analysis: Cal 74 (0% fat); Fat 0gm; Choles 0mg; Carbo 16gm; Dietary Fiber 1 gm; Prot 3gm; Sod 155mg; Diabetic Exchanges 1 starch.

Busy People's Fun, Fast, Festive Christmas Cookbook

Daniel D. Emmett, born in Mount Vernon in 1815, wrote "Old Dan Tucker" at age 15 and later penned "Turkey in the Straw." His best-known song is "Dixie," written in 1859 for a black minstrel show in which a freed slave sang of his birthplace.

Mashed Potatoes Deluxe

The perfect quickie substitute for those of you who like the traditional, high-fat twice-baked potatoes.

2 pounds red-skinned potatoes with skins on, washed, pierced with fork
1 (8-ounce) package fat-free cream cheese, softened
½ cup fat-free butter spread
1¼–1½ cups skim milk
3 teaspoons garlic salt (optional)

Microwave whole potatoes in carousel microwave for 12 minutes or until fully cooked. Using a fork and sharp knife, cut cooked potatoes into cubes, leaving skins on. Put potatoes, cream cheese, butter spread, skim milk, and garlic salt, if using, into a medium-size mixing bowl. Mix on medium speed approximately 2 minutes or until desired creamy consistency. Microwave entire bowl of potato mixture an additional 1–2 minutes to reheat before serving. Serve additional butter spread on side, if desired. Yields 8 servings.

Note: If you do not have a carousel microwave, turn potatoes a quarter turn every 3 minutes.

Nutritional analysis: Cal 135 (0% fat); Fat 0gm; Choles 6mg; Carbo 27gm; Dietary Fiber 2gm; Prot 8gm; Sod 235mg.

Busy People's Low-Fat Cookbook

Potato Casserole

1 (30-ounce) bag frozen hash
browns
1 (10¾-ounce) can cream of
celery soup
1 (10¾-ounce) can cream of
potato soup

½ cup sour cream
½ cup shredded Cheddar
cheese

Thaw potatoes until they can be broken up. Mix all soups and sour cream. Stir in potatoes. Place mixture in a 9x13-inch pan sprayed with nonstick spray. Top with cheese; bake, uncovered at 350° for 1 hour.

Carroll County Humane Society Members & Friends
Cookbook Volume II

Potatoes au Gratin

The best potato dish I have ever tasted—and better yet, the easiest to prepare! The rich cheesy taste is great for a buffet.

1½ pounds frozen hash brown
potatoes
½ pint half-and-half or milk
¼ pound butter

½ pound American processed
cheese spread
4 ounces grated sharp Cheddar
cheese (1 cup)

Arrange frozen hash brown potatoes in a greased 9x9-inch baking dish. Melt all remaining ingredients in a saucepan; pour over potatoes; stir gently to mix. Cover and refrigerate 1 hour or longer. Bake uncovered in preheated 350° oven for 1 hour. Yields 9–12 servings.

Discover Dayton

Greek Oven Potatoes with Lemon Juice

1 cup chicken or beef broth
½ cup olive oil (or vegetable oil)
½ cup freshly squeezed lemon juice
1 teaspoon salt
½ teaspoon pepper
2 tablespoons dried oregano
1 tablespoon garlic powder (optional)
1 teaspoon dried dill (optional)
6 or 7 white baking potatoes, peeled, cut into quarters, lengthwise

Combine all ingredients except potatoes in a large bowl, until well blended. Add potatoes and coat thoroughly in mixture. Arrange potatoes in a greased 9x13-inch pan and pour juice remaining in the bowl over top. Cover with aluminum foil. Bake in preheated 375° oven for 1 hour. Uncover and continue baking another 30 minutes, or until potatoes are cooked through. Serves 6–8.

A Festival of Recipes

Stuffed Sweet Potatoes

6 medium sweet potatoes
Vegetable oil
2 cups firmly packed brown sugar, divided
2 eggs
¼ cup milk
1 teaspoon vanilla
1 cup butter, divided
1 cup walnuts
⅓ cup all-purpose flour

Rub potatoes with oil. Bake at 400° for 1 hour. Let stand until cool enough to handle. Cut slice from top of each potato and carefully scoop out pulp, leaving shells intact. Mash pulp until smooth. Add 1 cup brown sugar, eggs, milk, vanilla, and ½ cup butter, mixing well. Spoon mixture into potato shells.

Combine remaining 1 cup brown sugar, walnuts, flour, and remaining ½ cup butter, mixing to form crumbs. Sprinkle on stuffed potatoes and place in baking dish. Bake at 350° for 20 minutes. Serves 6.

I'll Cook When Pigs Fly

Zucchini Casserole

1 (14½-ounce) can chopped
  tomatoes
1 (15-ounce) can corn
1 zucchini, diced
1 cup cubed sharp Cheddar
  cheese

1 (4-ounce) can chopped green
  chiles
1 clove garlic, minced
1 small onion, chopped
Salt and pepper to taste

Combine all ingredients; mix well. Bake in 350° oven for 1 hour.

Note: If possible, use all fresh vegetables.

Sharing the Best from Our Kitchen

French Fried Zucchini

¾ cup all-purpose flour
1 teaspoon salt
¼ teaspoon garlic powder
Pepper to taste
¾ cup water or beer

2 eggs, separated
2 tablespoons oil
3 medium zucchini
Oil for frying

In medium bowl, combine flour, salt, garlic powder, and pepper.
In small bowl, combine water or beer, yolks, and oil. Combine
with flour mixture. Cover with plastic wrap. Set aside for 45 minutes.

Cut zucchini into julienne strips; set aside. Beat egg whites
until stiff. Fold into batter. In deep fat fryer, heat 1-inch oil to
375°. Place zucchini into batter to coat. Put into hot oil. Fry to
golden brown. Drain on paper towels. Makes 4 servings. Can be
used for appetizer also.

Favorite Recipes Home-Style

The nation's only manufacturer of metal whistles is located in Columbus,
where employees whistle while they work at American Whistle Corporation.

Creamed Spinach

Popeye would have gone nuts over this smooth and creamy spinach.

2 tablespoons cornstarch
1 tablespoon sugar
1 envelope Butter Buds, or 1
   tablespoon Butter Buds
   Sprinkles
1 (5-ounce) can evaporated
   skim milk

2 (10-ounce) packages frozen
   chopped spinach, excess water
   squeezed out
1/3 cup grated fat-free Parmesan
   cheese

In a large nonstick skillet, dissolve cornstarch, sugar, and Butter Buds in milk. Turn heat to medium. Add spinach; stir constantly and bring to a boil. Sprinkle with Parmesan cheese. Reduce heat to low; cover; let simmer 10 minutes. Yields 7 servings.

Nutritional analysis: Cal 67 (0% fat); Fat 0gm; Choles 5mg; Carbo 12gm; Dietary Fiber 2gm; Prot 6gm; Sod 129mg.

Busy People's Low-Fat Cookbook

Baked Herbed Spinach

1/4 cup finely chopped onion
Minced garlic, to taste
1/2 stick butter or margarine
2 (10-ounce) packages frozen
   chopped spinach, thawed,
   well drained
1 cup milk or cream

1/4 cup grated Parmesan cheese,
   plus additional 1/8–1/4 cup
   for topping
1/4 cup dry bread crumbs
1/2 cup crumbled marjoram
1/2 teaspoon salt
Pepper to taste

Sauté onion and garlic in butter or margarine. Add remaining ingredients; mix well. Place in greased 8x8-inch baking dish. Sprinkle top with additional Parmesan cheese. Bake in 350° oven for 30 minutes or until cheese on top is brown.

Sharing Our Best

Spring Asparagus

What a wonderful way to eat fresh asparagus.

1 tablespoon mustard
⅓ cup fat-free sour cream
⅛ teaspoon dried dill weed

2 pounds fresh asparagus,
steamed

Mix mustard, sour cream, and dill together until well blended. Toss gently with freshly steamed asparagus. Serve immediately. If needed, this dish can be microwaved for a few minutes to warm. Yields 6 servings.

Nutritional analysis: Cal 52 (0% fat); Fat 0gm; Choles 0mg; Carbo 24gm; Dietary Fiber 2gm; Prot 3gm; Sod 212mg.

Busy People's Low-Fat Cookbook

Asparagus with Vinaigrette Sauce

24–32 asparagus spears,
cleaned, scraped

Salt to taste

Place asparagus spears flat in skillet, cover with cold water, and add salt. Cover, bring to a boil, then simmer 1–3 minutes. Drain and chill.

VINAIGRETTE SAUCE:
1 tablespoon Dijon-style
mustard
2 tablespoons wine vinegar
Salt and ground pepper to taste

½ cup virgin olive oil
2 tablespoons chopped fresh
parsley

In small bowl, combine mustard, vinegar, salt and pepper. Whisk vigorously, gradually adding oil. Once blended, whisk in parsley. Arrange asparagus on serving platter and pour sauce over top, or serve on the side. Serve chilled. Yields 4–6 servings.

With Great Gusto

Asparagus Casserole

12 asparagus spears
2 tablespoons chopped onion
2 tablespoons chopped celery
3 tablespoons butter
2 tablespoons grated Parmesan
  cheese

¼ cup bread crumbs
½ teaspoon salt
⅛ teaspoon pepper

Layer spears, onion, and celery in a greased 8x8-inch baking dish. Melt butter and add cheese, bread crumbs, salt, and pepper. Spread over asparagus. Cover and bake at 375° for 45 minutes.

Feeding the Flock—First Church of God

Broccoli and Cauliflower Casserole

1 cup water
½ cup uncooked white rice
10 ounces broccoli florets
10 ounces cauiflower florets
½ cup butter
1 onion, chopped

1 pound processed cheese, cubed
1 (10¾-ounce) can condensed
  cream of chicken soup
5⅜ ounces milk
1½ cups crushed buttery round
  crackers

In a saucepan, bring water to a boil. Add rice and stir. Reduce heat, cover, and simmer for 20 minutes. Drain and set aside.

Steam broccoli and cauliflower florets in small amount of water for 10 minutes, or until crunchy. Preheat oven to 350°.

In a large saucepan, melt butter and sauté onion. Stir cauliflower, broccoli, and rice into saucepan. Once vegetables and rice are coated, stir in cheese, chicken soup, and milk. Transfer the entire mixture to a greased 9x13-inch baking dish and sprinkle crackers on top. Bake for 30 minutes.

Food for Thought

Spicy Carrots with Cumin Seeds

¼ cup olive oil
2 medium onions, coarsely
  chopped
1½ pounds carrots, peeled,
  cut into 1-inch pieces
1 teaspoon cumin seeds
¼ teaspoon hot Hungarian
  paprika

½ teaspoon sweet Hungarian
  paprika
2 teaspoons tomato paste
3 cloves garlic, unpeeled
Salt to taste
¼ cup beef broth or water, as
  needed

Heat oil in a large skillet over medium-high heat until a light haze forms about it. Add onions and sauté, stirring, until they begin to color, about 5 minutes. Add carrots and continue to sauté, stirring until onions and carrots are well colored, about 12 minutes. Reduce heat to low. Stir in cumin seeds, hot and sweet paprika, tomato paste, garlic, and salt. Add enough broth to barely cover vegetables. Simmer, covered, stirring occasionally, until carrots are tender and liquid has reduced, about 30 minutes. Remove and discard garlic. Serve dish at once. Serves 4–6.

Recipes and Remembrances: Around St. George's Tables

In 1883, Barney Kroger invested his life savings of $372 to open a grocery store in downtown Cincinnati. He was the first grocer to offer a bakery and to combine a meat market and grocery store under one roof. Today, Kroger is one of the nation's largest grocery retailers.

Baked Corn

2 eggs
1 tablespoon butter, melted
2 tablespoons flour
2 tablespoons sugar

1 cup milk
Salt and pepper to taste
1 (15-ounce) can cream-style
  corn

In mixing bowl, combine eggs, butter, flour, sugar, milk, and seasonings. Add corn and mix well. Pour into greased baking dish, and bake at 350° for 25–30 minutes.

Ohio State Grange Cookbook (Gold)

Havarti Tomato Pie

2 unbaked 9-inch pastry shells
¼ cup Dijon mustard
1 (8-ounce) package Havarti
  cheese with dill, sliced
4–6 tomatoes, sliced

⅓ cup olive oil
Garlic salt to taste
⅓ cup chopped fresh parsley
¼ cup chopped fresh dill

Partially bake pastry shells, using package directions, but reducing baking time by ½; pastry should be firm but not browned. Spread mustard in bottom of pastry shells; cover with cheese slices and add layers of tomato slices. Brush tomatoes with oil. Season with garlic salt and sprinkle with parsley and dill. Bake at 375° for 20–30 minutes. Serves 8–10.

I'll Cook When Pigs Fly

Pasta, Rice, Etc.

The Longaberger Company in Newark is a maker of handcrafted maple wood baskets. The company's corporate headquarters on State Route 16 is a local landmark and takes the shape of their biggest seller, the Medium Market Basket.

Unbelievable Lasagna

1 pound hamburger, cooked, drained
1 (26-ounce) jar spaghetti sauce
1 (6-ounce) can tomato paste
¾ teaspoon oregano
2 eggs, beaten
1 (16-ounce) container cottage cheese

1 teaspoon salt
⅛ teaspoon pepper
½ (8-ounce) package lasagna noodles
½ pound mozzarella cheese, shredded
1 cup grated Parmesan cheese

Combine meat, spaghetti sauce, tomato paste, and oregano in bowl, mixing well. In separate bowl, mix eggs, cottage cheese, salt, and pepper. Spread 1 cup sauce mixture in greased 9x13-inch baking pan. Arrange a layer of uncooked noodles over sauce. Layer small amount of sauce mixture, then ½ the cottage cheese mixture, and sprinkle with ½ the cheeses. Repeat layers. Top with final layer of noodles, sauce mixture, cottage cheese mixture, then cheeses, covering noodles completely. Bake at 350° for 45 minutes, or until brown and bubbly. Let stand 15 minutes.

Note: Additional spaghetti sauce may be used if too dry.

Cooking Along the Lincoln Highway in Ohio

Johnny Marzetti

Whether it's spelled Moussetti, Marziette, Mouzetti, Mousette, or Mousset, this dish is a basic guide for whipping up a quick casserole dinner from items you have on hand. Who is the infamous Johnny? No one seems to know, but he certainly got around.

2 cups chopped green bell
  peppers
1 cup chopped celery
2 cups chopped onions
1 pound ground beef
1 pound ground pork
¼ cup butter or margarine
2 teaspoons salt
½ cup chopped stuffed olives

1 (4-ounce) can sliced mushrooms,
  with liquid
1 (10½-ounce) can tomato soup
1 (8-ounce) can tomato sauce
1 (8-ounce) can tomato-mushroom
  sauce
1 pound broad noodles
2 cups grated American cheese

In a large skillet, sauté green peppers, celery, onions, and meats in hot butter. Add salt, reduce heat, and cook about 5 minutes. Stir in olives, mushrooms, and liquid, soup, and sauces. Cook another 5 minutes. Cook noodles according to package directions, undercooking them slightly. Drain. Turn noodles into a greased 10x14-inch roasting pan. Add meat mixture. Stir gently until well mixed. Sprinkle cheese on top. Bake 35 minutes at 350°. Yields 8 servings.

Cincinnati Recipe Treasury

Ohio's favorite inland vacation destination, Mohican Country is made up of five counties and includes the world's largest Amish settlement. It is also home to the Bridge to Yesteryear, which is located in the Mohican Wilderness campgrounds in Glenmont.

Spaghetti Patties

4 cups cooked spaghetti
3 eggs
4 bacon slices, fried, crumbled
¼ cup minced green onions
¼ cup grated Parmesan cheese
1 teaspoon salt
Dash of pepper

Combine all ingredients. Form into patties using ½ cup mixture per patty. Fry patties in oil over medium heat until brown and crispy. Makes 8–10 patties.

Editor's Extra: Break spaghetti into small pieces before cooking for neater patties.

Cooking Up a Cure

Spaghetti Pie

6 ounces spaghetti, cooked, drained
2 tablespoons butter
1 cup cottage cheese
½ cup grated mozzarella cheese
2 eggs, beaten
1 pound hamburger or sausage, browned, drained
½ cup chopped onion
¼ cup chopped green bell pepper
1 (8-ounce) can diced tomatoes
1 (6-ounce) can tomato paste
1 teaspoon sugar
1 teaspoon dried oregano
½ teaspoon garlic salt
⅓ cup grated Parmesan cheese

Mix spaghetti, butter, cottage cheese, and mozzarella cheese; add eggs. Mix together all ingredients, except Parmesan. Bake in greased 10-inch pie pan, uncovered, at 350° for 20 minutes. Sprinkle Parmesan cheese on top and bake 5 minutes longer. Makes 6 servings.

Food for Thought

Manicotti

6 eggs
¾ cup water
1 teaspoon oil

Pinch of salt
1½ cups all-purpose flour

Mix all ingredients together with beater. Mixture will be liquidy. Using a small 5-inch skillet or crêpe pan that has been coated with nonstick spray, pour 2 tablespoons batter and rotate pan quickly to spread batter evenly. Cook until edges start to curl, then flip to other side. Cook a few seconds. Must not get brown. Repeat with remaining batter. Stack each with wax paper in between.

FILLING:

1 (8-ounce) can tomato sauce
1½ pounds ricotta cheese
2 small eggs
¼ cup chopped celery

½ cup chopped parsley
½ cup grated Parmesan cheese
Salt and pepper to taste

Cover bottom of 11x15-inch baking dish with tomato sauce, reserving some for top. Mix remaining ingredients well—it should be firm. Fill one crêpe at a time with Filling across lower third of crêpe. Roll up and place with seam down in sauce. Make only one layer in baking dish. Cover top with tomato sauce and a sprinkle of Parmesan cheese. Serves 8.

Favorite Recipes Home-Style

Born in 1910 in New Carlisle, Roy Plunkett, a DuPont chemist, unintentionally invented Teflon in 1938 while working with refrigerants. It wasn't until the 1960s that the resin came into common use as a nonstick surface on pots and pans.

Linguine with Chicken, Caramelized Oranges and Pistachios

2 oranges
2 tablespoons butter
2 tablespoons sugar
8 ounces dry linguine
4 tablespoons olive oil, divided
2 boneless, skinless whole
   chicken breasts, cut into
   ¼-inch strips
2 shallots, chopped
8 ounces kalamata olives,
   pitted, quartered

2 green onions, diced
1 cup raw pistachio nuts, toasted,
   chopped, divided
1 teaspoon dried red pepper
   flakes, or to taste (optional)
½ cup grated Parmigiano-
   Reggiano cheese
Salt and pepper to taste
¼ cup chopped fresh parsley
¼ cup fresh chopped cilantro

Slice top and bottom off each orange and discard. Cut orange rind from top to bottom in 1-inch strips, removing any white pith. Cut rind into long thin strips. Squeeze juice from oranges and reserve. Cook orange rind strips in a pot of boiling water for 2 minutes. Drain and rinse under cold water; set aside.

Melt butter in a saucepan. Add reserved orange juice and sugar and simmer 5 minutes. Add reserved orange rind and cook until liquid reduces to a syrupy glaze.

Cook linguine until al dente. Drain and toss with 2 tablespoons olive oil. Place on a serving platter and keep warm.

Meanwhile, in a large skillet, sauté chicken in remaining 2 table-spoons olive oil 5–7 minutes. Add shallots, olives, green onions, and orange rind glaze. Sauté 2 minutes. Add ¾ cup pistachio nuts and pepper flakes, if desired; stir until well mixed. Spoon chicken mixture over linguine. Sprinkle with cheese. Season as needed with salt and pepper. Garnish with remaining ¼ cup pistachio nuts, parsley, and cilantro.

Crowd Pleasers

Tortellini in Tomato Cream Sauce

1 (10-ounce) package assorted
  tortellini
1 cup dry vermouth
⅔ cup minced sun-dried
  tomatoes in oil, drained
1½ cups chicken broth

2 cloves garlic, mashed
1½ cups sour cream (not
  fat-free)
6 scallions, minced
Fresh tarragon, fresh basil, and
  grated Parmesan to taste

Cook tortellini and reserve. Boil vermouth, tomatoes, broth, and garlic for 5 minutes; reduce heat to low, then stir in sour cream and scallions. Warm only. Serve over tortellini. Garnish with chiffonade of herbs and fresh Parmesan. Serves 4.

Note: Add cooked shrimp or chicken to increase protein.

Recipes and Remembrances: Around St. George's Tables

Greek-Style Shrimp with Pasta

1 teaspoon finely chopped garlic
5 tablespoons olive oil, divided
2 cups cubed peeled tomatoes
½ cup dry white wine
Salt and black pepper to taste
¾ cup finely chopped fresh
  basil
1 teaspoon dried crumbled
  oregano

1½ pounds medium shrimp,
  peeled, deveined
⅛ teaspoon hot red pepper
  flakes
8 ounces crumbled feta cheese
6 ounces rigatoni, cooked,
  drained

Sauté garlic in 2 tablespoons olive oil in a skillet. Add tomatoes. Cook 1 minute. Add wine, salt, pepper, basil, and oregano. Cook over medium heat 10 minutes. Season shrimp with salt and pepper. Heat remaining 3 tablespoons olive oil in large skillet. Add shrimp. Sauté 1 minute or until shrimp turn pink. Sprinkle with red pepper flakes. Spoon into a small, greased baking dish. Sprinkle with feta cheese. Spoon tomato sauce over top. Bake at 400° for 10 minutes or until bubbly. Spoon over hot pasta on a serving platter. Yields 4 servings.

America Celebrates Columbus

Joe Montana's Mom's Ravioli

FILLING:

1 medium onion, finely
  chopped
Butter for sautéing
2 pounds ground beef sirloin
1 pound regular ground beef
1 (10-ounce) package frozen
  chopped spinach, thawed,
  squeezed dry

2 eggs, beaten
½ cup grated Romano cheese,
  or to taste

Sauté onion in butter in a skillet until tender. Add meat and cook until browned; drain. Add spinach and mix well. Remove from heat.

In a separate skillet, cook scrambled eggs. Add eggs to meat mixture and quickly stir to mix. Stir in cheese.

DOUGH:

6 cups all-purpose flour
3 eggs

2 teaspoons salt
Water as needed

Mix all ingredients together until dough is firm and feels very smooth. Roll out dough until thin. Cut dough into circles with a glass. Spoon about 1 teaspoon Filling into each circle. Fold circle in half and seal with a fork. To cook, place the ravioli in a large pot of boiling salted water; when they rise to the top, they are ready.

Crowd Pleasers

Located in Ada, the Wilson Football Factory is the only dedicated football factory in the world and the only place where footballs are manufactured in the United States. Wilson has been the exclusive provider of footballs for the National Football League since 1941.

Linguine with Tomato and Basil Sauce

1 medium onion, chopped
1–2 garlic cloves, crushed
2 tablespoons vegetable oil
1 (28-ounce) can whole
 tomatoes, cut into quarters
2 tablespoons chopped sweet
 basil

1 tablespoon sugar
1 cup heavy cream
¼ cup butter
12–16 ounces linguine, cooked,
 drained
Grated Parmesan cheese
 (optional)

Sauté onion and garlic in vegetable oil in a skillet until onion is translucent. Add tomatoes, basil, and sugar. Cook 10 minutes. Add cream and butter. Cook 10 minutes or until heated through, stirring constantly. Pour over hot linguine in a large serving bowl and toss to coat well. Sprinkle with Parmesan cheese, if desired.

America Celebrates Columbus

Favorite Mac and Cheese

1½ cups cottage cheese
1½ cups sour cream
2 eggs
24 ounces sharp Cheddar
 cheese, shredded

2 cups cooked elbow macaroni
2 cups cooked mostaccioli rigati
Salt and pepper to taste

Mix all ingredients in a large bowl. Transfer to a greased 9x13-inch baking dish. Bake at 375° until golden and crusty, about 40 minutes.

Favorite Recipes from the Delaware Police Department

Terry's Original
Rice-Veggie-Cheese Casserole

3 cups cooked rice, divided
6 large mushrooms, sliced
½ yellow onion, sliced
Thyme
3 cups shredded Cheddar
   cheese, divided
Oregano
15 cauliflower florets

½ cup sliced cauliflower stems
15 broccoli florets
½ cup sliced broccoli stems
1 medium zucchini, sliced,
   divided
Basil
Chopped garlic

Layer ingredients in a greased casserole dish in the following order. Layer 1: rice, mushrooms, onion, thyme, cheese, and oregano. Layer 2: rice, cauliflower florets and stems, zucchini, basil, cheese, and oregano. Layer 3: rice, broccoli florets and stems, zucchini, basil, cheese, and oregano. Cover with foil and bake at 375° for 45 minutes. Remove foil and spread chopped garlic over top. Bake uncovered for 15 minutes more, or until top browns.

Ohio Traditions with P. Buckley Moss

Spanish Rice

2 cups tomatoes or tomato juice
1 cup hot water
⅓ cup margarine
1 small onion, chopped
¼ cup sugar

Salt and pepper to taste
6 tablespoons uncooked
  long-grain rice
3 slices American cheese

In a large skillet, combine all ingredients except cheese. Bring to a boil, then reduce heat to medium-low. Cook 1 hour or until rice is done. Stir frequently. Melt cheese slices on top before serving. Serves 4–6.

Ohio State Grange Cookbook (Blue)

Harvest Rice

This is a great addition to a Thanksgiving dinner, but great served anytime with roast chicken, turkey, or pork.

2 cups chicken broth
½ cup brown rice
½ cup wild rice
2 tablespoons butter
3 medium onions, sliced into
  small wedges (or green
  onions for additional color,
  if desired)

1 tablespoon brown sugar
1 cup dried cranberries
⅔ cup sliced mushrooms
½ cup toasted almond slivers
½ teaspoon finely grated orange
  zest
Salt and pepper to taste

Combine broth and rice in saucepan and bring to a boil. Reduce heat to low; cover and simmer 35–45 minutes until rice is tender and broth is absorbed.

In medium skillet, melt butter over medium heat. Add onions and brown sugar. Sauté until butter is absorbed and onions are translucent and soft. Lower heat and continue to cook onions until they caramelize. Stir in cranberries and mushrooms. Cover skillet and cook 10 minutes, or until berries start to swell. Stir in nuts and orange zest, then fold this mixture into cooked rice. Salt and pepper to taste, and serve.

The "Friends" Cookbook

Baked Antipasto

2 tubes refrigerated crescent
rolls, divided
¼ pound American cheese
¼ pound Swiss cheese
¼ pound provolone cheese
¼ pound salami, chopped
¼ pound pepperoni, chopped
¼ pound ham, chopped

2 eggs (save 1 yolk for top of
crescent rolls)
½ teaspoon garlic powder
½ teaspoon black pepper
1 (16-ounce) jar roasted red
peppers
2 tablespoons sliced black olives

In a 9x13-inch baking dish, layer 1 can crescent rolls. Alternate
cheeses and meats. Scramble eggs with garlic powder and pepper and pour over meats and cheeses. Top with roasted peppers
and sliced black olives. Cover with remaining tube crescent rolls
and brush tops of rolls with egg yolk. Bake at 350° for 30 minutes,
uncovered, then 30 minutes, covered.

Rose Hill Recipes

Easy Quiche

2 tablespoons flour
2 cups shredded cheese
(Cheddar and mozzarella or
all of one kind)
½ teaspoon salt

Dash of pepper
1 cup 2% milk
2 eggs
1 (9-inch) unbaked pie shell

Add flour to cheese and mix well. Blend in salt, pepper, milk, and
eggs. Pour into pie shell and bake at 350° for 45 minutes or until
nicely browned.

Variations: May sauté onion with sausage and/or cooked and drained
broccoli or spinach and put in bottom of pie crust before adding egg
mixture. Time may need to be increased 5–10 minutes with additional
ingredients.

Tasteful Treasures Cookbook

Crab Quiche in Bacon Crust
with Cheese Sauce

1 (9-inch) pie crust
5 slices bacon, cooked, drained,
　crumbled
6–12 ounces crabmeat, flaked
3 large eggs, slightly beaten
1½ cups milk or cream
1 tablespoon finely chopped
　fresh parsley
½ teaspoon ground nutmeg

½ teaspoon grated lemon peel
½ teaspoon Worcestershire
½ teaspoon dried thyme
⅛ teaspoon onion salt
⅛ teaspoon pepper
1 (1-pound) jar pasteurized
　processed cheese
2 tablespoons dry white wine

Line 9-inch pie pan with pie crust. Press bacon into bottom and sides. (Pie shell may then be covered with wax paper and refrigerated overnight, if desired.) Arrange crabmeat in bottom of pie shell. Combine eggs with milk, parsley, nutmeg, lemon peel, Worcestershire, thyme, onion salt, and pepper. Pour over crabmeat. Bake at 450° for 10 minutes. Reduce heat to 350° and bake 30 minutes longer, or until filling is set.

Serve with hot cheese sauce made by heating cheese over hot water in double boiler, adding wine, and stirring until smooth. Yields 6 servings.

With Great Gusto

Ohio and North Carolina both take credit for the Wright brothers and their world-changing inventions—Ohio because the brothers developed and built their design in Dayton, and North Carolina because Kitty Hawk was the site of the first flight. With a spirit of friendly rivalry, Ohio adopted the slogan "Birthplace of Aviation Pioneers," recognizing not only the Wright brothers, but also astronauts John Glenn and Neil Armstrong, both Ohio natives. The current license plates in Ohio carry the motto "Birthplace of Aviation." The current North Carolina license plates say "First in Flight."

Zucchini Quiche

1 tablespoon canola oil
4 cups thinly sliced, unpeeled
  zucchini (about 1½ pounds)
1 cup chopped onion, fresh or
  frozen
2 tablespoons dried parsley
  flakes
½ teaspoon black pepper
¼ teaspoon salt

¼ teaspoon garlic powder
½ teaspoon dried basil
¼ teaspoon dried oregano
2 large eggs
1½ cups shredded reduced-fat
  Muenster or mozzarella cheese
1 (9-inch) Brown Rice Crust
2 teaspoons Dijon mustard

Preheat oven to 375°. Spray a large skillet with cooking spray. Add oil to skillet; heat 1–2 minutes. Add zucchini and onion; cook until tender, about 10 minutes. Add parsley, pepper, salt, garlic powder, basil, and oregano; stir to mix.

In a large mixing bowl, blend eggs and cheese. Add zucchini mixture to egg-cheese mixture; stir to combine. Spread prepared Brown Rice Crust with mustard. Pour zucchini mixture evenly into crust. Bake in 375° oven for 18–20 minutes or until knife inserted in center comes out clean. Let stand 10 minutes before cutting into wedges to serve. Serve hot. Serves 6.

Nutritional analysis: Cal 252; Prot 15gm; Carbo 23gm; Dietary Fiber 3gm; Fat 12gm; Sat. Fat 4.5gm; Choles 122mg; Sod 352mg.

BROWN RICE CRUST:

2 cups cooked brown rice, or 1
  (8.8-ounce) package 90-second
  prepared brown rice

1 large egg, beaten
1 tablespoon grated Parmesan
  cheese

In mixing bowl, combine rice, egg, and Parmesan cheese; stir to mix. Press firmly into prepared 9-inch pie plate. Bake in 375° oven for 3 minutes. Fill with desired filling and continue baking according to recipe instructions.

Nutritional analysis: Cal 88; Prot 3gm; Carbo 15gm; Dietary Fiber 1gm; Fat 2gm; Sat. Fat .5gm; Choles 36mg; Sod 28mg.

More Nutritious Still Delicious

Ham and Cheese Picnic Pie

1 recipe (2-crust) pie pastry
3 eggs
1 (15-ounce) carton ricotta
  cheese
1 (15-ounce) carton small-curd
  cottage cheese, drained
½ cup seasoned bread crumbs
½ cup grated Parmesan cheese
¼ cup minced fresh parsley
1½ teaspoons Creole or Italian
  seasoning, divided

Salt to taste
½–1 teaspoon freshly ground
  pepper
2 or 3 dashes hot sauce
1 pound deli ham, cut into ¼-inch
  cubes
4 ounces mozzarella cheese, cut
  into ¼-inch cubes
1 bunch green onions, thinly
  sliced
1 egg, beaten

Roll half the pastry into an 11-inch circle. Fit into a 10-inch springform pan. Chill in refrigerator. Beat 3 eggs in a large bowl. Add ricotta cheese, cottage cheese, bread crumbs, Parmesan cheese, parsley, 1 teaspoon Creole seasoning, salt, pepper, and hot sauce, and mix well. Stir in ham, mozzarella cheese, and green onions. Pour into pastry-lined pan. Pull edge of pastry over filling. Brush with ½ of the beaten egg.

Roll remaining pastry into a 12-inch circle. Place over filling, crimping edges of pastry together; the edge will be inside the springform pan. Brush with remaining beaten egg. Sprinkle with remaining ½ teaspoon Creole seasoning. Bake at 375° for 1 hour and 10 minutes. Remove from oven. Let stand until cool. Chill in refrigerator. Serve at room temperature. Yields 12–15 servings.

America Celebrates Columbus

Singer Dean Martin was born in Steubenville in 1917. He earned the nickname "the Beatles buster" after his 1964 hit "Everybody Loves Somebody" knocked the Fab Four out of the top spot on the Billboard charts at the peak of Beatlemania. He is remembered with a festival each June.

Hawaiian Pizzas

The low-fat tortillas taste like a super-thin crispy pizza crust. Great served with a fresh red lettuce salad.

10 (10-inch) low-fat tortillas
½ cup teriyaki baste and glaze sauce
1 (8-ounce) bag shredded fat-free mozzarella cheese
1 (5.5-ounce) can pineapple tidbits in it's own juice, drained, juice discarded
½ cup chopped green onion
1 (8-ounce) bag extra lean ham, chopped

Spray bottoms of tortillas with nonfat cooking spray. Spread 2 teaspoons teriyaki sauce over each tortilla. Sprinkle 1 heaping tablespoon cheese evenly over each pizza. Top with 1½ tablespoons pineapple, 1 teaspoon green onion, and 1 tablespoon ham. Put each tortilla pizza directly on rack in oven. Bake at 400° for 7 minutes or until cheese is melted. Yields 10 individual serving-size pizzas.

Nutritional analysis: Cal 257 (6% fat); Total fat 2gm; Choles 16mg; Carbo 41gm; Dietary Fiber 4gm; Prot 18gm; Sod 1334mg; Diabetic Exchanges 2 starch, 1 other carbo, 2 very lean meat.

Busy People's Low-Carb Cookbook

Meats

One blimp is an unusual site in most cities. In Akron, some days you'll see four! Here, four Goodyear blimps fly in formation over the company's Wingfoot Lake airship hangar near Akron. The Goodyear Airdock has been home to the company's fleet of blimps since 1929 when it was constructed.

Ham Loaf

MEAT MIX:

1 pound ground smoked ham
1½ pounds ground lean pork
2 eggs
1 cup cracker crumbs
1 cup milk

½ teaspoon salt
Pepper to taste
6 slices pineapple
10 maraschino cherries

Mix together meats, eggs, crumbs, milk, salt, and pepper. Place pineapple in the bottom of a baking dish and put cherries in the center.

SAUCE MIX:

¾ cup brown sugar
1 teaspoon dry mustard

¼ cup vinegar

Mix ingredients, and spread ½ of Sauce Mix over pineapples. Over this, spread Meat Mix. Spread remaining Sauce Mix over top. Bake at 375° for 1½–2 hours. Serves 10.

Cooking Along the Lincoln Highway in Ohio

Ham Loaf

2 pounds ground ham
2 pounds ground pork
2 cups crushed graham
  crackers
½ cup milk
3 eggs, beaten

1 (10-ounce) can tomato soup
1 cup brown sugar
½ cup vinegar
½ cup cold water
½ teaspoon dry mustard

Mix ham, pork, crackers, milk, and eggs. Shape into loaf. Place in lightly greased baking dish. Mix tomato soup, brown sugar, vinegar, water, and dry mustard to make a sauce. Pour over ham loaf. Bake at 300° for 2 hours.

Love, Mom: Stories and Recipes from Kingston, Ohio

Traditional Baked Ham

I see so many recipes that call for needless, painstaking efforts. Once you see how easy this recipe is, you'll agree. When I tested this recipe using presliced ham, the ham was too dry.

1 (8-pound) fully cooked, hickory smoked, boneless honey ham (do not use presliced ham)
1 cup cherry cola soda

½ cup dark brown sugar
½ teaspoon ground allspice
1 (20-ounce) can pineapple slices in pineapple juice
10 maraschino cherries

Preheat oven to 275°. Place ham in a 9x13-inch casserole. Pour soda over entire ham in casserole dish. In a medium bowl, stir together dark brown sugar and allspice. Pat sugar mixture on ham. With toothpicks, secure pineapple rings to outside of ham (2 or 3 picks per ring). Using one toothpick, secure one cherry inside each ring of pineapple. Put 2 pieces of aluminum foil together lengthwise and seal to make a tent. Cover casserole dish with aluminum foil tent, securing it tightly around casserole dish, but do not puncture foil with toothpicks. Bake 4–5 hours or until a meat thermometer reads 160°. Let ham rest about 10 minutes before cutting. Pour ham juice into small bowl so that guests can serve themselves juice for their ham if they wish. Yields 30 (4-ounce) servings.

Busy People's Fun, Fast, Festive Christmas Cookbook

Located in Lima, Rudolph Foods Company is the world's largest producer of pork rind products, making 100 million pounds each year.

Baked Ham and Sweet Potatoes

2 medium-thick slices cured
  ham
4 or 5 medium sweet potatoes,
  peeled, sliced 1-inch thick

1 large orange
Brown sugar
Butter

In a large greased baking dish, lay one slice of ham. Place layer of potatoes. Cover potatoes with thin slices of orange, leaving 3 or 4 slices with peeling on them. Sprinkle with sugar and dot with butter. Lay second slice of ham on this and slice remaining orange over this. Sprinkle again with sugar and dot with butter. Arrange remaining potatoes around edges of pan. Add small amount of water. Cover and bake in 350° oven 1½ hours. Uncover last half hour. Serves 6–8.

Ohio State Grange Cookbook (Gold)

Spiced Pork Chops

½ cup all-purpose flour
1½ teaspoons garlic salt
1½ teaspoons ground mustard
1½ teaspoons paprika
½ teaspoon celery salt
¼ teaspoon ground ginger
⅛ teaspoon dried oregano
⅛ teaspoon dried basil

⅛ teaspoon salt
Dash of pepper
4 (¾-inch-thick) pork loin
  chops
2 tablespoons cooking oil
1 cup ketchup
1 cup water
¼ cup packed brown sugar

In a shallow dish, combine first 10 ingredients. Dredge chops on both sides. In a skillet, brown in oil on both sides. Place in greased 9x13-inch baking dish. Combine ketchup, water, and sugar. Pour over chops. Bake uncovered at 350° for 1 hour or until tender. Serves 4.

Sharing Our Best

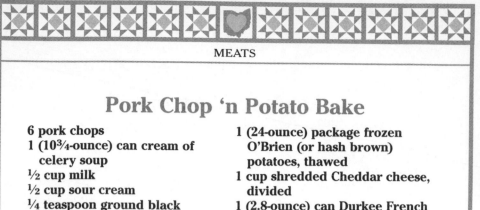

Pork Chop 'n Potato Bake

6 pork chops
1 (10¾-ounce) can cream of
  celery soup
½ cup milk
½ cup sour cream
¼ teaspoon ground black
  pepper
¼ teaspoon seasoned salt

1 (24-ounce) package frozen
  O'Brien (or hash brown)
  potatoes, thawed
1 cup shredded Cheddar cheese,
  divided
1 (2.8-ounce) can Durkee French
  Fried Onions, divided

Brown pork chops in lightly greased skillet. Combine soup, milk, sour cream, pepper, and seasoned salt. Stir in potatoes, ½ cup cheese, and ½ can fried onions. Spoon mixture into 9x13-inch baking dish. Arrange pork chops over potatoes. Bake, covered, at 350° for 40 minutes. Top with remaining cheese and onions, and bake, uncovered, 5 minutes longer. Makes 6 servings.

Carroll County Humane Society Members & Friends
Cookbook Volume I

My Best Spareribs

3 pounds western-style
  boneless ribs
1 stick margarine
1 teaspoon garlic powder
1 envelope Lipton onion
  mushroom soup mix

½ cup brown sugar
½ cup white vinegar
1½ cups ketchup
½ cup mild salsa

Preheat oven to 375°. Line a large baking pan with foil, or heavily grease a large baking pan. Place ribs in pan and bake uncovered for 20 minutes. In a saucepan, mix remaining ingredients and bring to a boil. Reduce heat and simmer until ribs have baked 20 minutes. Brush ribs generously with sauce and bake covered an additional 50 minutes or until done. Brush occasionally with more sauce during baking.

Feeding the Flock—First Church of God

Pork Tenderloin
with Raspberry Sauce Supreme

1 pound pork tenderloin,
  trimmed and cut into
  8 crosswise pieces

Cayenne pepper to taste
2 tablespoons margarine
2 kiwi fruit, peeled, thinly sliced

Press each pork tenderloin slice to 1-inch thickness. Lightly sprinkle both sides of each slice with cayenne pepper. Heat margarine in heavy skillet over medium-high heat. Add pork slices; cook 3 or 4 minutes on each side.

RASPBERRY SAUCE:

6 tablespoons red raspberry
  preserves
2 tablespoons red wine vinegar
1 tablespoon ketchup

½ teaspoon horseradish
½ teaspoon soy sauce
1 clove garlic, minced
Fresh raspberries

Combine all ingredients in small saucepan; simmer over low heat about 3 minutes, stirring occasionally. Keep warm. Place cooked pork slices on warm serving plate. Spoon Sauce over; top each pork slice with kiwi slice. Garnish serving plate with remaining slices and fresh raspberries, if desired.

The "Friends" Cookbook

The hot dog originated on a chilly day in 1907 by concessionaire Harry M. Stevens of Niles. His regular food items, especially soda and ice cream, weren't selling well. Fans wanted something hot. Stevens had an idea. He sent an associate to a local deli for a supply of dachshund sausages and long rolls. Stevens split the rolls, inserted the sausages, and offered them for sale. The sandwiches were an instant success. Their place in history was ensured the following day by a local cartoonist who had sampled the new sandwich and wanted to depict the scene, but he wasn't sure how to spell "dachshund." So he called the boiled sausages "hot dogs"—and the name stuck.

Tortellini Toss

1 small onion, chopped
1 clove garlic, minced
¼ cup butter or margarine
1½ pounds pork tenderloin
  or boneless chicken, cut into
  3-inch strips
1 teaspoon salt
1 teaspoon dried basil

½ teaspoon lemon pepper
¼ teaspoon dried marjoram
1 (14-ounce) package frozen sugar
  snap peas, partially thawed
1 (19-ounce) package frozen
  tortellini, cooked, drained
¼–½ cup grated Parmesan
  cheese

Sauté onion and garlic in butter until tender. Add meat and seasonings. Cook and stir 5 minutes or until meat is no longer pink. Add vegetables; reduce heat. Cover and simmer 2–3 minutes. Add tortellini and Parmesan cheese. Toss to coat. Yields 6 servings.

Cooking Up a Cure

Bratwurst Noodle Casserole

2 pounds bulk Carle's
  Bratwurst
1 medium onion, diced
12 ounces noodles, boiled,
  drained

1 pound sauerkraut, drained
2 (10¾-ounce) cans cream of
  mushroom soup
¼ cup grated Cheddar cheese
1 cup bread crumbs

Brown bratwurst in skillet until fully cooked, but still juicy. Add onion and sauté. In a bowl, mix bratwurst, onion, noodles, sauerkraut, and mushroom soup. Place into greased 9x13-inch baking pan or 2-quart casserole dish. Top with cheese and bread crumbs. Bake at 350° for 45 minutes.

Cooking Along the Lincoln Highway in Ohio

Pizza Meat Loaf Cups

1 egg, beaten
½ cup pizza sauce
¼ cup seasoned bread crumbs
½ teaspoon Italian seasoning

1½ pounds ground beef
1½ cups (6 ounces) shredded
  mozzarella cheese

In a bowl, combine egg, pizza sauce, bread crumbs, and Italian seasoning. Crumble beef over mixture and mix well. Divide between 12 greased muffin pans. Press onto bottom and up sides. Fill centers with cheese.

Bake at 375° for 15–18 minutes or until there is no pink in the meat. Place additional sauce over cups.

Cooking Along the Lincoln Highway in Ohio

Meat Porcupines

1 pound ground beef
1 tablespoon finely minced
   onion
2 teaspoons baking powder

¾ cup milk
½ cup uncooked rice
1 cup tomato soup or juice

Mix beef, onion, baking powder, milk, and rice. Mold into balls about 1½ inches in diameter. Pour tomato soup or juice over and bake in uncovered dish for 30 minutes at 350°.

Ohio State Grange Cookbook (Gold)

Beef Stroganoff

1 pound beef tenderloin,
   sirloin, or round steak
4 tablespoons flour, divided
¾ teaspoon salt, divided
4 tablespoons butter or
   margarine, divided
½ cup chopped onion
1½ cups sliced, fresh
   mushrooms

1 clove garlic, minced
1 tablespoon tomato paste
1 teaspoon instant beef bouillon
   granules
1½ cups water
1 cup dairy sour cream
2 tablespoons dry white wine
Hot cooked noodles

Partially freeze meat; thinly slice across grain into bite-size strips. Combine 1 tablespoon flour and ½ teaspoon salt; coat meat with flour mixture. In skillet, heat 2 tablespoons butter. Add meat and brown quickly on both sides. Add onion, mushrooms, and garlic. Cook 3–4 minutes or until onion is crisp-tender. Remove meat and mushroom mixture from pan. Add remaining 2 tablespoons butter to pan drippings; stir in 2 tablespoons flour. Add tomato paste, bouillon, and remaining ¼ teaspoon salt. Stir in water. Cook and stir over medium-high heat until bubbly. Cook and stir 1–2 minutes longer.

Combine sour cream and remaining 1 tablespoon flour. Return meat and mushrooms to skillet. Stir in sour cream mixture and wine. Heat thoroughly, but do not boil. Serve over noodles. Serves 4.

Camp Whitewood Camp Cookbook

Paprika Beef Roll

3 pounds round steak, cut in 2
  pieces
Salt and black pepper to taste
Paprika
¼ pound fresh mushrooms,
  finely sliced
1 large onion, sliced
1 (4-ounce) jar pimentos,
  drained, chopped
1 (12-ounce) package stuffing
  mix

½ cup butter, melted
1 tablespoon boiling water
1 egg, beaten
1 (6-ounce) jar pimento-stuffed
  green olives
¼ cup butter
6 whole mushrooms
1 cup red wine

Using mallet, pound steak until thin. Rub salt, pepper, and liberal amount of paprika into steaks. On each steak, layer sliced mushrooms, onion, and pimento. Crush stuffing mix and sprinkle evenly on vegetables.

In small bowl, whisk melted butter, boiling water, and egg. Quickly drizzle mixture on stuffing crumbs.

Arrange olives in row on long side of each steak; roll up from that edge. Secure firmly with string at each end and in center. Season with salt and black pepper. Sauté steak in ¼ cup butter in roasting pan, turning to brown on all sides. Place whole mushrooms around steak rolls and sprinkle lightly with salt, black pepper, and paprika. Add wine. Bake, covered, at 350° for 2 hours, basting with pan juices at 20-minute intervals. Serve hot or cold. Serves 6.

I'll Cook When Pigs Fly

Beef Roll-Ups

1 box beef flavor stuffing mix
6–8 thin slices beef
2 tablespoons olive oil

1 (14-ounce) can beef consommé
½ can water

Prepare stuffing mix as directed on package. Place ⅓ cup stuffing mix on each slice of beef. Roll up, tuck ends under, and secure with toothpicks. Heat oil in heavy skillet. Brown roll-ups in oil, then cover with consommé and water. Any extra stuffing can be mounded on top of beef. Cover skillet and bake in 350° oven for 1–1½ hours.

Columbus Colony Creations

Great Beef Stew

2 pounds beef, cut into 1-inch
  cubes
3 small onions, cut in quarters
½ bunch carrots, cut up
½ bunch celery, cut up
3 or more potatoes, peeled, cut
  up

3 tablespoons minute tapioca
3 tablespoons soy sauce
1 (14½-ounce) can tomatoes,
  peeled, mashed

In Dutch oven, layer ingredients in order given. Do not stir. Bake, covered, in 350° oven for 2½ hours.

Country Collections Cookbook II

Leonard Franklin Slye was born in Cincinnati on November 5, 1911. You may know him as Roy Rogers—famous singer and cowboy actor. He and his third wife Dale Evans, his golden palomino Trigger, and his German shepherd Bullet, were featured in over one hundred movies and *The Roy Rogers Show*.

Margaret's Sloppy Joes

1½ pounds ground beef
½–1 small onion, chopped
¼ teaspoon celery seed
   (optional)
1 tablespoon sweet pickle juice
¾ cup ketchup
3 tablespoons brown sugar

½–1 tablespoon mustard
1 tablespoon Worcestershire
½ teaspoon chili powder
½ green bell pepper, chopped
Salt and pepper to taste
Hamburger buns

In a skillet, combine beef, onion, and celery seed. Sauté until beef is browned; drain. Stir in remaining ingredients, except buns, seasoning with salt and pepper to taste. Simmer, uncovered, for approximately 1 hour. Continue cooking over low heat until desired consistency. Serve on hamburger buns. Serves 8–10.

Note: Vinegar or water may be substituted for sweet pickle juice. Also, thin sauce with tomato juice or water, if needed.

Ohio Cook Book

Roy's Meatballs

2 pounds ground beef (or half
   pork)
½ cup cracker crumbs
2 eggs, beaten
2 teaspoons salt
1 small onion, chopped, plus 1
   tablespoon chopped onion,
   divided

¼ teaspoon pepper
½ cup chopped pimentos
Flour
2 tablespoons butter
2 cups strained tomato juice

Combine beef, cracker crumbs, eggs, salt, 1 tablespoon chopped onion, pepper, and pimentos, and shape into balls the size of an egg. Roll in flour and brown in frying pan. Place in casserole dish. Melt butter in frying pan, add remaining onion, and brown; add tomato juice. Pour over meatballs in casserole dish. Bake, covered, in 400° oven for 1–1½ hours.

Mt. Zion Lutheran Church Cookbook

Carmela's Tomato Sauce

MEATBALLS:

1 pound ground chuck
2 eggs
Salt and pepper to taste
2 cloves garlic, chopped fine
½ cup chopped parsley

½ cup grated Parmesan cheese
½ cup bread crumbs, more if
 needed
¼ cup oil for frying

Mix ingredients, except oil, well. Roll into walnut-size balls. Fry in oil until lightly brown.

SAUCE:

1 (28-ounce) can tomato purée
1 (28-ounce) can crushed
 tomatoes
1 (6-ounce) can tomato paste

Salt and pepper to taste
¼ cup chopped parsley
2 tablespoons basil
Spaghetti noodles

In 6-quart pot, place purée, crushed tomatoes, and tomato paste; stir well. Add next 3 ingredients; mix well. Cook for 1 hour. Add Meatballs with oil in pan to Sauce. Cook for ½ hour. Cook spaghetti and put in large serving bowl. Put Sauce over spaghetti. Serve Meatballs separately. Serves 4.

Favorite Recipes Home-Style

Pasties

4 cups all-purpose flour
2 teaspoons salt
1½ cups shortening
10 tablespoons ice water
1 pound lean beef, cut into small cubes
1 pound coarsely ground lean beef
1 pound lean pork, cut into small cubes
5 large potatoes, peeled, chopped
1½ cups small cubes rutabaga
2 large onions, chopped
1 tablespoon salt
1 teaspoon ground pepper

Mix flour and salt in large chilled bowl. Cut in shortening with pastry blender until mixture is crumbly. Add ice water all at once. Mix well, adding additional water, if needed, to hold dough together. Divide dough into portions. Combine beef cubes, ground beef, pork, potatoes, rutabaga, onions, salt, and pepper in a bowl and mix well.

Roll each portion of dough into a ¼-inch thick circle on a lightly floured surface (approximately 8-inch diameter). Place 1 cup mixture in center of each dough circle. Fold up sides of dough to enclose filling, overlapping edges and pressing together to seal. Crimp edge and cut a vent. Place on a baking sheet. Bake at 400° for 45–50 minutes, or until golden brown. Serve with ketchup and dill pickles.

Note: May bake, cool, individually wrap, and freeze. May serve with beef gravy. One Pastie and a salad makes a great meal.

Variation: May add 2 or 3 chopped carrots to meat and vegetable mixture—adds color and flavor.

The "Friends" Cookbook

First envisioned in the late 1950s, the Buckeye Trail is a 1,450-mile trail that loops around the entire state of Ohio, reaching into every corner. From a beachhead on Lake Erie near Cleveland to a hilltop overlooking the Ohio River in Cincinnati, a hiker can experience the natural beauty of the state.

Country Sausage Gravy

This gravy can be served over biscuits or potatoes. It has a hearty flavor and is easy to prepare.

1 pound bulk sausage
1 (10¾-ounce) can cream of
  chicken soup
1 can milk

½ teaspoon dry mustard
¼ teaspoon seasoned salt
¼ teaspoon pepper
1 cup sour cream

In a heavy skillet, crumble sausage and cook over medium heat until browned; drain and set aside. In the same skillet, blend soup and milk together. Add mustard, salt, and pepper, and bring to a boil. Reduce heat and stir in sausage and sour cream. Simmer until heated through, but do not boil. Serves 4–6.

Ohio Cook Book

Hamburger Gravy

Here's an old-time favorite that many heart- and waist-conscious people probably thought they could never enjoy again.

1 pound ground beef (eye of
  round)
1 envelope Butter Buds, dry
2 teaspoons garlic salt (optional)

Dash of pepper (optional)
3 cups skim milk, divided
½ cup cornstarch

Combine ground beef, Butter Buds, garlic salt, and pepper, if using, in a large saucepan or Dutch oven over medium heat. Cook beef until browned. Stir 2 cups milk into seasoned beef. Mix cornstarch and remaining 1 cup milk in bowl, stirring until cornstarch is completely dissolved. Add cornstarch mixture to beef, stirring constantly. Cook 5 minutes longer or until thick and creamy. Yields 6 (¾-cup) servings.

Nutritional analysis: Cal 189 (17% fat); Fat 4g; Choles 43mg; Carbo 18gm; Dietary Fiber 0gm; Prot 1gm; Sod 193mg.

Busy People's Down-Home Cooking
Without the Down-Home Fat

Pepper Steak

1 tablespoon paprika
1 teaspoon ginger
1 pound round steak, cut into
  ¼-inch strips
2 cloves garlic, crushed
2 tablespoons butter
2 tablespoons bouillon granules
2 cups beef broth or stock,
  divided

½ cup sliced mushrooms
1 cup sliced onions
2 green bell peppers, sliced
  into strips
¼ cup soy sauce
3 tablespoons cornstarch
⅓ cup water
2 medium tomatoes, chopped
3 cups cooked rice

Combine paprika and ginger. Sprinkle over steak. Let stand. In large skillet, brown steak and garlic in butter. Combine bouillon and 1 cup beef broth and add to beef. Cover and simmer 20 minutes.

Combine remaining 1 cup beef broth, mushrooms, onions, peppers, soy sauce, cornstarch, and water. Pour over steak. Add tomatoes and stir to heat through. Serve over rice. Makes 6 servings.

Camp Whitewood Camp Cookbook

GOLFLEGENDS.ORG

Golf is bound to be king in Ohio since the master himself, Jack Nicklaus, is from Columbus. He is widely regarded as the greatest professional golfer of all time, in large part because of his records in major championships. Nicklaus accumulated a record eighteen Majors in a professional PGA career lasting from 1961 to 2005 when he played his last round in the British Open at the Old Course at St. Andrews. The Jack Nicklaus Museum, located in Ohio State University's sports complex, showcases the golf superstar's career through exhibits of trophies, photographs, and mementos from his major championships and 100 worldwide tournament victories.

Steak à la Pizzalo

1 large slice round steak, 1–2
  inches thick
Salt and pepper to taste
¼ cup chopped parsley
1 tablespoon dried basil
2 cloves garlic, finely chopped
½ cup grated Parmesan cheese
4–5 tablespoons olive oil

Water
1 (28-ounce) can crushed
  tomatoes with purée
1 (16-ounce) can mushrooms,
  or 1 pound fresh
¾ cup grated mozzarella cheese
  (optional)

Place steak in a 9x13-inch baking dish. Cover with next 6 ingredients. Place water in dish to come even to top of steak; add tomatoes. Bake, covered with foil, at 350° for 1½ hours or until steak is tender.

Ten minutes before the end of baking, add mushrooms and mozarella. If water is down, you may add a little. When cheese is melted, remove from oven. Cut into serving pieces. Serves 6.

Favorite Recipes Home-Style

Beef Burgundy

6 strips bacon or turkey bacon,
  cut up
3 pounds beef chuck roast,
  cut into 1-inch cubes
1 large carrot, sliced
1 medium onion, sliced
1 teaspoon salt
½ teaspoon pepper
3 tablespoons flour
2 (14-ounce) cans beef broth,
  divided

2 cups red burgundy wine
2 garlic cloves, minced
½ teaspoon thyme
1 bay leaf
10–12 small pearl onions
6 tablespoons butter or magarine,
  divided
2 tablespoons oil
1–2 pounds mushrooms

In Dutch oven, cook bacon till crisp. Remove bacon. Brown beef in bacon drippings. Remove meat. Brown carrots and onions, and spoon off fat. Return bacon and chuck to pan with vegetables. Add salt, pepper, and flour, stirring to coat meat lightly. Add 1½ cans beef broth, wine, garlic, thyme, and bay leaf. Cover and simmer about 3 hours.

Brown onions (can use bottled onions) in 3 tablespoons butter and 2 tablespoons oil. Add remainder of broth, cover, and simmer 10 minutes. Brown mushrooms in remaining 3 tablespoons butter or margarine. Add mushrooms and onions to beef. Cook together about 10 minutes. Serves 6–8.

Food, Glorious Food

McGill Masterpiece

1 pound mild bulk pork sausage
1 pound hot bulk pork sausage
1 medium onion, chopped
6 eggs, beaten
2 (10¾-ounce) cans cream of
  celery soup, undiluted

½ cup milk
6 cups crispy rice cereal, divided
1½ cups cooked rice
2½ cups grated Cheddar
  cheese
1 tablespoon butter, softened

Cook sausage, stirring to crumble, until browned. Remove from skillet and set aside. Sauté onion in sausage drippings until tender. In mixing bowl, combine eggs, soup, and milk, beating until foamy.

Spread 5 cups cereal in greased 9x13x2-inch baking pan. Spread cooked rice evenly on cereal. Layer sausage with onion on rice and sprinkle with cheese. Spoon egg mixture evenly on cheese layer. Toss remaining 1 cup cereal with butter and sprinkle on layered ingredients. Bake at 325° for 1 hour. Remove from oven, cover with aluminum foil, and let stand for 10 minutes before serving. Serves 8–10.

I'll Cook When Pigs Fly

Ohio's official flower, the scarlet carnation, is rooted in Alliance. In 1866, local green thumb and politician Dr. Levi Lamborn propagated the flower from French seedlings, calling it "Lamborn Red." Opposing William McKinley for the 18th Congressional District in 1876, Lamborn presented the future president with a "Lamborn Red" boutonniere before each debate. As McKinley's political star rose, he spoke of the scarlet carnation as a good-luck charm. When he became president, he took to wearing one at all times and presenting flowers from a bouquet on his desk to guests. On September 14, 1901, moments after removing the flower from his lapel and giving it to a young admirer at the Buffalo Exposition, McKinley was killed by an assassin's bullet.

Barbeque Brisket

1 (5- to 6-pound) beef brisket,
  not corned
Dash of liquid or dry smoke
Dash of celery salt
Dash of garlic powder

Dash of onion powder
Dash of Worcestershire
Dash of seasoned salt
Water, enough to cover bottom of
  pan

Place brisket in roasting pan. Sprinkle smoke, celery salt, garlic powder, and onion powder on both sides of brisket. Marinate in refrigerator overnight or 12 hours.

After marinated, sprinkle on Worcestershire and seasoned salt. Add enough water to cover bottom of pan about ½ inch deep. Cover with foil and bake at 250° for 8–12 hours, until tender. Slice and remove fat before serving. Serve with Barbeque Sauce.

BARBEQUE SAUCE:
1 cup drippings from brisket
1 (8-ounce) can tomato sauce
2 tablespoons brown sugar

4 tablespoons water
2 tablespoons flour

Combine drippings, tomato sauce, and brown sugar in a saucepan. Boil. Whisk together water and flour. Pour flour mixture into boiling drippings. Cook until thickened. Serve with brisket.

Favorite Recipes–First Church of God

Poultry

Cleveland was chosen as the location for the Rock and Roll Hall of Fame and Museum because Cleveland disc jockey, Alan Freed, is widely credited with promoting the new genre of music, and coining the term "rock and roll." Cleveland also held the first rock and roll concert, the Moondog Coronation Ball in 1952.

Best Roast Chicken

1 (5- to 6-pound) roasting
   chicken
Kosher salt to taste
Freshly ground pepper to taste
1 large bunch fresh thyme
1 lemon, halved

1 head garlic, cut in half
   horizontally
2 tablespoons butter, melted
1 Spanish onion, thickly sliced
1 cup chicken stock
2 tablespoons all-purpose flour

Preheat oven to 425°. Remove giblets and any excess fat from chicken. Rinse chicken inside and out and pat dry on outside. Place chicken in a roasting pan and liberally salt and pepper inside cavity. Stuff cavity with thyme, lemon halves, and garlic. Brush outside of chicken with butter and season with salt and pepper. Tie legs together with kitchen string and tuck wing tips under body of chicken. Scatter onion slices around chicken.

Roast at 425° for 1 hour and 30 minutes or until juices run clear when cut between leg and thigh. Transfer chicken to a cutting board and cover with foil to keep warm.

Remove fat from bottom of roasting pan, reserving 2 tablespoons in a small cup. Add chicken stock to pan and cook over high heat, scraping bottom of pan, for 5 minutes, or until reduced. Combine reserved 2 tablespoons chicken fat and flour and add to pan. Boil a few minutes or until gravy thickens. Strain gravy into a small saucepan and season to taste. Keep warm over very low heat. Carve chicken, placing meat on a serving platter. Serve chicken with gravy.

Crowd Pleasers

Columbus native Mary Campbell is the only person to win the Miss America Pageant two years in a row (1922 and 1923) and she was first runner-up in 1924. After that, the rules were changed so a contestant could compete only once.

Roast Chicken with
Orange, Lemon, and Ginger

1 (6-pound) roasting chicken
1 navel orange
2 lemons, divided
3 tablespoons peeled, finely
  grated fresh ginger, divided
Freshly ground black pepper to
  taste

Salt to taste
5 tablespoons butter, melted, or
  olive oil
¼ cup fresh lemon juice
½ cup fresh orange juice
3 tablespoons honey

Preheat oven to 350°. Pat chicken dry. Put chicken on a rack in a roasting pan. Grate zest of orange and 1 lemon and cut zested lemon into quarters. Rub outside of chicken with lemon quarters and discard them. Cut orange and remaining lemon into quarters. In a small bowl, stir together zests and 1 tablespoon ginger. Rub zest mixture evenly inside cavity of chicken. Put orange and lemon quarters inside body and neck cavities of chicken and season chicken with pepper and salt.

In a small bowl, stir together butter or oil, juices, honey, and remaining 2 tablespoons ginger. Truss chicken, if desired, and roast in middle of oven, basting with juice mixture at least 4 times during roasting (if chicken is browning too quickly, tent with foil), 2–3½ hours, or until a meat thermometer inserted in fleshy part of thigh registers 170° and juices run clear. Transfer chicken to a cutting board and let stand 15 minutes before carving. Serve with defatted pan drippings as a sauce. Serves 6.

Recipes and Remembrances: Around St. George's Tables

Beer Butt Bird

2 (3½- to 4-pound) chickens
1 teaspoon sugar
1 teaspoon onion powder
1 teaspoon cayenne pepper
1 teaspoon paprika
1 teaspoon dry yellow mustard

1 tablespoon finely ground sea
salt
1 cup apple cider
1 tablespoon balsamic vinegar
2 (12-ounce) cans beer

Wash, dry, and season chickens generously inside and out with rub. Work mixture well into skin and under breast skin as much as possible. Cover and set aside at room temperature for an hour or so.

Drink (if desired) or do away with ½ the beer in each can. Place the can with remaining ½ inside, upright on smoker or grill, and lower chicken body cavity onto can (make sure can is covered with aluminum foil just on the outside only); the steam from the beer helps cook and keep the chicken tender.

Smoke for 2–2½ hours on slow, low heat. Meat thermometer should read 180° to be thoroughly done. (We used our gas grill, took the top rack off, covered bottom rack with foil, and cooked on lowest setting.) Cooked 2 fryer chickens for 2 hours. Remove cans with mitts.

Asthma Walk Cook Book

Honey-Glazed Baked Chicken

⅓ cup all-purpose flour
1 teaspoon garlic salt
Pinch of pepper
1 (3-pound) chicken, quartered
6 tablespoons butter or
   margarine, divided

¼ cup honey
3 tablespoons lemon juice
2 tablespoons soy sauce
Pinch of ground ginger

Mix flour, garlic salt, and pepper, then coat chicken quarters thoroughly. As oven preheats to 350°, melt 2 tablespoons butter in a shallow baking dish just large enough to hold chicken in a single layer. Arrange chicken, skin side down in butter. Bake, uncovered, 30 minutes. Meanwhile, melt remaining 4 tablespoons butter with honey, lemon juice, soy sauce, and ginger. When chicken has baked 30 minutes, turn it skin side up. Evenly pour on butter mixture. Continue baking, brushing occasionally with sauce, until chicken is tender. Serves 4.

50 Years and Still Cookin'!

Herbed Chicken Breasts

4 chicken breasts
½ cup olive oil
Flour
Juice from 3 lemons

4 garlic cloves
2 large sprigs rosemary
1 teaspoon salt and pepper

Coat chicken breasts with olive oil and refrigerate overnight or longer.

Coat chicken with flour and bake in flat, greased pan at 375°, covered, for 45 minutes. Remove drippings and add lemon juice, garlic, rosemary, salt and pepper. Bake, covered, an additional 15 minutes.

Ohio Traditions with P. Buckley Moss

Garlic Roast Chicken
with Rosemary and Lemon

2½ pounds boneless, skinless
  chicken breasts, cut into large
  chunks
6 cloves garlic, crushed
3 tablespoons fresh rosemary
  leaves, stripped from stems
3 tablespoons extra virgin olive
  oil

1 lemon, zested, juiced
1 tablespoon grill seasoning
  blend, or coarse salt and
  black pepper
½ cup dry white wine or
  chicken broth

Preheat oven to 450°. Arrange chicken in a 9x13-inch baking dish. Add garlic, rosemary, olive oil, lemon zest, and grill seasoning or salt and pepper to dish. Toss and coat chicken with all ingredients, then place in oven. Roast 20 minutes. Add wine and lemon juice to dish and combine with pan juices. Return to oven and turn oven off. Let stand 5 minutes longer, then remove chicken from oven. Place baking dish on trivet and serve, spooning pan juice over chicken pieces.

Tasteful Treasures Cookbook

Apricot Chicken with Almonds

4 skinless, boneless chicken
  breast halves
⅝ teaspoon salt, divided
½ teaspoon black pepper,
  divided
⅓ cup sliced almonds

½ cup apricot preserves
1½ tablespoons soy sauce
1 tablespoon whole-grain
  mustard
1 tablespoon unsalted butter

Put oven rack in lower third of oven and preheat oven to 400°. Lightly oil a 9x13-inch flameproof baking dish (not glass). Pat chicken dry and sprinkle all over with ½ teaspoon salt and ¼ teaspoon pepper, then arrange at least ¼ inch apart in baking dish. Bake 10 minutes. While chicken is baking, toast almonds in a small baking pan in oven, stirring twice, until golden, 8–10 minutes. Meanwhile, cook apricot preserves, soy sauce, mustard, butter, and remaining ⅛ teaspoon salt and ¼ teaspoon pepper in a small saucepan over moderate heat, stirring until preserves are melted. Pour sauce over chicken and continue to bake until chicken is just cooked through, about 10 minutes more. Turn on broiler and broil chicken 4–6 inches from heat, basting once, until chicken is glazed and browned in spots, about 3 minutes. Serve sprinkled with almonds.

Franklin County 4-H Favorites

The WACO Aircraft Company of Troy was the nation's leading aircraft manufacturer of civilian aircraft from 1928–1935. Beginning in 1921 as the Weaver Aircraft Company in Lorain, they moved to Troy in 1924 and became the Advance Aircraft Company but kept the WACO logo. In 1934/35, the company originally produced the WACO YMF model, which was unquestionably regarded as the finest open sport aircraft. When production was reestablished in 1986 with the WACO YMF Classic, many updated features were incorporated. Today's production aircraft offers a complete array of features, making it the finest sport biplane anywhere. The WACO YMF has and always will represent the essence of true aviation pleasure.

Chicken for Company

7 chicken breasts	1 cup sour cream
1 carrot	1 sleeve Ritz or Town House
1 stalk celery	crackers
1 (10¾-ounce) can cream of	1 stick margarine, melted
chicken soup	Poppy seeds

Boil chicken breasts with carrot and celery until chicken is tender. Remove and discard skin, bones, carrot, and celery. Heat soup and sour cream and mix thoroughly. (A small amount of chicken stock may be added to thin slightly.) Cut up chicken in bite-size pieces and add to soup mixture. Place chicken mixture in greased baking dish. Crush crackers and add melted margarine. Mix until crumbly and place crumbs on top of chicken. Sprinkle with poppy seeds. Bake at 350° for 30–35 minutes or until topping is golden brown. Serves 6–8.

Entertaining Made Easy

Party Chicken

1 (4-ounce) package chipped	8 slices bacon
beef	1 (10¾-ounce) can cream of
8 boneless, skinless chicken	mushroom soup
breasts	1 cup sour cream

Spray bottom of an 8x12-inch baking dish with Pam, or grease with margarine. Tear or cut up chipped beef into small pieces and put in bottom of dish. Wrap chicken breasts with bacon and arrange on the chipped beef. Mix soup and sour cream; pour over all. Refrigerate until ready to bake, or bake immediately.

Bake at 275° for 3 hours, uncovered. You can use less chicken and the same amount of soup and sour cream. The soup and sour cream make a tasty gravy, and can be served over chicken on a bed of rice.

Feeding the Flock—Trinity United Methodist Women

Chicken with Feta and Tomatoes

¼ pound plain, dried bread
crumbs
2 tablespoons fresh oregano
leaves, chopped, divided
¾ teaspoon salt, divided
¾ teaspoon pepper, divided
4 (5-ounce) boneless, skinless
chicken breast halves

2 tablespoons olive oil, divided
½ cup diced red onion
2 teaspoons chopped garlic
¼ cup ouzo (or dry white wine)
2 pounds plum tomatoes, peeled,
seeded, cut into ¼-inch strips
½ cup crumbled feta cheese
2 tablespoons chopped fresh dill

In food processor, process bread crumbs, 1 tablespoon oregano, and ¼ teaspoon salt and pepper. Place mixture on wax paper and coat chicken breasts on both sides. In large skillet, heat 1 tablespoon olive oil over medium-high heat. Add chicken and cook for 7 minutes, turning once. Remove chicken to plate.

In same skillet, add remaining 1 tablespoon olive oil, onion, and garlic, and sauté 1 minute. Pour in ouzo. Raise heat to high. Add tomatoes and remaining ½ teaspoon salt and pepper. Cook until tomatoes are soft, about 3 minutes. Stir in remaining oregano. Spoon sauce over 4 dinner plates. Slice chicken, place on top of sauce, and sprinkle with feta cheese and chopped dill. Serves 4.

A Festival of Recipes

In New Straitsville, there's a fire that won't go out. In 1884, angry coal miners started the fire by putting timbers in coal cars, soaking them with oil, igniting them, and pushing them into the mine on Plumber's Hill. The coal caught fire and no one has been able to extinguish it. As the coal burnt out under the ground, roads collapsed and flames shot out of the ground. It is said that one water well was so hot that you could make coffee directly with water drawn from the well. The fire in the New Straitsville mine burns to this day, making it the longest-duration conflagration in the world.

Buttermilk Fried Chicken with Rosemary-White Wine Gravy

This recipe is a Murphin Ridge classic, and a favorite among our Amish neighbors. It's delicious any time of the year with mashed potatoes and old-fashioned green beans.

4 boneless, skinless, butterflied chicken breasts
1 cup buttermilk
1 cup plus 2 tablespoons flour, divided
1 tablespoon kosher salt
1 teaspoon freshly ground pepper
2 tablespoons butter

1 teaspoon chopped fresh rosemary, or ½ teaspoon dried rosemary leaves
¼ cup dry white wine
1 cup chicken stock, or 1 teaspoon chicken base paste mixed with 1 cup water
1 cup milk
¾ cup vegetable shortening

Soak breasts in buttermilk for no longer than 15 minutes. Mix 1 cup flour with kosher salt and pepper.

Heat a small saucepan over medium-high heat. Add butter; when melted, add remaining 2 tablespoons flour. Whisk to form a smooth paste. Using a wooden spoon, continue to stir paste in saucepan another minute. Add rosemary, then remove from heat and stir in wine and chicken stock or base. Switch back to whisking the mixture and return it to heat. Add milk and bring to a simmer; the gravy should be thickening. Taste it and season with salt and pepper. Continue to simmer gravy gently while you cook the chicken.

Heat a skillet large enough to hold all 4 pieces of chicken. Add shortening to skillet and let it heat to 325°, or until flour sprinkled on it sizzles and bubbles. Pull 1 piece of chicken out of buttermilk and dip into flour, coating it well. Gently slide it into skillet, and repeat with remaining 3 pieces. Cook chicken until golden, then flip it and cook other side. Continue frying and flipping until chicken is firm to the touch and juices run clear when meat is pierced. Pour used oil into a suitable metal can or container. Pour a little more wine, stock, or water into skillet and use a wooden spoon to scrape up remaining chicken drippings; add them to gravy. Serve chicken with a generous ladle of gravy and a heap of mashed potatoes. Yields 4 servings.

A Taste of the Murphin Ridge Inn

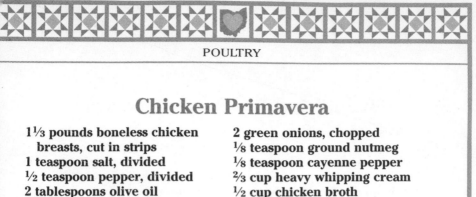

Chicken Primavera

1⅓ pounds boneless chicken
   breasts, cut in strips
1 teaspoon salt, divided
½ teaspoon pepper, divided
2 tablespoons olive oil
1 medium sweet red pepper,
   julienned
1 cup sliced fresh mushrooms

2 green onions, chopped
⅛ teaspoon ground nutmeg
⅛ teaspoon cayenne pepper
⅔ cup heavy whipping cream
½ cup chicken broth
8 ounces uncooked linguine
½ cup frozen peas

Sprinkle chicken with ½ teaspoon salt and ¼ teaspoon pepper. In large skillet, cook chicken in oil over medium heat 8–10 minutes. Remove and keep warm.

In same skillet, sauté red peppers, mushrooms, onions, nutmeg, and cayenne until tender. Add cream and broth. Bring to a boil; cook until sauce is reduced by a third. Meanwhile, cook linguine according to package directions; drain. Add chicken, linguine, peas, and remaining salt and pepper to sauce; heat through. Yields 4 servings.

Food for Thought

Chicken with Purple Onions

2 large purple onions
2 pounds boneless, skinless
   chicken breasts
6 tablespoons Parmesan cheese
   dressing

8 ounces grated Parmesan
   cheese
Cayenne pepper to taste
Parsley, chopped

Peel onions. Cut into 6 (½-inch-thick) slices. Place on ungreased baking sheet. Trim chicken of any visible fat and cut breasts lengthwise into ½-inch strips. Lay chicken strips on onion rounds to solidly cover onion slice. Drizzle 1 tablespoon dressing over each serving. Generously sprinkle Parmesan cheese and add cayenne pepper to taste. Sprinkle with parsley. Bake at 425° for 25–30 minutes. Serves 6.

A Treasury of Recipes for Mind, Body & Soul

Oven Fried Parmesan Chicken

1½ tablespoons canola oil
6 ounces plain nonfat yogurt
4 boneless, skinless chicken
   breasts (about 1¼ pounds)
½ cup plain dry bread crumbs
4 tablespoons grated Parmesan
   cheese

2 tablespoons all-purpose flour
2 teaspoons chili powder
½ teaspoon onion powder
¼ teaspoon garlic powder
⅛ teaspoon cayenne pepper

Preheat oven to 425°. Spray a 9x13x2-inch baking pan with cooking spray. Drizzle canola oil over bottom of pan.

In a medium bowl, mix yogurt and chicken until chicken is coated. Cover bowl with plastic wrap; refrigerate until needed.

In a gallon-size, resealable plastic bag, combine bread crumbs, cheese, flour, chili powder, onion powder, garlic powder, and cayenne pepper; seal. Shake gently to combine. Remove chicken from yogurt. Place chicken in bag one piece at a time. Shake gently to coat. Place coated chicken in prepared baking pan. Bake uncovered in 425° oven for 20 minutes or until chicken is cooked through and juices run clear. Makes 4 servings.

More Nutritious Still Delicious

Patricia's Chicken

1 (2-pound) package chicken
  tenders
2 eggs, beaten
1 cup plain bread crumbs
1 cup Italian bread crumbs

1 cup grated Parmesan cheese
Butter or margarine
2 large jars sliced mushrooms
1 pound grated Muenster cheese
1 (14-ounce) can chicken broth

Cut chicken into 1-inch squares. Place in medium bowl with eggs, enough to cover chicken. Soak 1 hour. Mix bread crumbs and Parmesan cheese and bread the chicken. Fry chicken in butter or margarine, not oil. Drain. In 9x13-inch pan, layer chicken, mushrooms, and cheese; repeat twice. Pour broth over all. Bake at 350° for 45 minutes, uncovered, and serve.

Sharing the Best from Our Kitchen

Chicken Waikiki

4 chicken legs and breasts
½ cup flour
⅓ cup vegetable oil

1 teaspoon salt
¼ teaspoon pepper

Wash chicken and pat dry. Coat with flour. Brown chicken 25 minutes in oil and arrange in a shallow roasting pan. Sprinkle with salt and pepper.

SAUCE:
1 (16-ounce) can pineapple
  slices or chunks
1 cup sugar
1 tablespoon cornstarch
¾ cup cider vinegar

1 tablespoon soy sauce
¼ teaspoon ground ginger
1 chicken bouillon cube
1 large green bell pepper, cut
  crosswise into ¼-inch circles

Preheat oven to 350°. Drain pineapple and pour syrup into a 2-cup measure. Add water to 1¼ cups. In saucepan, mix sugar, cornstarch, pineapple syrup, vinegar, soy sauce, ginger, and bouillon cube. Bring to a boil and stir 2 minutes. Pour over chicken. Bake uncovered 30 minutes. Add fruit and green pepper and bake 30 minutes longer. Serve with rice.

Camp Whitewood Camp Cookbook

Chicken and Egg Mold

2 tablespoons unflavored gelatin
½ cup cold water
1 cup hot chicken broth or
    liquid from cooking chicken
1 cup mayonnaise or salad
    dressing
1 teaspoon curry powder, or to
    taste

¾–1 cup finely chopped green
    bell pepper and/or celery
2 cups shredded cooked chicken
3 hard-cooked eggs, chopped
Salt (optional)

In large bowl, soften gelatin in cold water. Add hot broth and stir until gelatin is dissolved. Stir in mayonnaise until evenly distributed in small clumps. Add curry powder and chopped vegetables; stir. Add shredded chicken and eggs, and salt, if desired. Leave in mixing bowl or pour into wet mold; chill until firm, 2 hours minimum.

Scoop directly from bowl or unmold onto large plate to serve. If using circular form, center may be filled with grape tomatoes, vegetable sticks, olives, etc. for added color. Recipe will need to be doubled for large bowl or mold form. Serves 6–8.

Food, Glorious Food

The man who taught America to write in cursive, Platt Rogers Spencer, was living in Geneva when he created the Spencerian style of penmanship in the 1840s, which was soon adopted by schools nationwide. Spencerian Script became the standard across the United States. The spreading popularity of the typewriter in the 1920s nearly rendered it obsolete. (The Coca-Cola logo is a notable example of Spencerian Script.) It was gradually replaced with a simpler and less elegant style developed by A. N. Palmer.

Chicken Enchiladas

1 (10¾-ounce) can cream of
   chicken soup
1 cup sour cream
1½ cups grated Cheddar cheese,
   divided

2 cups cooked chicken or
   turkey
½ (4-ounce) can green chiles
8 large flour tortillas
Sliced onions (optional)

Combine soup, sour cream, and ¾ cup cheese, and divide mixture in half. To one half of the mixture, add chicken and chiles. Fill tortillas with chicken mixture and roll up. Place side-by-side in a 9x13-inch pan. Spread remaining mixture over enchiladas. Sprinkle remaining cheese and onions on top. Cover loosely with foil and bake at 325 ° for 25 minutes.

Feeding the Flock—First Church of God

Chicken Enchiladas Supreme

2 cups cooked, chopped
   chicken or turkey meat
1 (4-ounce) can chopped,
   mild green chiles
1 (7-ounce) can green chile
   salsa

½ teaspoon salt
2 cups sour cream
12 corn tortillas
1½ cups grated Monterey Jack
   cheese

Combine chicken, green chiles, and green chile salsa, and mix well. Mix salt and sour cream in a medium bowl. Heat about ½ inch oil in a small skillet. Dip each tortilla into hot oil for about 5 seconds, just to soften. Drain on paper towels.

Dip each fried tortilla into bowl containing cream and salt, coating each side. Fill each tortilla with chicken mixture. Roll and place in ungreased flat baking dish. Pour remaining cream over enchiladas and sprinkle with cheese. Bake uncovered at 350° for 20–25 minutes. Makes 6 servings.

Tasteful Treasures Cookbook

Chicken Casserole

4 cups chopped cooked chicken
breasts
1 (10¾-ounce) can cream of
chicken soup
1 (10¾-ounce) can cream of
celery soup

2 cups grated Cheddar cheese
1 cup Miracle Whip
2 cups chicken broth
2½ cups broken uncooked
vermicelli spaghetti
Crumbled herbed croutons

Combine all ingredients, except croutons. Mix well. Pour into a 9x13-inch baking dish. Sprinkle croutons on top and bake at 350° for 45–60 minutes or until bubbly.

Sharing Recipes Cookbook

Chicken Cobbler

Country cooking at its best.

1 pound boneless, skinless
chicken breasts, cut into
bite-size pieces
1 (1-pound) package mixed
vegetables
½ cup chopped frozen onion,
or 1 medium onion, chopped

2 (12-ounce) jars fat-free chicken
gravy
1½ cups dry pancake mix
¾ cup fat-free, low-sodium
chicken broth

Spray a slow cooker with nonfat cooking spray. In cooker, stir together chicken, frozen vegetables, onion, and gravy until well mixed. Cover and cook on HIGH for 2 hours. In a medium bowl, stir pancake mix and broth together to make a thick batter. Spread batter over boiling gravy in slow cooker. Cover and cook on HIGH another ½ hour. Yields 5 servings.

Nutritional analysis: Cal 315 (4% fat); Fat 2gm; Choles 53mg; Carbo 49gm; Dietary Fiber 7gm; Prot 29gm; Sod 1137mg.

Busy People's Slow Cooker Cookbook

Chicken à la King

This very tasty dish is creatively made. By allowing pasta to sit with the other ingredients overnight, it becomes a thick, creamy base for our Chicken à la King.

1 (12½-ounce) can chicken
  breast in water, not drained
1 (15-ounce) can sweet peas
1 (7¼-ounce) box macaroni
  and cheese (use pasta only)
1½ cups hot water
1 (10¾-ounce) can 98% fat-free
  condensed cream of mushroom
  soup, undiluted

1 cup refrigerated fat-free
  nondairy creamer
¼ cup chopped pimientos
  (optional)

Spray a slow cooker with nonfat cooking spray. In the cooker gently stir together chicken breast with its water, sweet peas, macaroni, hot water, and mushroom soup. Cover and place entire slow cooker in refrigerator for 8–12 hours or overnight.

Remove cooker from refrigerator. Cook on HIGH for 2½–3 hours. Gently stir for 2–4 minutes or until pasta dissolves and gets thick and creamy. Gently stir in creamer until well blended. Stir in chopped pimientos, if using. Serve over toast or baked biscuits. Yields 14 (½-cup) servings.

Nutritional analysis: Cal 122 (9% fat); Fat 1gm; Choles 12mg; Carbo 18gm; Dietary Fiber 1 gm; Prot 7gm; Sod 313mg.

Busy People's Slow Cooker Cookbook

Teddy Boor of Ashville invented and built the nation's oldest working traffic light in the early 1930s. This bullet-shaped light hung at the corner of Main and Long for more than fifty years before being replaced by a more modern signal. The light is now on display as the main attraction at the Ashville Museum.

Southern-Style Chicken Gravy

There is something comforting about this meal that warms you to the heart.

1 (14½-ounce) can chicken
   broth
1 cup skim milk
¼ cup cornstarch
1 tablespoon garlic salt
   (optional)

Dash of pepper (optional)
3 (8-ounce) cans no-salt mixed
   vegetables, drained
1½ pounds boneless, skinless
   chicken breasts, cooked,
   chopped

Combine broth, milk, and cornstarch in a Dutch oven. Add garlic salt and pepper, if using, and mix well to dissolve cornstarch completely. Turn heat to medium. Add vegetables and chicken. Cook for 10–12 minutes or until thick and creamy, stirring occasionally. Yields 10 servings.

Note: Serve a half cup gravy over a couple of biscuits for a hearty breakfast treat.

Nutritional analysis: Cal 126 (10% fat); Fat 1gm; Choles 40mg; Carbo 9gm; Dietary Fiber 2gm; Prot 18gm; Sod 256mg.

Busy People's Down-Home Cooking
Without the Down-Home Fat

Chicken Tetrazzini

This is so flavorful that it can be "dressed up" with a spinach salad and wine for company.

4 whole chicken breasts	1 cup sliced mushrooms (fresh or
1 onion, chopped	canned)
¾ pound very thin spaghetti,	2 tablespoons butter
broken into thirds (4 cups	2 tablespoons sherry
cooked)	2 cups Velouté Sauce

Put chicken in foil with chopped onion; bake at 350° until chicken is tender, about 30 minutes. Cook spaghetti according to package directions. If using fresh mushrooms, sauté in butter. Season with sherry, and set aside. If using canned mushrooms, drain liquid and add sherry to can to marinate until needed.

VELOUTÉ SAUCE:

4 tablespoons melted butter	½ cup heavy cream
6 tablespoons all-purpose flour	1 cup grated Romano or
½ teaspoon salt	Parmesan cheese
½ teaspoon paprika	4 dashes paprika
2 cups canned chicken broth	

In a medium-size saucepan, melt butter over low heat. Stir in flour, salt, and paprika. Cook, stirring, until it makes a smooth paste. Slowly add broth, stirring to mix very well. Cook over medium heat until sauce thickens to very heavy cream consistency. Remove from heat; add cream a little at a time, stopping before sauce becomes too soupy or thin. Put all the spaghetti in a greased, shallow 3-quart baking dish; spoon ½ sauce on top; arrange chicken, torn into pieces, mushrooms, sherry, and onions. Top with remaining sauce. Sprinkle with Romano or Parmesan cheese; add paprika for color. Bake in a preheated 400° oven for 20 minutes. May be frozen before baking. Thaw and heat to serving temperature. Yields 8 servings.

Discover Dayton

Grandma Ratliff's Chicken & Dumplings

1 (5-pound) stewing chicken   **1 cup milk**
1 teaspoon salt

Place whole chicken in a large soup kettle and cover with water; add salt. Cook over low heat for approximately 3 hours or until meat is tender; remove chicken, reserving broth, and let chicken cool; debone. Heat chicken broth over medium heat; add milk and enough water to equal 2 gallons; bring to a boil. Carefully drop dumpling dough by large spoonfuls into boiling broth and cook for 20 minutes, stirring frequently. Reduce heat to low, add chicken back to kettle, and continue to cook for 5–10 minutes, or until broth thickens into a gravy. Serves 8–10.

GRANDMA'S DUMPLINGS:
4 cups self-rising flour   **¼ cup cooking oil**
3 cups milk   **12 drops yellow food coloring**
1 cup chicken broth   **Salt and pepper to taste**

In a mixing bowl, combine all ingredients. Mix well, then let rise for 5 minutes before adding to broth.

Ohio Cook Book

The Soap Box Derby is a youth racing program that has run nationally since 1934. World Championship finals are held each August at Derby Downs in Akron. The idea of the Soap Box Derby grew out of a photographic assignment of Dayton newsman Myron Scott. He covered a race of cars built by young boys in his home community and was so impressed with this event that he acquired a copyright for the idea and began development of a similar program on a national scale.

Chicken Couscous Sandwiches

3 cups chicken broth
4 tablespoons butter
2 cups couscous
2–3 scallions, thinly sliced
1 bell pepper, red or orange, chopped
1 small zucchini, chopped
2 medium carrots, chopped

1 pound boneless, skinless chicken breasts
Butter for sautéing chicken
6 ounces Monterey Jack cheese, finely shredded
⅓ cup ranch dressing
4 whole-wheat pita breads
Cayenne pepper to taste

Bring broth and butter to a boil. Remove from heat. Add couscous and cover. Let stand 5 minutes. In large bowl, combine couscous and prepared vegetables. Trim chicken of any visible fat. Sauté chicken in butter approximately 7 minutes. Cut chicken into small cubes and add to couscous mixture. Season to taste. After mixture has cooled, stir in cheese. Add only enough dressing to achieve desired moistness and flavor. Fill pita bread halves with mixture. Sprinkle with cheese. Bake sandwiches in a 350° oven 7–10 minutes or until heated through and bread is slightly crispy. Serves 8.

A Treasury of Recipes for Mind, Body & Soul

Turkey Tetrazzini

7 ounces whole-wheat blend
  spaghetti
1 tablespoon butter
½ pound mushrooms, sliced
  (use ½ shiitake, if desired)
3 tablespoons all-purpose flour
¼ teaspoon salt
¼ teaspoon freshly ground
  black pepper

1½ cups evaporated skim milk
1 cup reduced-sodium chicken or
  turkey broth
3 tablespoons sherry (optional)
1 medium red bell pepper, diced
4 green onions, sliced
2 cups cooked turkey, cut in small
  cubes
½ cup grated Parmesan cheese

Spray a 2-quart casserole with cooking spray. Break spaghetti into 2-inch pieces; cook according to package directions, omitting salt. Drain; set aside.

Preheat oven to 350°. In a large saucepan, melt butter. Add mushrooms; sauté until tender, stirring often. Add flour, salt, and pepper; stir to combine. Gradually add milk, stirring until mixture has thickened. Add chicken broth; simmer until slightly thickened. Blend in sherry. Remove from heat. Add red pepper, green onions, spaghetti, and chopped turkey to sauce; stir to combine. Pour into prepared casserole. Sprinkle with Parmesan cheese. Bake, uncovered, in 350° oven for 25–30 minutes. Remove from oven; let stand 10 minutes before serving. Makes 8 (1-cup) servings.

Nutritional analysis: Cal 226; Prot 20gm; Carbo 30gm; Dietary Fiber 4gm; Fat 4gm; Sat. Fat 2gm; Choles 38mg; Sod 312mg.

More Nutritious Still Delicious

Herbed Turkey

This is probably one of the moistest turkeys you will ever eat. The spices are wonderful. I will be making my turkey like this from now on.

1 (7½-pound) whole turkey
   breast (on the bone)
½ teaspoon rubbed thyme
1 teaspoon Cajun seasoning

1 teaspoon paprika
1 teaspoon black pepper
½ cup fat-free zesty Italian salad
   dressing

Spray a large slow cooker with nonfat cooking spray. Place turkey on a cutting board and remove skin by pulling it off with your hands. Discard skin. In a small mixing bowl, stir together thyme, Cajun seasoning, paprika, and black pepper. With your hands, press spices onto outside of turkey until they lightly cover the whole turkey breast. Place turkey in slow cooker.

Lightly drizzle Italian dressing over top and into bottom of slow cooker. If you pour slowly, the spices will stay on outside of turkey breast. Cover and cook on HIGH for 3½–4 hours or until meat is completely white. When turkey is completely cooked, place on platter. Yields 16 (4-ounce) servings.

Nutritional analysis per serving: Cal 166 (8% fat); Fat 1gm; Choles 100mg; Carbo 1gm; Dietary Fiber 0gm; Prot 35gm; Sod 152mg; Diabetic Exchanges 4 very lean meat.

Busy People's Fun, Fast, Festive Christmas Cookbook

Was Ohio the 17th state or the 47th state to be admitted to the Union? History tells us it was the 17th, but a little digging shows that on the eve of its 2003 bicentennial, Ohio discovered that Congress never officially voted on statehood in 1803, and didn't formally do so until 1953. That makes it the 47th state, not the 17th! Well, Ohio decided to go ahead and celebrate its bicentennial in 2003, rather than wait another 150 years.

Cheesy Turkey Bake

3 cups diced cooked turkey
2 cups cooked rice
1 medium onion, chopped
½ cup chopped celery
1 (10¾-ounce) can cream of
  mushroom soup
1 cup mayonnaise
1 (15-ounce) can mixed
  vegetables, drained

4 tablespoons lemon juice
2 teaspoons salt
1 cup grated smokey Cheddar
  cheese
2 (9-inch) deep-dish pie shells
4 tablespoons butter, melted
2 cups crushed cornflakes

In large bowl, mix all ingredients except pie shells, cornflakes, and butter. Refrigerate overnight or several hours.

Precook pie shells 10 minutes at 400°. Fill pie shells with turkey mixture and bake 40 minutes at 350°. Melt butter and sauté cornflakes. Sprinkle this topping over pies and bake 5 more minutes. Each pie serves 6.

Dawn to Dusk

Seafood

Marblehead Lighthouse is the oldest operating lighthouse on the Great Lakes, dating back to 1821. The historic structure offers one of the most scenic views of the Lake Erie Islands across the bay. Its green light distinguishes the lighthouse signal from white lights coming from air beacons.

Shrimp Sautéed in White Wine and Garlic

2 tablespoons unsalted butter, divided
1 teaspoon extra virgin olive oil
2 tablespoons finely chopped shallots
2 cloves garlic, finely chopped
1 cup dry white wine

2 pounds raw medium-size shrimp, shelled, deveined
¼ cup chopped fresh parsley
¼ cup chopped fresh basil, or 1 tablespoon dried
Salt and pepper to taste

In large heavy skillet, melt 1 tablespoon butter with olive oil over medium heat. Add shallots and garlic, and sauté until shallots are transparent and soft, being careful not to burn garlic. Increase heat to high, and add wine, shrimp, parsley, and basil. As liquid comes to a boil and shrimp turn color, remove shrimp with slotted spoon and set aside. (Be careful not to overcook.) Rapidly boil wine and herbs until ½ cup liquid remains. Add salt and pepper. Remove from heat and stir in remaining 1 tablespoon butter. Add shrimp and return to heat briefly to warm. Yields 4 servings.

With Great Gusto

Born on September 4, 1932, in Hammondsville, Clarence "Bevo" Francis became one of the greatest scorers in college basketball history during his career at Rio (pronounced RYE-oh) Grande College in Rio Grande. In 1953, Bevo averaged 48.3 points a game, which is an NCAA record. This included a record 113 points in a single game. He actually averaged 50.1 points per game over the season, but the NCAA excluded some of his best games because they were against lesser competition, such as junior colleges. One of the games that did not count during his career was a 116-point game against Ashland Junior College (Kentucky).

Shrimp Scorpio

3 tablespoons olive oil
2 cups minced onion
2 teaspoons minced garlic
¼ cup minced fresh parsley
1 tablespoon minced dill
¼ teaspoon sugar

2 cups chopped, peeled tomatoes
   (fresh or canned)
½ cup tomato sauce
1 pound medium shrimp, peeled,
   deveined
1 cup crumbled feta cheese

Heat oil in saucepan, add onions, and cook until golden brown. Stir in garlic, parsley, dill, sugar, tomatoes, and tomato sauce; simmer 30 minutes. Add shrimp to sauce and cook 3 minutes. Pour mixture into a 1½-quart casserole and sprinkle top with crumbled feta cheese. Bake in a preheated 425° oven for 5 minutes or until cheese melts.

A Festival of Recipes

Basil and Garlic Shrimp and Scallops

The mild flavors of these ingredients compliment each other.

1 tablespoon light butter
1 teaspoon Mrs. Dash Tomato
   Basil Seasoning Blend
1 tablespoon minced garlic
1 (20-ounce) bag frozen bay
   scallops, thawed

1 (16-ounce) bag frozen fully
   cooked and cleaned salad
   shrimp, thawed

In large, 12-inch nonstick skillet over medium heat, melt butter with seasoning blend and garlic. Add scallops. Cook 2–3 minutes. Turn scallops; continue cooking another 2–3 minutes or until scallops are white throughout. Add shrimp; cover; reduce heat to low. Cook 1 minute or until shrimp are fully heated. Remove from heat; serve immediately. Yields 4 (⅔-cup) servings.

Nutritional analysis: Cal 253 (14% fat); Total fat 4gm; Choles 273mg; Carbo 4gm; Dietary Fiber 0gm; Prot 48gm; Sod 500mg; Diabetic Exchanges 6 very lean meat.

Busy People's Low-Carb Cookbook

Broccoli and Shrimp Stir-Fry

1 tablespoon vegetable oil
12 ounces peeled deveined
  shrimp
2 cups fresh or frozen broccoli
1 medium red bell pepper, cut
  into thin 2-inch strips
½ cup snow peas
½ cup sliced fresh mushrooms
¼ cup sliced water chestnuts

2 teaspoons instant chicken
  bouillon
½ cup boiling water
1 tablespoon cornstarch
1 teaspoon lemon juice
1 teaspoon dried basil leaves
½ cup cold water
½ cup sliced green onions
Cooked rice

Heat oil in a wok over medium heat. Add shrimp. Stir-fry for 4 minutes or until shrimp turn pink. Remove shrimp to a heated dish. Add broccoli, red pepper, snow peas, mushrooms, and water chestnuts to the wok. Stir-fry until vegetables are tender-crisp. Dissolve instant bouillon in boiling water. Stir cornstarch, lemon juice, and basil into cold water. Add bouillon mixture and cornstarch mixture to the vegetables. Cook until thickened, stirring constantly. Add green onions and shrimp. Stir-fry until heated through. Serve over cooked rice. Yields 4 servings.

America Celebrates Columbus

Lake Erie Potato-Fried Fish

1½ pounds white bass, yellow
   perch, or other fillets
1 teaspoon salt
¼ teaspoon pepper
1 egg, beaten

1 tablespoon water
1 cup instant mashed potatoes
1 package onion or Italian salad
   dressing mix
Cooking oil

Sprinkle fish fillets with salt and pepper. In a bowl, beat together egg and water. In another bowl, combine potato flakes and dressing mix. Dip fish into egg mixture to coat, then dredge in potato flake mixture. Heat ⅛ inch oil in a skillet. Add fish and over moderate heat, fry for 4–5 minutes per side. Drain on paper towels.

Ohio Cook Book

Baked Orange Roughy

Butter
6 orange roughy fillets

Cayenne pepper
Tarragon leaves, crushed

Butter a large baking sheet. Lay fillets in a single layer on sheet. Sprinkle with pepper and crushed tarragon. Bake at 425° for 10–12 minutes. Melon Salsa dressing is served on the side. Serves 6.

MELON SALSA:

½ honeydew, finely chopped
½ cantaloupe, finely chopped
1 jalapeño pepper, seeded,
   minced

2 tablespoons fresh lime juice
2 tablespoons olive oil
2 tablespoons minced fresh mint

Combine all ingredients. Let stand 15 minutes to allow flavors to blend. You may want to drain off some of the liquid before serving. Serves 6.

A Treasury of Recipes for Mind, Body & Soul

Pan-Fried Halibut à la Sherry

As far as I am concerned, the best way to eat fish is fried. I love the eastern shore where people don't turn up their noses at frying fish. The fish should be crunchy on the outside and moist and juicy on the inside. Halibut is not usually fried, but I love my recipe for preparing it this way.

4 halibut fillets
1 cup white wine
1 cup heavy cream
1 teaspoon salt
1 teaspoon pepper
1 cup all-purpose flour

¼ cup fresh but dry bread
   crumbs (or Japanese panko
   crumbs)
Canola oil
Lemon wedges

Drip fillets in white wine and then cream. Season filets with salt and pepper, then dip in flour and crumbs; shake off any excess breading. Pour ¼ inch canola oil in a pan and fry fillets until golden on both sides. Serve with lemon and tartar sauce. Yields 4 servings.

TARTAR SAUCE:

½ small yellow onion, minced
2 tablespoons apple cider
   vinegar
3 tablespoons sugar
½ cup chopped sweet pickles

Dash of Tabasco
1 cup mayonnaise
1 teaspoon freshly chopped dill,
   or ¼ teaspoon dried

Mix onion, vinegar, and sugar in a medium mixing bowl and let it sit for 5 minutes. Stir in rest of ingredients. Season to taste with salt, pepper, and a few drops of Tabasco. Store in refrigerator until fish is ready.

A Taste of the Murphin Ridge Inn

Life Savers were invented in 1912 by Clarence Crane, a Cleveland chocolate maker who wanted a sweet product that wouldn't melt in the summer heat. He decided on a hard candy in the shape of a circle with a hole in the middle. Since the new candy looked like miniature life preservers, he called them Life Savers.

Thyme-Scented Salmon with Tuscan White Bean Salad

SALAD:

1 tablespoon extra virgin olive oil
⅓ cup finely chopped celery
½ cup finely chopped carrot
½ cup finely chopped shallots
2 cloves garlic, minced
3 tablespoons fresh lemon juice

2 teaspoons chopped fresh parsley
2 teaspoons chopped fresh mint
2 teaspoons chopped fresh basil
2 tablespoons water
1 (15-ounce) can cannellini beans or other white beans, drained

Preheat oven to 375°. Heat oil in a medium nonstick skillet; add celery, carrot, shallots, and garlic. Cook 4 minutes or until tender; add lemon juice, parsley, mint, basil, water, and beans. Cook bean mixture 2 minutes or until thoroughly heated, stirring constantly. Remove from heat and cover.

SALMON:

2 teaspoons chopped fresh thyme
1 teaspoon chopped fresh parsley
½ teaspoon salt

⅛ teaspoon black pepper
4 (6-ounce) salmon fillets, about 1 inch thick
3 tablespoons fresh lemon juice

Combine thyme, parsley, salt, and pepper in a small bowl; sprinkle evenly over fish. Place fish on a foil-lined baking sheet or broiler pan. Bake at 375° for 14 minutes or until fish flakes easily when tested with a fork. Remove from oven; sprinkle evenly with lemon juice. Serve with bean salad. Serves 4.

50 Years and Still Cookin'!

Salmon with Fresh Herb Pesto

2½ ounces roasted cashews, divided
1 cup panko bread crumbs
½ ounce grated fresh Parmesan cheese
3–4 sprigs fresh thyme
3–4 leaves fresh sage
2 cups loosely packed fresh basil leaves

1 clove garlic
1 tablespoon fresh lemon juice
⅓ cup extra virgin olive oil
Salt and pepper to taste
4 (8-ounce) salmon fillets
¼ pound clarified butter

Place 2 ounces cashews in a food processor. Process 30 seconds or until cashews are chopped medium fine. Mix with panko bread crumbs and set aside.

Place remaining ½ ounce cashews and Parmesan cheese in food processor. Process 30–40 seconds, until mixture is finely chopped. Add thyme, sage, basil, garlic, and lemon juice. Process 15–20 seconds, then add olive oil and process 45 seconds more. Salt and pepper to taste.

Brush each salmon fillet with clarified butter. Dip fillet in cashew crust and place skin side up in a hot pan. Cook about 4 minutes, then turn salmon and finish cooking 4–5 minutes more. Place salmon on a plate and put a dollop of pesto on center of the fillet. Yields 4 servings.

Don't Forget the INNgredients!

The Celina Rotary Lighthouse is a unique light, not because of its age or history, but because of its location. While lighthouses are usually constructed to provide aid to vessels navigating dangerous open waters or shores, Celina stands on the west bank of Grand Lake St. Marys, a 13,500-acre man-made lake near the city of Celina. Built in 1986 as a project of the local Rotary Club, this 40-foot lighthouse is functional, but acts more as an observation tower than a navigational aid.

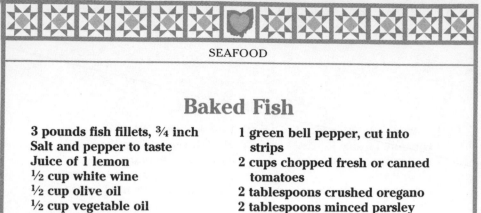

Baked Fish

3 pounds fish fillets, ¾ inch
Salt and pepper to taste
Juice of 1 lemon
½ cup white wine
½ cup olive oil
½ cup vegetable oil
2 cloves garlic, minced

1 green bell pepper, cut into
strips
2 cups chopped fresh or canned
tomatoes
2 tablespoons crushed oregano
2 tablespoons minced parsley
Bread crumbs

Place fish on greased baking dish and sprinkle with salt, pepper, and fresh lemon juice. In saucepan, combine remaining ingredients except bread crumbs. Pour sauce over fish. Sprinkle bread crumbs on top. Bake, uncovered, in preheated 400° oven for 45 minutes or until fish is nice and brown. Serves 5–6.

A Festival of Recipes

Steamed Sole

1½–2 pounds fillet of sole
8 romaine lettuce leaves
1 (7.5-ounce) can salmon,
  drained
5 tablespoons minced green
  onions

1 clove garlic, minced
2½ tablespoons chili sauce
Juice of ½ lemon
2 tablespoons minced parsley
⅛ teaspoon cayenne pepper

Separate fillets into 8 equal portions, allowing 3–4 for each lettuce leaf. Steam lettuce leaves for 3–4 minutes or until pliable (reserve water for second steaming). Combine salmon, green onions, garlic, chili sauce, lemon juice, parsley, and cayenne pepper. On each softened lettuce leaf, place a fillet and spoon on about 3 tablespoons of the salmon mixture. Roll up jellyroll-style, folding the ends in. Steam, seam side down over rapidly boiling water for 10 minutes. Remove from heat and place on plate.

LEMON BUTTER SAUCE:
4 tablespoons butter   1 tablespoon lemon juice

Melt butter. Remove from heat and stir in lemon juice. Place juice in individual containers to serve as a thin sauce over sole. Serves 4.

A Treasury of Recipes for Mind, Body & Soul

If you wear shoelaces, chances are they were made in Portsmouth. The nation's largest manufacturer of shoelaces, Mitchellace, Inc., produces more than four million pairs of shoelaces every week!

Thai Crab Cakes
with Cilantro-Peanut Sauce

A new twist on an old standby!

CRAB CAKES:

1¼ cups fresh bread crumbs
1 cup chopped fresh bean
sprouts
¼ cup finely chopped green
onions
¼ cup coarsely chopped fresh
cilantro

2 tablespoons fresh lime juice
⅛ teaspoon cayenne pepper
1 egg, lightly beaten
1 egg white, lightly beaten
1 pound lump crabmeat, picked
over
2 tablespoons olive oil, divided

Combine bread crumbs, bean sprouts, onions, cilantro, juice, cayenne pepper, egg, egg white, and crabmeat in a medium bowl. Cover and chill 1 hour. Divide mixture into 8 equal portions. Shape each portion into a ½-inch-thick patty. Heat 1 tablespoon oil in a large nonstick skillet over medium heat. Add 4 patties and cook 3 minutes on each side or until lightly browned. Remove patties and keep warm. Wipe skillet clean with paper towels. Re-coat skillet with remaining tablespoon oil and cook remaining 4 patties. Serve with Cilantro-Peanut Sauce.

CILANTRO-PEANUT SAUCE:

¼ cup balsamic vinegar
2½ tablespoons granulated
sugar
2 tablespoons brown sugar
2 tablespoons low-sodium soy
sauce
½ teaspoon dried red pepper
flakes

⅛ teaspoon salt
1 clove garlic, minced
2 tablespoons creamy peanut
butter
½ cup chopped fresh cilantro
2 tablespoons chopped fresh
mint

Combine vinegar, sugars, soy sauce, pepper flakes, salt, and garlic in a small saucepan. Bring to a boil, stirring frequently. Remove from heat. Add peanut butter and stir with a whisk until smooth; cool. Stir in cilantro and mint. Yields 4 servings.

Note: Fresh bread crumbs make the difference in this recipe—don't use dried!

Causing a Stir

Scalloped Oysters

6 tablespoons butter
2 cups fine cracker crumbs
1 pint oysters

Salt and pepper to taste
½ cup milk

Melt butter; add crumbs and mix well. Divide oysters for 2 layers. Place a layer on bottom of baking dish. Sprinkle with ½ of crumb mixture. Season with salt and pepper to taste; repeat layers. Pour milk over top. Bake at 350° for 30 minutes or until brown. Serves 6.

Columbus Colony Creations

Fried Oysters

2 dozen oysters
Bread crumbs, finely crushed,
  seasoned

2 eggs, beaten

Pat each oyster dry. Dip into seasoned bread crumbs, then into beaten eggs, and again into bread crumbs. Shake gently to remove any loose crumbs. Fry in deep fat fryer (375°–390°) or deep skillet till golden brown. (Always use bread crumbs because cracker crumbs will absorb the grease and bread crumbs will not.) Yields 4 servings.

Favorite Recipes–First Church of God

Cakes

Cuyahoga Valley Scenic Railroad is one of the oldest, longest, and most scenic excursion railways in the country, running through the heart of beautiful Cuyahoga Valley National Park, along the Cuyahoga River and the historic Ohio and Erie Canalway between Cleveland and Akron, and on to Canton.

Ancestor Apple Cake

4 cups peeled, chopped apples
2 cups sugar
2 eggs
½ cup oil
2 cups all-purpose flour

1 teaspoon baking soda
2 teaspoons cinnamon
1 teaspoon salt
1 teaspoon vanilla
1 cup or more chopped walnuts

Mix all ingredients together until well blended. Bake in greased round cake pan at 350° until knife inserted comes out clean, 25–30 minutes.

Cooking Up a Cure

Apple Baba

4 tart apples, such as Granny
  Smith, peeled, cored,
  quartered, thinly sliced
  crosswise
2¼ cups sugar, divided
1 teaspoon ground cinnamon
4 large eggs

1 cup vegetable oil
½ cup fresh orange juice
2 teaspoons vanilla extract
4 cups unbleached flour
1 teaspoon baking powder
Confectioners' sugar for
  garnish

Preheat oven to 350°. Grease a 10-inch tube pan. Place apples in a large bowl; sprinkle with ¼ cup sugar and cinnamon; set aside. In a large bowl, beat eggs and remaining 2 cups sugar with electric mixer until pale yellow and thick. Gradually beat in oil, orange juice, and vanilla extract.

Sift together flour and baking powder. Gradually add to egg mixture, stirring with a large wooden spoon. You will have a batter the consistency of thick honey. Fold apples into batter, making sure they are well distributed. Pour apple batter into prepared pan, and smooth top with rubber spatula. Bake until top is well browned and splitting, about 1¼ hours. Invert baba onto a rack and cool. Sprinkle with confectioners' sugar before serving. Serves 8–10.

Recipes and Remembrances: Around St. George's Tables

Apple Dapple

¼ cup butter, softened
1 cup sugar
1 egg
1 cup all-purpose flour
1 teaspoon baking soda

½ teaspoon salt
¾ teaspoon cinnamon
½ teaspoon nutmeg
2 cups grated apple
½ cup chopped nuts

In a mixing bowl, cream together butter and sugar; add egg and beat well. In a separate bowl, sift together flour, baking soda, salt, cinnamon, and nutmeg. Add flour mixture to creamed mixture; stir in apples and nuts. Pour into a buttered 8-inch baking pan. Bake at 350° for 45 minutes.

SAUCE:
½ cup butter
½ cup cream

1 cup sugar

In a saucepan, combine butter, cream, and sugar. Bring mixture to a boil; reduce heat and simmer for 20 minutes, stirring constantly. Serve warm over cake squares.

Ohio Cook Book

Mandarin Orange Cake

This three-layer cake is made to order for Easter. It's not only pretty, but very easy to make.

1 (18¼-ounce) yellow cake mix (no pudding)
1 (11-ounce) can Mandarin oranges, undrained
4 eggs
½ cup vegetable oil

1 (15-ounce) can crushed pineapple, undrained
1 (9-ounce) carton whipped topping, thawed
1 (3-ounce) package vanilla instant pudding

Combine cake mix, oranges, eggs, and oil. Beat for 2 minutes at high speed with a mixer. Reduce speed to low and beat for 1 minute. Pour mixture into 3 greased and floured cake pans. Bake at 350° for 25 minutes or until tester comes out clean. Cool 10 minutes; remove and cool completely.

Combine pineapple, whipped topping, and pudding, and blend with mixer. Let stand 5 minutes or until mixture is of spreading consistency. Spread between layers and on top and sides of cake. Chill before serving.

50 Years and Still Cookin'!

Peach Kuchen

1 (18¼-ounce) package white cake mix
½ cup flaked coconut
½ cup margarine
1 (29-ounce) can sliced peaches, drained

2 tablespoons sugar
½ teaspoon cinnamon
1 cup sour cream
1 egg, slightly beaten

Combine cake mix and coconut; cut in margarine. Press onto bottom and 1 inch up sides of a 9x13-inch pan. Bake at 350° for 10–15 minutes. Arrange peach slices on top of baked cake. Combine sugar and cinnamon and sprinkle over peaches. Blend sour cream and egg. Pour over all. Bake an additional 15 minutes at 350° until set. Cool and keep refrigerated.

Cooking Up a Cure

Blueberry Upside Down Cake

Home run. Yes, sir. I hit a home run when I created this winner. Absolutely delicious and oh, so pretty.

6 egg whites
1 cup water
⅓ cup applesauce
1 (18¼-ounce) box French
  vanilla cake mix, dry

1 (21-ounce) can blueberry pie
  filling
Fat-free whipped topping
  (optional)

Preheat slow cooker to HIGH. Spray cooker with nonfat cooking spray. In a large bowl, beat egg whites on high speed with a mixer for 1–2 minutes or until soft peaks form. Reduce speed to MEDIUM and mix in water, applesauce, and cake mix. Mix another minute, scraping sides of bowl often. Pour pie filling into bottom of prepared slow cooker. Pour cake batter over pie filling. Do not stir.

Place a paper towel on top of slow cooker and put lid on paper towel to cover. Cook on HIGH for 2 hours. Take lid and paper towel off. Take crock out of slow cooker, if possible. Let it cool for 10 minutes. Place a large serving plate with an edge (so sauce won't overflow off the plate) upside down on top of slow cooker. Holding slow cooker and plate firmly together, carefully flip cake upside down. It will be steamy hot so be very careful. The berries will ooze down the sides of the cake. Serve hot, chilled, or at room temperature with fat-free whipped topping, if desired. Yields 12 servings.

Nutritional analysis: Cal 243 (15% fat); Fat 4gm; Choles 0mg; Carb 48gm; Dietary Fiber 2gm; Prot 4gm; Sod 311mg.

Busy People's Slow Cooker Cookbook

Martha Finley, creator of the *Elsie Dinsmore* series of children's books, was born in 1828 in Chillicothe. Finley's tales of the pious Elsie struck a chord with young readers and were popular through twenty-seven sequels. *Elsie Dinsmore* was published in 1868, and became the publisher's best-selling book that year, spawning a series that sold over five million copies. *Elsie Dinsmore* remained in print for fifty years, and outsold every other novel for juveniles for three generations, with the exception of *Little Women*.

Linda's Carrot Cake

2 cups all-purpose flour, sifted
2 teaspoons baking powder
1½ teaspoons baking soda
1 teaspoon salt
2 teaspoons cinnamon
2 cups sugar

4 eggs
1¼ cups oil
2 carrots, grated
1 (30-ounce) can crushed
   pineapple, well drained
½ cup chopped nuts

Grease and lightly flour a 9x13-inch baking pan. Mix flour, baking powder, baking soda, salt, cinnamon, and sugar. Set aside. In mixing bowl, beat eggs; add oil. Slowly beat in flour mixture; mix well. Add carrots, pineapple, and nuts. Beat 2 minutes. Pour into prepared pan, and bake at 350° for 35–45 minutes or until cake springs back.

ICING:
1 (8-ounce) package cream
   cheese, softened
½ cup margarine, softened

1 pound confectioners' sugar
1 teaspoon vanilla

Combine cream cheese and margarine; add sugar and vanilla; beat together. Spread on cake.

Favorite Recipes–First Church of God

"Disorderly Conduct" Cake

1 cup flaked coconut
1 cup chopped pecans
1 (18¼-ounce) package German
   chocolate cake mix

1 stick butter, softened
1 (8-ounce) package cream
   cheese, softened
1 pound confectioners' sugar

Grease and flour a 9x13-inch pan. Spread coconut and pecans in pan. Prepare cake mix according to package directions. Pour batter over pecans and coconut. Mix butter, cream cheese, and sugar. Drop by teaspoons over batter. Bake at 350° for 45 minutes. Cake will be shaky but will set up.

Favorite Recipes from the Delaware Police Department

Filled Kugelhopf

5 egg yolks
½ cup sweet butter, softened
2 tablespoons sugar
2½ cups all-purpose flour,
   sifted
1 cake yeast, dissolved in
   ¼ cup milk

1 teaspoon vanilla
¼ teaspoon salt
Luke-warm sweet cream
Powdered sugar for dusting

Cream egg yolks, butter, and sugar until thick. Add flour, yeast, vanilla, salt, and enough cream to make a very delicate soft dough. Beat with a wooden spoon until dough is smooth, shiny, and no longer sticks to spoon. Cover and allow to rise double in size.

Now place half the dough into a large, well-buttered, deep, round cake or tube pan.

Spread Filling evenly over dough, then cover with the other half of dough. Cake pan should be half full. Allow to rise again for 20 minutes, until pan is filled. Bake in 325°–350° oven for 40–45 minutes or until fully baked. Remove immediately from pan to cool. Dust with powdered sugar and serve.

FILLING:

1 cup ground almonds or
   walnuts
½ cup finely chopped raisins

3 tablespoons sugar
½ teaspoon cinnamon
½ lemon rind, grated

Combine ingredients well.

Aunt Paula's American Hungarian Cookbook

Located at the Toledo Zoo, the world's only Hippoquarium offers visitors a chance to observe Nile hippos in a natural setting as they lope along underwater in their crystal-clear pool. The Hippoquarium was rated by *USA Today* as one of the nation's ten best animal exhibits, and was also featured in *National Geographic*. Despite the hippo's cuddly portrayal in fiction, the hippopotamus is among the most dangerous and aggressive of all mammals.

Moravian Sugar Cake

CAKE:

¾ cup margarine, softened
1 cup sugar
2 eggs
1 cup potato water (drained
   from potatoes)
1 cup mashed potatoes

2 teaspoons salt
2 packages yeast, dissolved in
   warm water and 1 teaspoon
   sugar
8 cups all-purpose flour, or
   enough to make soft dough

Cream shortening and sugar. Beat in eggs, potato water, potatoes, and salt. Add yeast mixture. Add flour to make a soft dough. Let stand 2–3 hours in a warm place to rise until doubled. Flatten out dough in 8 greased pans and let rise again. Use fingers to punch holes in dough.

TOPPING:

2⅔ cups brown sugar
2 tablespoons plus 2 teaspoons
   all-purpose flour
1½ teaspoons cinnamon
⅔ cup butter, melted (no
   substitute)

1 cup whipping cream
   (half-and-half or condensed
   milk can be used)

Mix brown sugar, flour, and cinnamon. Add melted butter and mix well. Divide into 8 portions; sprinkle a portion in holes of each portion of dough. Drizzle ⅛ cup whipping cream over each portion, preferably in the holes. Bake in 350° oven for 20–30 minutes until light brown. Makes 8 (8-inch) round pans.

Country Collections Cookbook II

Almond Cake

The almond filling makes a winning frosting.

1 (12-ounce) can almond filling
    for pastries, cakes, and
    desserts
3 egg whites
1 (18¼-ounce) box butter-
    flavored cake mix, dry

1 cup water
⅓ cup applesauce
2 teaspoons almond extract

Preheat a slow cooker to HIGH. Spray slow cooker with nonfat cooking spray. Spread almond filling in bottom of prepared slow cooker. In a large bowl, beat egg whites about 2 minutes or until soft peaks form. Stir in cake mix, water, applesauce, and almond extract until well mixed. (There may be some small lumps in batter—that's okay.) Pour cake batter over almond filling. Do not stir.

Place a paper towel on top of slow cooker. Place the slow cooker lid on top of paper towel to cover. Cook on HIGH for 1¾ hours or until a knife inserted in middle comes out clean. Remove lid and paper towel. If possible, remove the crock from slow cooker. Let it cool for 15 minutes.

Place a large serving plate with an edge (so the sauce won't overflow off the plate) upside down on top of slow cooker. Holding slow cooker and plate firmly together, carefully flip cake upside down. It will be steamy hot so be very careful.

Frost sides of cake with almond filling from top of cake, leaving some almond filling on top. Serve warm or chilled. Yields 12 servings.

Nutritional analysis: Cal 279 (17% fat); Fat 5gm; Choles 0mg; Carbo 55gm; Dietary Fiber 2gm; Prot 3gm; Sod 321mg.

Busy People's Slow Cooker Cookbook

Black Forest Upside Down Cake

I'm so very, very excited about this cake. It looks beautiful and is very impressive. Tastes great.

6 egg whites
½ cup applesauce
1 cup water
1 (18¼-ounce) box chocolate cake
mix, dry

1 (20-ounce) can light cherry pie
filling

Preheat slow cooker on HIGH. Spray slow cooker with nonfat cooking spray. In a large mixing bowl, with a hand mixer, beat egg whites, applesauce, and water together on medium speed until soft peaks form. Gently fold cake mix into peaks. Pour pie filling into bottom of cooker. Pour batter over pie filling. Do not stir.

Place a paper towel on top of slow cooker and place lid over paper towel to cover. Cook on HIGH for 2½–3 hours or until knife inserted in center comes out clean. Turn off cooker. If possible, take crock out of slow cooker. Let it sit 10 minutes. Remove paper towel. Run a knife along edge of slow cooker to loosen cake. Place a large serving plate with an edge (so sauce won't overflow off the plate) upside down on top of slow cooker. Holding slow cooker and plate firmly together, carefully flip cake upside down. It will be steamy hot so be very careful. If desired, serve with fat-free whipped topping or fat-free vanilla ice cream. Good served hot, cold, or at room temperature. Yields 12 servings.

Note: Be careful lifting slow cooker since hot cherry pie filling will ooze down over cake and onto large serving plate. You may want to serve this dessert with a spoon from slow cooker if you are concerned about inverting the cake.

Nutritional analysis: Cal 213 (17% fat); Fat 4gm; Chole 0mg; Carb 39gm; Dietary Fiber 2gm; Prot 4gm; Sod 364mg.

Busy People's Slow Cooker Cookbook

Cappuccino-Chocolate Coffee Cake

⅓ cup flaked coconut
¼ cup chopped nuts
½ cup sugar, divided
3 tablespoons butter or margarine, melted, divided
2 cups Bisquick mix

⅔ cup milk
1 egg
⅓ cup semisweet chocolate
  chips, melted
2 teaspoons powdered instant
  coffee

Heat oven to 400°. Grease an 8x8-inch square pan. Mix coconut, nuts, ¼ cup sugar, and 1 tablespoon butter. Set aside. Beat remaining ingredients, except chocolate chips and coffee, in large bowl on low speed 30 seconds, scraping bowl constantly. Beat on medium speed 4 minutes, scraping bowl occasionally. Pour into pan.

Stir together chocolate and coffee; spoon over batter. Lightly swirl chocolate mixture through batter several times with knife for marbled effect. Sprinkle coconut mixture evenly over top. Bake 20–25 minutes or until golden brown. Serve warm.

Food for Thought

In 1972, Vincent Marotta of Cleveland invented Mr. Coffee, the first home drip coffee maker. Prior to this, coffee was usually perked, either on stove top or in an electric percolator.

Milky Way Cake

This recipe is a hit with anyone who tries it. And the cake gets better with age because it gets more moist the longer it sits. It's really easy to make and tastes great when served with whipped topping. The original recipe has been around for quite a while, because it called for $0.25 candy bars!

5 Milky Way Candy Bars
1 cup margarine, divided
2 cups sugar
4 eggs
2½ cups all-purpose flour

1 cup buttermilk
½ teaspoon baking soda
2 teaspoons vanilla
½ cup chopped nuts (optional)

Melt candy bars and ½ cup margarine in top of a double boiler. Mix until smooth; set aside. Cream sugar and remaining margarine; add eggs one at a time, beating until smooth. Add flour, buttermilk, and baking soda. Mix well. Add candy bar mixture, vanilla, and nuts. Mix well. Turn into greased and floured tube pan or fluted tube pan. Bake at 350° about 60 minutes, or until cake tests done. Remove from oven and cool. Turn cake out onto a plate.

MILKY WAY CAKE ICING:
This icing is an option to use for the cake. In fact, I don't think Mom ever made the icing. She usually just served the Milky Way Cake with whipped topping.

3 Milky Way Candy Bars
1 stick butter or margarine

1 teaspoon vanilla
2 cups confectioners' sugar

Melt candy bars and margarine in top of double boiler until smooth. Add vanilla and confectioners' sugar, stirring constantly until icing is smooth. Add a small amount of milk to icing mixture if it is too thick to spread. Spread over cooled cake.

Love, Mom: Stories and Recipes from Kingston, Ohio

Kahlúa Mousse Cake

CRUST:

½ cup graham cracker crumbs
½ cup finely chopped walnuts
1 cup finely chopped almonds

½ cup sugar
1 stick unsalted butter, melted

Preheat oven to 350°. Lightly oil a 9½ x 2-inch springform pan. In a bowl, stir together ingredients until combined well; press onto bottom of pan. Bake Crust in middle of oven 15 minutes, or until pale golden. Cool in pan on a rack.

CHOCOLATE LAYER:

2 cups heavy cream
16 ounces semisweet chocolate,
  chopped coarsely

2 tablespoons light corn syrup
1 stick unsalted butter, cut into
  pieces

In a saucepan, heat cream, chocolate, and corn syrup over moderately high heat, stirring occasionally, until chocolate is melted and mixture just comes to a boil. Remove pan from heat and stir in butter, one piece at a time, until smooth. Pour mixture over Crust in pan and chill, until firm, about 3 hours.

BUTTER CREAM LAYER:

1½ cups sugar
½ cup water
6 large egg yolks
3 sticks unsalted butter,
  softened

½ cup Kahlúa
4 ounces semisweet chocolate,
  chopped, melted, cooled

In a saucepan, cook sugar and water over moderately high heat, stirring occasionally, until sugar is melted. Simmer syrup, undisturbed, until a candy thermometer registers 240°.

In a bowl with an electric mixer, beat yolks until smooth. Add hot syrup in a stream, beating on high speed until thickened and cooled. Reduce speed to medium and beat in butter, a little at a time. Beat in Kahlúa and chocolate until combined well. Spread Butter Cream over Chocolate Layer and chill until firm, about 3 hours. Run a knife around edge of pan and carefully remove side of pan. Serves 6–8.

Recipes and Remembrances: Around St. George's Tables

Century-Style Chocolate Sheet Cake

A tester could have sworn she was eating the cake from the Old Century Bar in downtown Dayton!

CAKE:

2 sticks butter
1 cup water
2 tablespoons cocoa
2 cups all-purpose flour
2 cups sugar

1 teaspoon baking soda
1 teaspoon salt
2 eggs, lightly beaten
½ cup buttermilk

Preheat oven to 375°. Combine butter, water, and cocoa in a large saucepan. Bring to a boil; immediately remove from heat. Stir in flour, sugar, baking soda, and salt. Mix thoroughly. Add eggs and buttermilk; stir. Pour into a greased jellyroll pan. Bake 20 minutes.

ICING:

1 stick butter
6 tablespoons milk
¼ cup cocoa
1 (1-pound) package powdered
  sugar

Pinch of salt
1 teaspoon vanilla
½–1 cup chopped pecans

Melt butter in a saucepan. Mix in milk, cocoa, powdered sugar, salt, and vanilla. Pour Icing over Cake while still hot. Spread Icing evenly and sprinkle with pecans. Yields 20 servings.

Causing a Stir

Fluffy Sponge Cake

This is an awesome cake. When we were kids, Mom often made this cake. We would sit down when we came home from school and eat a slice of sponge cake with whipped topping on it. It was also one of Dad's favorite cakes and he especially liked it topped with fresh strawberries.

1½ cups all-purpose flour	⅓ cup cold water
1 teaspoon baking powder	2 teaspoons vanilla
½ teaspoon salt	1 teaspoon lemon flavoring
6 eggs, separated	1 teaspoon grated lemon rind
1½ cups sugar	½ teaspoon cream of tartar

Blend flour, baking powder, and salt; set aside. Beat egg yolks in a small bowl until very thick and lemon-colored. Pour beaten egg yolks in a large bowl and gradually beat in sugar. Alternate adding flour mixture and water, flavorings, and rind to egg/sugar mixture.

In another bowl, mix egg whites and cream of tartar. Beat mixture until egg whites form stiff peaks. Gradually and gently fold egg yolk mixture into batter. (Do not overmix this!) Pour into ungreased 4x10-inch tube pan. Bake at 325° for 60–65 minutes. (Cake is done when it springs back when touched.) Remove from oven and invert pan over neck of funnel or bottle. Let cool. Remove from pan.

Love, Mom: Stories and Recipes from Kingston, Ohio

Angel Food Cake

1 cup sifted cake flour
1½ cups sifted confectioners'
  sugar
1½ cups egg whites
1½ teaspoons cream of tartar

⅓ teaspoon salt
1½ teaspoons vanilla
½ teaspoon almond extract
1 cup granulated sugar

Measure and sift together cake flour and confectioners' sugar. In mixing bowl, beat egg whites, cream of tartar, salt, vanilla, and almond extract with wire whip until foamy. Gradually add sugar 2 tablespoons at a time, and continue beating until meringue holds stiff peaks. Sift flour mixture over meringue. Fold in gently just until flour/sugar mixture dissappears. Keep turning your mixing bowl while folding in the sugar and flour. Push batter into ungreased 10-inch tube pan. Gently cut through the batter with spatula. Bake 45 minutes or more at 350° till cake tests done. Invert on bottle neck and let hang till cold.

Mt. Zion Lutheran Church Cookbook

Lemon Custard Cake Dessert

1 prepared angel food cake
1 (6-ounce) package lemon
   instant pudding
3 cups cold milk

2 cups sour cream
2 (21-ounce) cans cherry,
   strawberry, or blueberry pie
   filling

Tear cake into bite-size pieces. Place in 9x13-inch pan or trifle bowl. In a mixing bowl, combine pudding mix, milk, and sour cream. Beat until thickened, about 2 minutes. Spread over cake. Spoon pie filling on top. Chill until time to serve.

Sharing Recipes Cookbook

Vanilla Wafer Cake

2 sticks margarine, softened
1½ cups sugar
½ cup milk
6 eggs

1 (12-ounce) box vanilla wafers,
   crushed
1 (7-ounce) can flaked coconut
1 cup chopped pecans

Beat margarine and sugar until creamy. Add milk, eggs (one at a time), vanilla wafers, coconut, and pecans. Bake in greased Bundt pan for 2 hours in 275° oven.

Sharing Our Best

Quilt patterns are appearing on rural barns throughout southern Ohio. The idea originated with Donna Sue Groves, who purchased a barn in Adams County that had the "Chew Mail Pouch Tobacco" slogan painted on it. She wanted to replace the slogan with a painted quilt square, to honor her mother, Nina Maxine Groves, a noted quilter who learned the craft from her mother and grandmother. Through funding from the Ohio Arts Council and community support, Groves accomplished her wish and now her quilt barn idea appears on additional barns in several Ohio counties and other states. The barns are forming a "Clothesline of Quilts in Appalachia," the name of the regional project.

Easy and Delicious Amaretto Cake

1½ cups chopped toasted
  almonds, divided
1 (18¼-ounce) package yellow
  cake mix (without pudding)
1 (4-ounce) package vanilla
  instant pudding mix
4 eggs
½ cup vegetable oil

¾ cup water, divided
¾ cup amaretto, divided
1½ teaspoons almond extract,
  divided
½ cup sugar
2 tablespoons butter or
  margarine

Sprinkle 1 cup almonds in bottom of well-greased and floured 10-inch tube pan. Set aside. In mixing bowl, combine cake mix, pudding mix, eggs, oil, ½ cup water, ½ cup amaretto, and 1 teaspoon almond extract. Beat on low speed of electric mixer until dry ingredients are moistened. Beat on medium speed for 4 minutes. Stir in remaining ½ cup almonds. Pour batter into prepared tube pan. Bake at 325° for 1 hour, or until toothpick inserted in center comes out clean. Cool in pan for 10–15 minutes. Remove from pan and cool completely.

For glaze, combine sugar, remaining ¼ cup water, and butter in small saucepan. Bring to a boil, reduce heat to medium, and gently boil, stirring occasionally, for 4–5 minutes (until sugar dissolves). Remove from heat and cool 15 minutes. Stir in remaining ¼ cup amaretto and remaining ½ teaspoon almond extract. Punch holes in top of cake with wooden pick. Slowly spoon glaze on top of cake, allowing it to soak into cake. Yields 16 servings.

With Great Gusto

Scottown is one of only three communities in the nation with a sequential zip code—45678. The other two are Virginia Beach, Virginia (23456), and Schenectady, New York (12345).

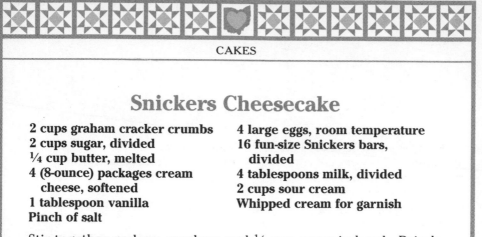

Snickers Cheesecake

2 cups graham cracker crumbs
2 cups sugar, divided
¼ cup butter, melted
4 (8-ounce) packages cream
  cheese, softened
1 tablespoon vanilla
Pinch of salt

4 large eggs, room temperature
16 fun-size Snickers bars,
  divided
4 tablespoons milk, divided
2 cups sour cream
Whipped cream for garnish

Stir together graham crackers and ¼ cup sugar in bowl. Drizzle in butter and stir well with fork. Press evenly into 10-inch springform pan.

Beat cream cheese and 1½ cups sugar at medium speed until softened and fluffy. Add vanilla and salt, and blend. Add eggs one at a time on lowest speed. Pour over crust. Chop 10 candy bars. Combine with 2 tablespoons milk. Cook and stir over very low heat until smooth. Spoon over cheesecake batter in parallel stripes. With a knife, cut across the strips to swirl melted candy into batter. Bake at 350° for 1 hour or until done. Edges should be firm and center moves slightly. Cool 10 minutes.

Chop remaining 6 candy bars and melt with remaining 2 tablespoons milk over low heat. Beat together with sour cream and remaining ¼ cup sugar. Spread sour cream mixture over cheesecake. Bake at 350° for 10 minutes. Remove from oven and drizzle sour cream in a decorative pattern. Return to oven 3 minutes. Refrigerate immediately. May serve with whipped cream and whole candy bars for decoration

50 Years and Still Cookin'!

Festive Piña Colada Cheesecake

CHEESECAKE:

6 tablespoons unsalted butter, melted

1¾ cups graham cracker crumbs

¾ cup chopped pecans, toasted

1 tablespoon sugar plus ½ cup, divided

3 (8-ounce) packages cream cheese, softened

5 large eggs

1 (8-ounce) can crushed pineapple, drained

1 cup cream of coconut

1 cup sour cream

⅓ cup light rum

4 teaspoons coconut extract

Whipped cream and toasted coconut for garnish

Stir together butter, cracker crumbs, pecans, and 1 tablespoon sugar. Press into bottom and 1½ inches up side of a lightly greased 10-inch springform pan. Beat cream cheese and remaining ½ cup sugar at medium speed with an electric mixer 3 minutes or until fluffy. Add eggs, one at a time, beating well after each addition. Add pineapple and next 4 ingredients, beating until blended. Pour mixture into crust. Bake at 325° for 1 hour and 14 minutes or until center is almost set. Cool on a wire rack. Spread Glaze over top of cheesecake. Cover and chill at least 8 hours. Garnish, if desired.

GLAZE:

1 tablespoon cornstarch

1 tablespoon water

1 (8-ounce) can crushed pineapple

¼ cup sugar

2 tablespoons lemon juice

Stir together cornstarch and water until smooth. Combine cornstarch mixture, crushed pineapple, sugar, and lemon juice in a saucepan over medium heat; cook, stirring constantly, 5 minutes, or until mixture is thickened and bubbly. Remove from heat; let cool completely before glazing cheesecake.

Ohio Traditions with P. Buckley Moss

Flourless Chocolate Raspberry Truffle Torte

RASPBERRY SAUCE:

¾ pound fresh or frozen
  raspberries, thawed
1 orange, juiced (¼ cup)

½ lemon, juiced (1½ tablespoons)
½ cup sugar

Put all ingredients in blender and process until smooth. Strain and refrigerate until ready to use. Any remaining Sauce can be frozen for months.

TORTE:

1¼ pounds bittersweet or
  semisweet chocolate
2 sticks butter

1¼ cups Raspberry Sauce
8 eggs
½ cup sugar

Spray a springform pan with nonstick spray. Line bottom with parchment or wax paper to fit. Spray paper with spray. Preheat oven to 425°.

  Melt chocolate and butter over double-boiler. Add Raspberry Sauce when melted. Whip eggs with sugar in electric mixer until triple in volume. Pour chocolate mixture into eggs and fold until blended and smooth. Pour batter into pan and tap on counter to release any air bubbles. Set on a baking sheet tray with edges or in a baking dish with sides and pour about ¼ inch of hot water into tray or dish to create a water bath. Be careful not to get any water into the chocolate torte. Bake at 425° for 10–12 minutes until outside edges just start to pull away from pan. Torte will set once it is cooled. Refrigerate until completely cooled. Serves 8–10.

Food, Glorious Food

Low-Fat Sugar-Free Cheesecake

2 (8-ounce) packages fat-free
  cream cheese, softened
1 (8-ounce) package low-fat
  cream cheese, softened
2 teaspoons vanilla

4 teaspoons lemon juice
3½ teaspoons or 12 packets
  aspartame sweetener
1 cup fat-free egg product

Combine all ingredients in food processor. Process until smooth, scraping down sides as needed. Pour into lightly greased spring-form pan and bake at 375° for 30 minutes or until center is set.

Ohio State Grange Cookbook (Blue)

Cookies *and* Candies

The Pro Football Hall of Fame is located in Canton. The American Professional Football Association, later renamed the National Football League, was founded in Canton on September 17, 1920. More than eight million fans have visited the museum since its opening in September 1963.

Potato Chip Cookies

1 cup shortening
1 cup brown sugar
1 cup white sugar
2 eggs
1 teaspoon vanilla
2 cups all-purpose flour

½ teaspoon salt
1 teaspoon baking soda
2 cups slightly crushed potato chips
1 cup chopped nutmeats

Cream shortening and sugars. Add eggs and vanilla; beat well. Add flour, salt, and baking soda; stir until well mixed. Add chips and nuts. Drop on ungreased cookie sheets with a teaspoon. Bake at 350° for 12 minutes. Makes 5 dozen cookies.

Note: If weather is warm, try chilling dough awhile and make small balls by rolling, instead of dropping by teaspoon.

Cookies & Tea

Potato Chip Cookies

1 pound butter, softened
1 cup sugar
2 teaspoons vanilla

1 cup crushed potato chips
3½ cups all-purpose flour
Confectioners' sugar

Cream butter, sugar, and vanilla. Stir in chips and flour. Drop by heaping teaspoon onto greased baking sheet. Bake at 350° for 12 minutes. Cool. Sprinkle with confectioners' sugar.

Entertaining Made Easy

In celebration of the 150th anniversary of the potato chip in 2003, five Ohio potato chip companies constructed the world's largest bag of (edible) potato chips, weighing 1,082 pounds and serving 16,000 people. "Chipping in" were Ballreich's in Tiffin, Conn's in Zanesville, Jones' in Mansfield, Shearer's in Brewster, and Mike-Sell's in Dayton. Ingredients included 4,250 pounds (more than two tons) of Ohio "Superior"-variety potatoes, 700 pounds of hydrogenated soybean oil, and 80 pounds of salt. The bag's dimensions were 8x5x5 feet.

Best Cookies in the World

2 sticks butter, softened
1 egg
1 cup sugar
1 cup brown sugar
3½ cups all-purpose flour

1 cup oil
1 cup rolled oats
1 cup crushed cornflakes
½ cup flaked coconut, or more
½ cup finely chopped pecans

Cream butter, egg, and sugars; mix well. Add flour alternately with oil. Add remaining ingredients. Roll ¾ teaspoonful into balls and place 2 inches apart on greased cookie sheets. Dip fork into cold water and press down on each cookie. Bake at 325° for 10–15 minutes or until lightly golden tan. Let cookies sit on baking sheets for a few minutes to set. Cool on paper. Yields 6 dozen cookies.

Cookies & Tea

Moravian Molasses Cookies

1¼ cups light brown sugar,
  firmly packed
6 tablespoons margarine
6 tablespoons solid shortening
2 cups dark molasses
1 tablespoon baking soda

¼ cup boiling water
6⅔ cup all-purpose flour, sifted
1 tablespoon ground cloves
2 tablespoons ground ginger
1 tablespoon ground cinnamon

In a heavy saucepan, combine brown sugar, margarine, shortening, and molasses. Heat until brown sugar is dissolved.

Dissolve baking soda in boiling water and stir into molasses mixture. (The mixture will bubble up.) Remove from heat. Sift flour and spices together and gradually add to saucepan, stirring with a wooden spoon until well incorporated. Form dough into a rectangle, wrap and let sit overnight. Do not refrigerate.

The next day, preheat oven to 275° and line baking sheets with parchment paper. On a floured board, roll small pieces of dough as thin as possible. (Dough should be thin enough to see one's hand through it.) Cut with cookie cutter and set 1–2 inches apart on baking sheet. Bake exactly 10 minutes and allow to cool on baking sheets.

Country Collections Cookbook II

Granny's Iced Shortbread Cookies

This is my most treasured recipe—a tradition as long as I can remember. I serve them with Irish coffee every Christmas Eve, and they look and taste magnificent!

SHORTBREAD:

1 pound butter, room
  temperature
1 cup superfine granulated
  sugar

3¼ cups all-purpose flour

Beat butter well, until light and fluffy. Add sugar and flour gradually. Generously sprinkle flour on a cloth-covered pastry board; knead dough well with your hands. Flour cloth-covered rolling pin and roll dough until about ¼ inch thick. Dip cookie cutters in flour; cut out dough (suggested shape: star, bell, cross) and place cookies on lightly greased cookie sheet. Bake in a preheated 225° oven about 1 hour, or until edges of cookie become beige. Cool before icing and decorating.

BUTTER ICING:

¼ pound (1 stick) butter,
  softened
1 pound confectioners' sugar
1 teaspoon almond extract

2–3 teaspoons half-and-half, or
  enough to reach spreading
  consistency

Mix icing ingredients until smooth. Spread onto cookies. Decorate immediately with gold dragées (little gold balls made of sugar for use in decorating). Store in tin boxes. Yields 4 dozen cookies.

Discover Dayton

Sugar Cookies

This soft sugar cookie reminds our children of an old family recipe, Madeline Cookies. They are lightly sweetened.

2¼ cups all-purpose flour
1½ cups confectioners' sugar
1 cup applesauce
2 egg whites

1½ teaspoons baking soda
1 teaspoon cream of tartar
1½ teaspoons almond extract

Preheat oven to 375°. Spray 2 cookie sheets with nonfat cooking spray. Combine flour, confectioners' sugar, applesauce, egg whites, baking soda, cream of tartar, and almond extract in a medium bowl; mix well. Drop by rounded teaspoonfuls onto prepared cookie sheets. Bake for 7–8 minutes or until golden brown. Yields 48 cookies.

Note: This dough can be refrigerated for weeks until ready to use. If desired, sprinkle with colored sugar before baking.

Nutritional analysis: Cal 40 (0% fat); Fat 0gm; Choles 0mg; Carbo 9gm; Dietary Fiber 0gm; Prot 1gm; Sod 42mg

*Busy People's Down-Home Cooking
Without the Down-Home Fat*

Linda's Christmas Sugar Cookies

Great for all holidays . . . not just Christmas.

1½ cups sugar
1 cup Crisco
2 eggs
1 teaspoon vanilla
1 cup sour milk (add 1
   tablespoon vinegar if milk
   is sweet)

1 teaspoon salt
1 teaspoon baking soda
2 teaspoons baking powder
4½ cups all-purpose flour

Cream sugar and Crisco together. Add eggs, vanilla, and milk. Add salt, baking soda, baking powder, and flour. Mix all ingredients thoroughly. Use quite a bit of flour under the dough and on top when rolling out. Roll out to about same thickness as pie crust. Cut out with favorite cookie cutters. Bake at 350° for 10 minutes. Allow to cool; frost and decorate, if desired. Makes about 100 small cookies.

Feeding the Flock—First Church of God

No-Bakes

2 cups sugar
½ cup milk
3 tablespoons cocoa
1 stick butter, softened

½ cup peanut butter
2¾ cups quick oats
1 teaspoon vanilla

Boil sugar, milk, and cocoa for 1 minute. Remove from heat; add butter, peanut butter, oats, and vanilla. Stir until mixed well. Drop onto wax paper by tablespoon.

Columbus Colony Creations

Outrageous Chocolate Chip Cookies

1 cup regular sugar
¾ cup brown sugar
2 eggs
2 sticks butter, softened
1 cup peanut butter
1 teaspoon vanilla

½ teaspoon salt
1 teaspoon baking soda
2 cups all-purpose flour
1 cup oatmeal
1 (12-ounce) bag chocolate chips

Cream together first 4 ingredients. Add peanut butter and vanilla. Sift salt and baking soda with flour. Add flour mixture, oatmeal, and chocolate chips. After stirring, drop by rounded teaspoons about 2 inches apart onto a lightly greased cookie sheet. Bake 10 minutes at 350°. Makes 5–6 dozen cookies.

Feeding the Flock—Trinity United Methodist Women

White Chocolate Chunk Cookies

½ cup butter, softened
½ cup vegetable shortening
¾ cup granulated sugar
½ cup packed brown sugar
1 egg
1¾ cups all-purpose flour
1 teaspoon baking soda

½ teaspoon salt
2 teaspoons vanilla
10 ounces white chocolate,
  chopped
½ cup chopped macadamia nuts,
  toasted

Cream butter and shortening. Gradually add sugars, beating at medium speed until mixed well. Add egg and beat well. In a separate bowl, combine flour, baking soda, and salt. Add dry ingredients to creamed mixture and mix well. Stir in vanilla. Add white chocolate and nuts, and mix. Chill dough 1 hour.

When ready to bake, preheat oven to 350°. Drop dough by 2 tablespoonsful, 3 inches apart, onto lightly greased baking sheets. Bake at 350° for 10–12 minutes; cookies will be soft. Cool slightly on baking sheet. Remove to wire rack to cool completely.

Crowd Pleasers

Caramel-Filled Chocolate Cookies

2½ cups all-purpose flour
¾ cup unsweetened cocoa
  powder
1 teaspoon baking soda
1 cup plus 1 tablespoon
  granulated sugar, divided
1 cup packed brown sugar
1 cup margarine or butter,
  softened

2 teaspoons vanilla
2 eggs
1 cup chopped pecans, divided
48 Rolo Chewy Caramels in Milk
  Chocolate (9-ounce package)
4 ounces vanilla candy coating,
  melted

Preheat oven to 375°. In a small bowl, combine flour, cocoa, and baking soda. Blend well. In a large bowl, beat 1 cup granulated sugar, brown sugar, and margarine until light and fluffy. Add vanilla and eggs and beat well. Mix in dry ingredients. Stir in ½ cup pecans. For each cookie, using floured hands, shape about 1 tablespoon of dough around 1 caramel candy, covering completely.

In a small bowl, combine remaining ½ cup pecans and remaining 1 tablespoon sugar. Press one side of each dough ball into pecan mixture. Place, nut-side up, 2 inches apart on ungreased baking sheets. Bake at 375° for 7–10 minutes or until set and slightly cracked. Cool 2 minutes. Remove from baking sheet and cool completely on wire racks. Drizzle melted vanilla coating over cookies.

Crowd Pleasers

Born in Geneva in 1864, Ransom Olds built a three-wheeled steam-driven carriage in 1887, a four-wheeled steam-driven car in 1893, and the first Oldsmobile car in 1896. He began mass production of cars in Detroit in 1901. Olds created the assembly line in 1901, although most credit Henry Ford, whose contribution was to refine the process and perfect the standardization of components. This new assembly-line approach enabled Olds to more than quadruple his factory's output, from 425 cars in 1901 to 2,500 in 1902. In 1908, the cash-strapped company was acquired by General Motors. The Oldsmobile brand, after a production run of 107 years, was discontinued in 2004.

Lemonade Cookies

1 cup butter, softened
1 cup sugar
2 eggs, beaten
3 cups sifted all-purpose flour

1 teaspoon baking soda
1 (6-ounce) can frozen lemonade,
   thawed

Cream butter and sugar. Add eggs and blend. Combine flour and soda. Add to mixture and mix well. Add 4½ ounces (¾ can) lemonade; mix well. Drop by teaspoonful on ungreased cookie sheet. Bake at 350° for 10–12 minutes.

The "Friends" Cookbook

Orange Drop Cookies

1 cup margarine, softened
2 cups sugar
2 eggs, beaten
Juice from 1 orange
Grated rind from 1 orange

1 teaspoon baking soda
1 cup milk
4¾ cups all-purpose flour
2 teaspoons baking powder

Cream margarine, sugar, and eggs. Add juice and grated rind. Mix baking soda with milk and add to margarine mixture. Add flour and baking powder. Mix well. Drop by teaspoonfuls onto an ungreased baking sheet. Bake at 375° for 12–15 minutes. When cookies are completely cool, ice with Orange Drop Cookie Icing.

ORANGE DROP COOKIE ICING:
Juice from 1 orange
2 teaspoons butter, softened

1 (1-pound) box confectioners'
   sugar

Mix juice, softened butter, and confectioners' sugar together; spread on cookies.

Love, Mom: Stories and Recipes from Kingston, Ohio

Old-Fashioned Sour Cream Cookies

½ cup soft shortening
1½ cups sugar
2 eggs
1 cup thick sour cream
1 teaspoon vanilla

2¾ cups sifted flour
½ teaspoon baking soda
½ teaspoon baking powder
½ teaspoon salt

Preheat oven to 425°. Mix together shortening, sugar, and eggs. Stir in sour cream and vanilla. Sift dry ingredients together and stir into other mixture. Chill at least 1 hour. Drop rounded teaspoonfuls about 2 inches apart on lightly greased baking sheet. Bake 8–10 minutes, until lightly browned and when touched with finger, almost no imprint remains. Frost with Butter Icing.

BUTTER ICING:
3 cups sifted confectioners'
    sugar
⅓ cup soft or melted butter

About 3 tablespoons cream
1½ teaspoons vanilla

Combine ingredients until smooth.

Ohio State Grange Cookbook (Blue)

Grandma's Date Pinwheel Cookies

2 cups all-purpose flour
½ teaspoon baking soda
½ teaspoon salt
¼ teaspoon cinnamon
¼ teaspoon cloves

½ cup margarine, softened
1 cup brown sugar
1 egg, unbeaten
1 teaspoon vanilla

Sift flour, soda, salt, cinnamon, and cloves. Cream margarine and brown sugar. Add unbeaten egg and vanilla and beat well. Blend in dry ingredients. Roll out half of dough on floured surface to a 8x10-inch rectangle. Spread with half of Date Filling. Roll as a jellyroll, starting with 10-inch side. Wrap in wax paper. Repeat with remaining dough. Chill 2 hours.

Cut into slices about ¼ inch thick and place on lightly greased baking sheet. Bake at 375° for about 9 minutes.

DATE FILLING:
1¼ cups chopped dates
½ cup sugar

½ cup water
½ cup chopped nuts

Cook dates, sugar, and water on low heat until thick. Cool thoroughly; add nuts.

Sharing Recipes Cookbook

Ohio has the largest Amish population in the world—more than 35,000. The Darwin D. Bearley Collection of Antique Ohio Amish Quilts contains some 150 quilts ranging from the 1880s through the 1940s. The Ohio Amish Quilts went through three phases. The first was the quilts produced in the late 19th century (1870–1900). These were made mostly in brown and other earth tones and occasionally reds, blues, and greens. In the second phase, which started at the turn of the century, black became a dominant color and was used until 1930. At this point, the third phase began and pastel colors were used exclusively. Colors like lavender, pink, pale green, and yellow are commonly found in the quilts from this period. These colors were also used in the Amish clothing of the same periods.

Mocha Crinkles

1⅓ cups firmly packed light brown sugar
½ cup vegetable oil
¼ cup low-fat sour cream
1 egg
1 teaspoon vanilla
1¾ cups all-purpose flour
¾ cup unsweetened cocoa powder

2 teaspoons instant espresso or coffee granules
1 teaspoon baking soda
¼ teaspoon salt
⅛ teaspoon ground black pepper
½ cup powdered sugar

Beat brown sugar and oil in medium bowl with electric mixer. Mix in sour cream, egg, and vanilla. Set aside. Mix flour, cocoa, espresso, baking soda, salt, and pepper in another medium bowl. Add flour mixture to brown sugar mixture; mix well. Refrigerate dough until firm, 3–4 hours.

Preheat oven to 350°. Pour powdered sugar into shallow bowl. Set aside. Cut dough into 1-inch pieces. Roll into balls. Roll balls in powdered sugar. Bake on ungreased cookie sheets 10–12 minutes or until tops of cookies are firm to touch. Do not overbake. Cool on wire racks. Makes 6 dozen cookies.

Don't Forget the INNgredients!

In 1958, seventeen-year-old high school student Robert Heft from Lancaster High School designed a fifty-star flag to represent the new states of Hawaii and Alaska. It was accepted by Congress as the new U.S. flag. He originally received a "B-" for the project, but after discussing the grade with his high school teacher, Stanley Pratt, it was agreed that since the flag was accepted by Congress, his grade should be changed to an "A."

Mother Always Called Them "Sand Tarts"

½ cup butter
1 cup sugar
1 egg, well beaten
1 tablespoon cream

1 teaspoon vanilla
2 cups all-purpose flour
½ teaspoon salt
1 teaspoon baking powder

Cream butter and sugar. Add egg, cream, and vanilla. Sift flour, salt, and baking powder and add to creamed mixture, mixing well. Refrigerate overnight.

Using a small quantity at a time, roll out very thin on slightly floured board. Cut with small cutters and place on cookie sheets. Decorate as desired or sprinkle with sugar. Bake at 350° for 5 minutes. Yields 10 dozen.

With Great Gusto

Moonbeams

½ cup smooth or crunchy
   peanut butter
½ cup crinkled rice cereal,
   divided

¼ cup quick cooking oats,
   uncooked
¼ cup nonfat dry milk powder
¼ cup honey

Combine peanut butter, ¼ cup crinkled rice cereal, oats, milk powder, and honey. Mix with a large spoon until well blended. Place remaining ¼ cup crinkled rice cereal in a shallow bowl or on paper plate. Roll cookie dough into 1-inch balls, then roll in remaining cereal to coat the outside of each cookie.

Nutritional analysis: Cal 50; Prot 2gm; Carbo 5gm; Dietary Fiber <1gm; Fat 3gm; Sat. Fat .5gm; Choles <1mg; Sod 34mg.

More Nutritious Still Delicious

Hawthorn Hill Coconut Macaroons

These cookies were always served to the elementary school children who were carollers at Hawthorn Hill (Wright Brothers' home) at Christmastime twenty years or more ago. My father requested the recipe from the National Cash Register Company for me to use in a 4-H foods demonstration at the County Fair. It was a winner then, and it is still a winner today.

½ cup egg whites (about 4 large egg whites), room temperature
1 cup sugar

2½ cups granulated coconut, or flaked coconut granulated in food processor or blender
1 teaspoon vanilla

Beat egg whites until stiff peaks form when beaters are raised. Add sugar very slowly with beater at medium speed. By hand, fold in coconut carefully. Fold in vanilla carefully. Drop by table-spoonfuls onto a Teflon cookie sheet or a regular cookie sheet covered with parchment or brown wrapping paper. Bake in a pre-heated 325° oven for about 18 minutes or until light golden in color. Cool slightly before removing from paper with a stiff spatula. Yields about 2½ dozen cookies.

Discover Dayton

Cherry Coconut Bars

CRUST:

1 cup all-purpose flour
3 tablespoons powdered sugar

½ cup butter, softened

Preheat oven to 350°. Blend ingredients thoroughly. Press into 8-inch-square pan. Bake for 25 minutes.

FILLING:

1 egg, lightly beaten
1 cup sugar
¼ cup all-purpose flour
½ teaspoon salt
1 teaspoon vanilla

¾ cup chopped nuts
½ cup flaked coconut
½ cup maraschino cherries,
   drained, quartered

Combine ingredients; spread over hot baked Crust. Bake 30 minutes or until brown. Cool and cut into bars.

Cookies & Tea

Cherry Filled White Chocolate Squares

½ cup butter
2 cups vanilla chips, divided
2 eggs
½ cup sugar
1 cup all-purpose flour

½ teaspoon salt
½ teaspoon almond extract
½ cup cherry jam
½ cup shredded coconut
¼ cup sliced almonds

In a small saucepan, melt butter over low heat. Remove from heat and add 1 cup vanilla chips; do not stir. In a mixing bowl, beat eggs and gradually add sugar until blended; stir in vanilla chip mixture. Add flour, salt, and extract and stir well. Spread ½ of batter in a greased and floured 8x8-inch baking pan. Bake at 325° for 20 minutes.

In a small saucepan, melt jam over low heat, then spread evenly over baked mixture. Top with remaining batter, remaining vanilla chips, coconut, and almonds. Bake at 325° for 20–25 minutes or until light brown. Allow to cool before cutting into squares.

Ohio Cook Book

Cream Cheese Bars

These taste similar to cheesecake filling between two flaky layers of pastry.

1 (16-ounce) box filo dough
  sheets
1 (8-ounce) package low-fat
  cream cheese
1 (8-ounce) package fat-free
  cream cheese

1 cup plus ¼ cup Splenda
  granular, divided
3 egg whites, divided
1 teaspoon vanilla
¼ teaspoon lemon flavoring

Preheat oven to 375°. Spray a 9x13-inch pan with cooking spray. Cut filo dough sheets in half to fit pan. Use 10 (½ sheets). Wrap and refrigerate remaining sheets for later use. Spray 5 (½ sheets) with cooking spray, then stack sheets on top of each other in prepared pan. Bake at 375° for 7 minutes.

In meantime, with electric mixer in medium-size bowl, beat together on medium speed cream cheeses, 1 cup Splenda, 2 egg whites, vanilla, and lemon flavoring until smooth and creamy. Spread on baked filo. Spray remaining ½ sheets, one at a time, with nonfat cooking spray, then stack sheets on top of each other over cream mixture. Beat remaining egg white until frothy. Spread on top of filo. Bake an additional 15 minutes at 375°. Let bars cool before cutting.

Sprinkle top of cut bars with remaining ¼ cup Splenda. Do not sprinkle Splenda on before cutting into bars because the Splenda will make the top too sticky and difficult to cut. Cover and keep refrigerated until ready to serve. Yields 24 bars.

Tip: If you have lemon-flavored cooking spray, use it instead of plain cooking spray for added lemon flavor.

Nutritional analysis: Cal 71 (30% fat); Total fat 2gm; Choles 8mg; Carbo 8gm; Dietary Fiber 0gm; Prot 3gm; Sod 132mg; Diabetic Exchanges ½ starch, ½ lean meat.

Busy People's Low-Carb Cookbook

Caramel Choco-Bars

1 (14-ounce) bag Kraft caramels
⅔ cup evaporated milk, divided
1 (18¼-ounce) box German
   chocolate cake mix
¾ cup butter, melted
½ cup chopped nuts
1 (12-ounce) package chocolate
   chips

Melt caramels and ⅓ cup evaporated milk over low heat, keeping warm. Combine cake mix, butter, remaining ⅓ cup evaporated milk, and nuts. Mix well. Spread half of batter in greased 9x13-inch pan. Bake 6 minutes at 350°. Remove from oven; sprinkle with chocolate chips and drizzle with melted caramel mixture. Sprinkle remaining batter over caramel mixture. Bake 15–18 minutes at 350°. Cool 2 hours before cutting. Makes 4 dozen bars.

Ohio Traditions with P. Buckley Moss

Pumpkin Bars

BARS:

4 eggs, beaten
1 cup vegetable oil
2 cups white sugar
1 cup pumpkin
2 cups all-purpose flour
½ teaspoon salt
2 teaspoons cinnamon
1 teaspoon baking powder
1 teaspoon baking soda
1 cup chopped walnuts or raisins

Mix all ingredients in order given but do not overbeat. Pour into lightly greased floured jellyroll pan. Bake at 350° for 20–25 minutes. Frost warm bars with Cream Cheese Icing.

CREAM CHEESE ICING:

1 (3-ounce) package cream
   cheese, softened
1 tablespoon vanilla
6 tablespoons butter, softened
1 tablespoon milk
¾ pound confectioners' sugar

Mix ingredients until smooth and creamy.

Franklin County 4-H Favorites

Reese Cup Bars

BARS:

1 cup sugar
1 cup margarine, softened
2 cups flour
1 egg yolk

1 teaspoon vanilla
Enough creamy peanut butter to
  cover

Combine sugar and margarine. Add flour, egg yolk, and vanilla. Mix well and pour into greased 9x13-inch pan; bake at 375° for 15–20 minutes. Let cool, then cover with layer of peanut butter.

FROSTING:

3 cups powdered sugar
2 tablespoons cocoa
1 teaspoon vanilla

2 tablespoons milk
6 teaspoons brewed coffee

Combine all ingredients and spread over top of peanut butter. Cut into bars to serve.

Asthma Walk Cook Book

Blonde Brownies

1 cup sifted cake or all-purpose
  flour
½ teaspoon baking powder
⅛ teaspoon baking soda
½ teaspoon salt
½ cup chopped nuts (optional)
⅓ cup butter

1 cup firmly packed brown
  sugar
1 egg, slightly beaten
1 teaspoon vanilla
½ (6-ounce) package chocolate
  chips

Sift flour once and measure; add baking powder, baking soda, and salt. Sift again. Add nuts, if using, and mix well. Set aside. Melt butter in saucepan; remove from heat; add sugar and mix well. Cool slightly. Add egg and vanilla. Add flour mixture, a small amount at a time, mixing well after each addition. Turn into greased 9x9x2-inch pan. Sprinkle chocolate chips over top. Bake at 350° for 20–25 minutes. Cool in pan. Cut into 1½x2½-inch bars. Makes 2 dozen.

Cookies & Tea

Nut Cups

FILLING:

2 cups chopped pecans
2 eggs, beaten
1½ cups brown sugar

Pinch of salt
1 teaspoon vanilla
2 tablespoons melted butter

Combine all ingredients thoroughly. Set aside.

PASTRY:

2 (3-ounce) packages cream
  cheese, softened
2 sticks butter or margarine,
  softened

2 cups all-purpose flour
Powdered sugar (optional)

Combine cream cheese and butter; gradually add flour, mixing with hands. Divide dough into 4 equal parts. Each quarter of the dough will be enough for 12 mini-muffin cups. Divide each quarter into 12 balls and place one ball in each mini-muffin cup. Press with thumb or finger into bottom and around sides to form cup. Fill each with 1 teaspoon nut Filling. Bake at 350° for 15–20 minutes. When cool, you may sprinkle with powdered sugar, if desired. Makes 48 cookies that melt in your mouth. They keep well.

Cookies & Tea

Established in 1795, Jackson was one of the earliest settlements in the Northwest Territory. It was first named "Salt Lick Town" because it was the location of the Scioto Salt Works, Ohio's first industry. The salt licks were a prime reason the Ohio Territory was made into a state. From 1820, when there were five furnaces in operation, their numbers declined. Eventually production stopped altogether when other sources were found.

Almond Brittle

½ cup margarine
1 tablespoon light corn syrup

½ cup sugar
1 cup sliced almonds

Melt margarine in heavy skillet and add corn syrup and sugar. Stir and bring to a boil. Add almonds. Stir constantly and cook till golden (not dark) brown. Pour onto foil that has been buttered or sprayed with Pam.

Entertaining Made Easy

Coconut-Peanut Butter Snow Balls

1 cup peanut butter
1 tablespoon butter, softened

1 cup powdered sugar
1 cup Rice Krispies

Mix peanut butter and butter. Add powdered sugar and mix thoroughly. Add Rice Krispies. Shape into balls. Add more Rice Krispies if dough is not the right consistency to shape easily.

FROSTING:
⅔ cup powdered sugar
8 teaspoons milk

1⅓ cups flaked coconut
Raisins or nuts (optional)

Mix powdered sugar and milk. Roll balls in Frosting, then in coconut. A raisin or nut can be placed inside each ball for variety, if desired. Yields 2 dozen.

Cookies & Tea

Did you know that the founder of the Wendy's restaurant chain, Dave Thomas, got his start working with KFC founder Col. Harland Sanders? Col. Sanders hired Dave to turn a failing KFC store around, and that he did—he turned four of them into million-dollar successes. That success led Thomas to start a restaurant of his own, which he named after his eight-year-old daughter Melinda Lou, whose nickname is Wendy. The first Wendy's restaurant opened in 1969 in Columbus. Today, Dublin is home to Wendy's International, owner of Wendy's Old Fashioned Hamburgers, one of the largest restaurant-franchising companies with more than 6,000 Wendy's franchises around the world.

Scottish Haystacks

1 (12-ounce) can salted peanuts   3 cups butterscotch chips
1 (7-ounce) can potato sticks   3 tablespoons peanut butter

Combine peanuts and potato sticks in a bowl; set aside. In a microwave, heat butterscotch chips and peanut butter at 70% power for 1–2 minutes or until melted, stirring every 30 seconds. Add to peanut mixture; stir to coat evenly. Drop by rounded tablespoonfuls onto wax paper-lined baking sheets. Refrigerate until set, about 5 minutes. Store in an airtight container.

Crowd Pleasers

Lebkuchen

½ cup honey   ½ cup baking soda
½ cup molasses   1 teaspoon cinnamon
¾ cup brown sugar   1 teaspoon allspice
1 egg, beaten   1 teaspoon cloves
1 tablespoon lemon juice   1 teaspoon nutmeg
1 tablespoon grated lemon rind   ⅓ cup chopped nuts
2¾ cups all-purpose flour   ⅓ cup chopped citron

Combine honey and molasses, and bring to a boil. Cool and add brown sugar, beaten egg, lemon juice, and lemon rind. Then add flour, baking soda, spices, nuts, and citron. Chill overnight.

Roll about ¼ inch thick and cut into 1½- to 2½-inch squares and bake at 400° for 10–12 minutes or until no imprint remains when touched lightly with finger.

FROSTING:
1 cup sugar   ¼ cup powdered sugar
½ cup water

Boil sugar and water to 250° or indication of a thread appears. Remove from heat and add powdered sugar. Brush Frosting thinly on cookies just out of the oven. If Frosting gets sugary, reheat and add a little more water. Makes about 6 dozen.

Cooking Along the Lincoln Highway in Ohio

Popcorn Balls

2 cups sugar
1 cup light Karo syrup
½ cup water
1 tablespoon butter

½ teaspoon salt
1 heaping teaspoon baking soda
5 quarts popped corn

In large saucepan cook sugar, syrup, and water until reaches 260° on candy thermometer. Add butter and salt; mix well. Cook to 280°. Remove from heat. Add baking soda. Stir over heat again until golden brown. Remove from heat and stir in popped corn. Form into balls as soon as possible.

Sharing Recipes Cookbook

Fudge

The very best.

5 cups sugar
1 stick butter or margarine
1 (12-ounce) can evaporated
  milk
Dash of salt
1 (18-ounce) package chocolate
  chips (3 cups)

1–2 cups chopped nuts
  (optional)
1 (7-ounce) jar marshmallow
  crème
1 cap vanilla

In medium saucepan, bring sugar, butter, milk, and salt to a boil. Stir constantly until it forms a soft ball, about 5 minutes; remove from heat. Combine chocolate chips, nuts, marshmallow crème, and vanilla in bowl. Pour hot mixture over and stir until chips are melted, and shiny look leaves and becomes a little dull. Pour into buttered sheet pan, spread and refrigerate until it sets, then cut and put in plastic container to keep refrigerated; take out as needed.

Sharing the Best from Our Kitchen

Buckeyes from Ohio

1 pound butter, softened
2 (16-ounce) jars creamy
  peanut butter
2–3 pounds powdered sugar,
  sifted

24 ounces semisweet chocolate
  chips
½ bar paraffin wax

Mix butter, peanut butter, and sugar together. Roll into bite-size balls. Refrigerate on cookie sheets for several hours.

In double boiler, melt chocolate chips and paraffin. With a toothpick, dip each ball into chocolate mixture, coating well. Close toothpick hole and refrigerate. Can be frozen. Makes 150–180 small candies.

Hint: Soften peanut butter in jar in a microwave oven for easier mixing. Put powdered sugar in food processor for a few seconds to "sift" it.

50 Years and Still Cookin'!

Designated as Ohio's state tree in 1953, the buckeye tree gets its name from its large brown seeds that resemble the eyes of the male white-tailed deer, also called bucks. The buckeye tree provides Ohio with its nickname—the Buckeye State—due to the many buckeye trees that once covered the state. The nickname is thought to have originated around the time of the presidential election of 1840, when Ohio resident William Henry Harrison won the presidency. His supporters carved campaign souvenirs out of buckeye wood to show their support for their fellow Ohioan.

No Fail Divinity

4 cups sugar
1 cup light corn syrup
¾ cup water
Salt

3 egg whites
1 teaspoon vanilla
½ cup chopped nuts

Mix sugar, corn syrup, water, and salt in a 2-quart microwave-safe bowl. Cook in microwave 19 minutes. Stir every 5 minutes till candy thermometer reads 260°. Cook 1–2 minutes longer if needed to reach temperature.

While syrup cooks, beat egg whites very stiff in large bowl. Gradually add hot syrup over egg whites and continue beating at high speed until thick and candy loses gloss. Beating may require 12 minutes. Add vanilla and nuts to beaten mixture. Drop by teaspoon onto wax paper. Candy can be tinted with food coloring, if desired.

Mt. Zion Lutheran Church Cookbook

Pies *and* Other Desserts

A waterfall spills over a cliff and creates an unforgettable scene at Rock House in Hocking Hills State Park. The extreme topography in this area is due to the Blackhand Sandstone, a particular formation that is thick, hard, and weather-resistant, and so forms high cliffs and narrow, deep gorges.

Fluffy Cranberry Cream Cheese Pie

1¼ cups cranberry juice
cocktail
1 (3-ounce) package raspberry
gelatin
⅓ cup plus ¼ cup sugar,
divided
1 cup ground fresh cranberries
1 (3-ounce) package cream
cheese, softened

1 tablespoon milk
1 teaspoon vanilla extract
½ cup whipping cream
1 (9-inch) pie shell, baked, cooled
Whipped Cream
Whole cranberries

Bring cranberry juice to a boil in a saucepan and remove from heat. Combine gelatin and ⅓ cup sugar in a bowl. Add hot cranberry juice, stirring until sugar and gelatin are dissolved. Stir in ground cranberries. Chill until partially set.

Beat cream cheese, remaining ¼ cup sugar, milk, and vanilla in a mixer bowl until fluffy. Beat whipping cream in a mixer bowl until soft peaks form. Fold into cream cheese mixture. Place bowl of chilled cranberry mixture in a larger bowl filled with ice water and beat until fluffy. Let stand until mixture mounds.

Layer cream cheese mixture and cranberry mixture in baked pie shell. Garnish with additional whipped cream piped around edge and whole cranberries. Yields 6–8 servings.

America Celebrates Columbus

Johnny Vander Meer was a pitcher in Major League Baseball. From 1937–1949, he played for the Cincinnati Reds. A four-time All-Star, Vander Meer is the only pitcher in Major League history to pitch two consecutive no-hitters. On June 11, 1938, he no-hit the Boston Bees at Crosley Field. Four nights later, in the first night game played at Ebbets Field, he no-hit the Brooklyn Dodgers. After his double no-hit achievement, Reds' management wanted Vander Meer to change his uniform number to "00." He politely refused. Vander Meer was inducted into the Cincinnati Reds Hall of Fame in 1958.

Heavenly Cream Cheese Pie

CHOCOLATE NUT CRUST:

1 (6-ounce) package semisweet chocolate chips

1 tablespoon shortening
1½ cups chopped nuts

Line a 9-inch pie pan with foil. Over hot (not boiling) water in a double boiler, melt chocolate chips and shortening. Stir in nuts. Spread in pie pan over bottom and sides. Chill in refrigerator until firm, about 1 hour. Lift out of pan and peel off foil. Replace crust in pan; chill until ready to fill.

FILLING:

1 (6-ounce) package semisweet chocolate chips
1 (8-ounce) package cream cheese, softened
¾ cup sugar, divided

⅛ teaspoon salt
2 eggs, separated
1 cup whipping cream
3 tablespoons brandy, or 2 tablespoons Grand Marnier

Melt chocolate chips over hot (not boiling) water in a double boiler. Cool 10 minutes. In a large bowl, combine cream cheese, ½ cup sugar, and salt; beat until creamy. Beat in egg yolks one at a time. Stir into cooled chocolate; set aside.

In a small bowl, beat egg whites until foamy. Gradually beat in remaining ¼ cup sugar, and beat until stiff, glossy peaks form. Set aside.

In another small bowl, beat 1 cup whipping cream and brandy until soft peaks form. Fold flavored whipped cream and beaten egg whites into chocolate mixture. Pour into crust. Chill in refrigerator 3 hours or until firm.

TOPPING:

1 cup whipping cream
1 tablespoon brandy or Grand Marnier

Beat whipping cream and brandy until soft peaks form. Garnish on top of pie before serving.

Country Collections Cookbook II

Sugar Cream Pie

4 tablespoons butter
2 heaping tablespoons
  all-purpose flour
2 cups cold milk

1 cup sugar
1 (9-inch) pie shell, unbaked
Nutmeg

Melt butter in skillet. Add flour, stirring until smooth but not brown. Add milk, stirring constantly until mixture is thick (similar to a white sauce). Add sugar; stir until dissolved. Pour into unbaked pie shell. Sprinkle with nutmeg. Bake 35–40 minutes at 350°.

Love, Mom: Stories and Recipes from Kingston, Ohio

Brown Butterscotch Pie

6 tablespoons butter
1 cup brown sugar
1 cup boiling water
3 tablespoons cornstarch
2 tablespoons flour
Pinch of salt

3 egg yolks, slightly beaten
1⅔ cups milk
1 teaspoon vanilla
1 (9-inch) pie shell, baked
Whipped topping

Melt butter in large heavy skillet; cook until golden brown. Add brown sugar and cook stirring constantly until mixture comes to a boil. Stir in boiling water and remove from heat. Mix together cornstarch, flour, and salt; add egg yolks and milk, and stir until smooth. Add flour/egg mixture to brown sugar mixture and cook over medium heat until thickened. Add vanilla and cool. Pour into baked pie shell. Cover with whipped topping.

Ohio State Grange Cookbook (Blue)

Nutter Butter
Frozen Peanut Butter Pie

24 Nutter Butter Sandwich
  Cookies
5 tablespoons butter, melted
1 (8-ounce) package cream
  cheese, softened

1 cup creamy peanut butter
¾ cup sugar
1 tablespoon vanilla
1 (8-ounce) tub whipped topping,
  thawed, divided

Crush cookies in zipper-style plastic bag with rolling pin, or in food processor. Mix cookie crumbs and butter. Press onto bottom and sides of 9-inch pie plate.

Mix cream cheese, peanut butter, sugar, and vanilla with electric mixer on medium speed until blended. Gently stir in 1½ cups whipped topping. Freeze 4 hours or overnight until firm.

Let stand ½ hour or until pie can be cut easily. Garnish with remaining whipped topping and additional cookies, if desired. Makes 8 servings.

The "Friends" Cookbook

Buckeye Pie

4 large egg yolks
2½ cups milk
¼ cup cornstarch
1 cup light brown sugar

2 teaspoons vanilla
½ cup creamy peanut butter
1 (9-inch) pie shell, baked,
  cooled

Whisk egg yolks and milk in a bowl. In saucepan, combine milk mixture, cornstarch, and brown sugar. Cook over medium heat, stirring constantly, until mixture thickens and boils. Remove from heat and add vanilla. Stir in peanut butter. Cover pudding with plastic wrap to prevent skin from forming. Cool to room temperature. Spread in pie shell and cover with Topping.

TOPPING:

2 tablespoons unsalted butter
2 tablespoons corn syrup
1 tablespoon water

2 ounces semisweet chocolate
1 ounce milk chocolate
Whipped cream

Combine butter, corn syrup, and water in saucepan. Bring to a boil and remove from heat. Add both chocolates. Wait 5 minutes for chocolate to melt, then whisk until smooth. Cool 15 minutes and spread over filling. Refrigerate. Remove from refrigerator about 20 minutes before serving. Serve with whipped cream.

Entertaining Made Easy

The world's fastest electric car is the Buckeye Bullet, which holds the U.S. land speed record of 314.958 mph and the international record of 271.737 mph. The car was designed and built by engineering students at Ohio State University's Center for Automotive Research (CAR) in Columbus.

Pecan Pumpkin Pie

This is an old recipe. My friend was making pecan pies and pumpkin pies and had a little of each left. She put them together and it made a delicious pie. Not as rich as plain pecan pie.

3 eggs, beaten	½ cup canned pumpkin
1 cup dark Karo	3 tablespoons butter, melted
Pinch of salt	¼ cup canned milk
1 teaspoon vanilla	1 teaspoon pumpkin pie spice
1 cup sugar	2 (8-inch) pie crusts
1 cup chopped pecans	Whipped cream for garnish

Combine all ingredients and pour into pie crusts. Bake on bottom rack at 400° for 15 minutes. Reduce heat to 325° for 30–35 minutes, or until knife comes out clean. When cool, garnish with whipped cream.

Sharing Recipes Cookbook

Pecan Pie

3 eggs	1 cup dark corn syrup
⅔ cup sugar	1 cup pecan halves
⅓ teaspoon salt	1 (9-inch) pie shell, baked
⅓ cup butter, melted	

Beat together eggs, sugar, salt, melted butter, and corn syrup. Place pecans in bottom of pie shell. Pour in filling. Bake at 375° for 40–50 minutes. To prevent burning, cover crust with foil while baking.

Feeding the Flock—First Church of God

Easiest Apple Pie

This is one of the flakiest pie crusts I've ever eaten. I like it better than the traditional pie crust.

6 Granny Smith apples, peeled, thinly sliced
1 cup plus 1 tablespoon Splenda, divided
2 tablespoons cornstarch
¾ teaspoon ground cinnamon
⅛ teaspoon ground cloves
1 (16-ounce) box filo dough sheets
1 egg white, beaten

Preheat oven to 425°. Place apples in a microwave-safe bowl. Toss apples gently with 1 cup Splenda, cornstarch, cinnamon, and cloves. Cover and microwave 5–7 minutes, stirring every couple of minutes until apples are tender and fully heated.

While apples are cooking, cut filo dough in half to form a rectangle. Wrap one stack and save to use another time. Spray each sheet of dough with nonfat cooking spray before stacking 10 sheets of filo on top of each other to form bottom of pie crust. Place sheets across pie plate like tire spindles crossing in the center. Allow extra length to hang over edge of pie plate. Put cooked sweetened apples into pie plate.

With remaining 10 sheets of dough, make top crust by doing the exact same thing as for bottom crust. Do not press dough into bottom of plate. With scissors, cut dough hanging off the edge of pie plate. If needed, spray in between layers of filo dough sheets with nonfat cooking spray and tightly squeeze sheets together to help seal top and bottom layers of crust together. Brush top with beaten egg white. Cover edge with aluminum foil. Bake at 425° for 10 minutes. Remove foil; bake another 5–7 minutes or until top is light golden brown. Once removed from oven, sprinkle remaining 1 tablespoon Splenda on top.

Nutritional analysis: Cal 141 (5% fat); Total Fat 1 gm; Choles 0mg; Carbo 32gm; Dietary Fiber 2gm; Prot 2 gm; Sod 99mg; Diabetic Exchanges 1 starch, 1 fruit.

Busy People's Low-Carb Cookbook

Cranberry-Apple Pie

4 medium Golden Delicious
  apples, peeled, cored, sliced
½ cup water
1¾ cups sugar
2 tablespoons cornstarch
¼ teaspoon salt

2½ cups whole cranberries,
  fresh or frozen
2 tablespoons grated orange peel
3 tablespoons butter
Pastry for double-crust 9-inch pie
  (shell and lattice top)

Combine apples and water in large saucepan. Place over medium heat and cook, uncovered, until apples are slightly soft, 5–8 minutes. Preheat oven to 425°. Combine sugar, cornstarch, and salt, and blend thoroughly into apples. Add cranberries, orange peel, and butter. Cook, uncovered, medium heat until cranberries start to pop, about 5 minutes. Spoon into shell and top with lattice crust. Bake 20 minutes. Reduce heat to 350° and bake until golden brown, about 25 minutes. Serve warm or at room temperature. Serve with whipped cream, if desired.

Rose Hill Recipes

Elderberry Pie

CRUST:

½ cup Crisco
1½ cups all-purpose flour

Pinch of salt
Water to moisten

Cut shortening into flour and salt. Add just enough cold water to moisten. Divide in half. Roll out bottom crust and place in pie pan.

FILLING:

2⅔ cups elderberries
¾ cup sugar

1 tablespoon lemon juice
3–4 tablespoons flour

Cook enough to thicken before placing into pie crust. Fill bottom crust; cover with top crust. Slash top crust in several places. Bake at 425° for 15 minutes. Reduce heat to 325°; bake 25–35 more minutes.

A Taste of Faith

Buttermilk Berry Pie

3 large eggs
1 cup sugar
2 cups buttermilk
1 tablespoon butter, melted,
  cooled

1 teaspoon orange zest
¾ teaspoon cinnamon
⅛ teaspoon nutmeg
1 teaspoon vanilla extract
1 (9-inch) ready-made pie crust

Preheat oven to 425°. Beat all ingredients together. Pour batter into pie crust. Bake for 35 minutes. Serve with fresh berries and Berry Sauce.

BERRY SAUCE:
1 pint sliced strawberries
1 pint raspberries

¼ cup seedless raspberry jam

Purée berries and jam; strain. Yields 6 servings.

A Taste of the Murphin Ridge Inn

Grandma Hike's Blackberry Cobbler

2¼ cups sugar
5⅔ cups all-purpose flour,
  divided
2 quarts blackberries

1 tablespoon salt
1¾ cups vegetable shortening
¾ cup ice water
Butter patties

Mix sugar and ⅔ cup flour together; add to berries. Mix well; let stand. Mix remaining 5 cups flour and salt together. Cut shortening into flour mixture, forming small crumbs. Make a well and add ice water. Mix well. Split dough into 3 portions, with one portion being large enough to roll out to fit the bottom and sides of a 9x13-inch pan. Add ½ the berries. Top with pats of butter.

Roll out second portion of dough to just cover berries. Add remaining berries and top with pats of butter. Roll out remaining dough to top berries. Do not pinch dough together. Bake in 400° oven for 15 minutes, then 350° for 60 minutes.

Favorite Recipes from the Delaware Police Department

Apple Dumplings

SYRUP:

1½ cups sugar
1½ cups water
¼ teaspoon cinnamon
¼ teaspoon nutmeg
8 drops red food coloring

3 tablespoons butter plus extra
   for dotting, divided
2 or 3 apples, peeled, sliced
Additional sugar, cinnamon, and
   nutmeg for sprinkling

Combine sugar, water, cinnamon, nutmeg, and food coloring in saucepan and bring to a boil. Remove from heat and add 3 tablespoons butter.

PASTRY:

2 cups all-purpose flour
2 teaspoons baking powder
1 teaspoon salt

⅔ cup shortening
½ cup milk

Sift together dry ingredients. Cut in shortening till mixture resembles coarse crumbs. Add milk all at once. Roll out on lightly floured surface. Cut into 4- to 5-inch squares. Place apples on squares and sprinkle with additional sugar, cinnamon, and nutmeg. Place a dot of butter on each and form dumplings into small balls. Place in ungreased cake pan. Pour syrup over dumplings and sprinkle with sugar. Bake at 375° for 35 minutes. Yields about 12 dumplings.

Mt. Zion Lutheran Church Cookbook

Apple Pudding

¾ cup sugar
¼ cup brown sugar
3 tablespoons butter
1 egg
¾ cup all-purpose flour

2 teaspoons baking powder
¼ teaspoon salt
1 teaspoon vanilla
¼ cup chopped nuts
1 cup chopped apples

Combine all ingredients in a large pie plate. Bake at 350° for 30 minutes.

A Taste of Faith

Butterfinger Trifle

4 cups skim milk, divided
2 (3-ounce) boxes sugar-free
vanilla instant pudding mix
1 (16-ounce) container frozen
whipped topping, thawed,
divided
2 (2.1-ounce) Butterfinger candy
bars, divided

1 (12-ounce) fat-free pound cake,
broken in pieces
1 (3-ounce) box sugar-free
chocolate instant pudding mix
1 (3-ounce) box sugar-free
butterscotch instant pudding
mix

With a whisk, beat 2 cups milk and vanilla pudding mixes together for 1 minute. Stir in half the whipped topping and 1½ of the candy bars, crushed. Save remaining ½ bar for later. Gently stir in cake pieces. With a whisk, beat remaining 2 cups milk and chocolate and butterscotch pudding mixes together for 1 minute. Stir in remaining 8 ounces whipped topping. In bottom of a glass bowl, spread half the chocolate-butterscotch pudding mixture. Top with half the cake mixture. Smooth on remaining chocolate-butterscotch mixture. Spread with remaining cake mixture on top. Sprinkle with remaining crushed candy bar. Keep chilled until ready to serve. Yields 16 servings.

Nutritional analysis: Cal 187 (9% fat); Fat 2gm; Choles 1mg; Carbo 36gm; Dietary Fiber 0gm; Prot 4gm; Sod 427mg.

Busy People's Low-Fat Cookbook

Strawberry Cream Trifle

Enjoy fresh strawberries in a cloud of strawberry-flavored cream that are gently nestled between layers of soft cake.

1 pound (½ quart) fresh strawberries, cleaned, sliced
½ cup Splenda granular
1 (0.32-ounce) box sugar-free strawberry-flavored gelatin, dry
1 cup boiling water
1 cup cold water
1 (0.9-ounce) box sugar-free, fat-free banana cream pudding mix, dry
1¾ cups skim milk
1 (10.5-ounce) angel food cake, cut into thirds horizontally

Gently toss strawberries with Splenda in a medium bowl and set aside. In another medium bowl, stir gelatin into boiling water; stir for 2 minutes or until completely dissolved. Stir in cold water (or 6 large ice cubes). Stir until ice cubes are dissolved or until well mixed. Freeze for 5 minutes to soft-set.

In the meantime, in a medium bowl, mix pudding and milk together with a mixer on medium speed for 2 minutes. Refrigerate 5 minutes to soft-set.

Arrange 1 layer of angel food cake into bottom of a trifle bowl. Tear one of the remaining layers of angel food cake into pieces. Use ½ of torn cake pieces to fill in any gaps between layer of angel food cake and side of trifle bowl itself. Also fill in the round hole in the middle of cake. Set aside.

Remove gelatin and pudding from freezer and refrigerator. Stir together until well blended. Gently stir in sliced strawberries. Spoon half the strawberry mixture over cake in trifle bowl. Arrange remaining angel food cake layer on top of strawberry mixture and fill in gaps with remaining torn pieces of cake, just like you did for first layer. Spoon remaining strawberry mixture over second layer of angel food cake. Cover and refrigerate 2–3 hours or until completely set. Serve chilled. Garnish with additional fresh strawberries, if desired. Yields 20 (½-cup) servings.

Nutritional analysis: Cal 61 (0% fat); Fat 0gm; Choles 0mg; Carbo 13gm; Dietary Fiber 1gm; Prot 2gm; Sod 187mg; Diabetic Exchanges 1 other carbo.

Busy People's Diabetic Cookbook

Chocolate Pâte

PÂTE:

15 ounces semisweet chocolate
1 cup heavy cream
4 tablespoons unsalted butter
4 egg yolks

¾ cup powdered sugar
6 tablespoons dark rum
Sweetened whipped cream for
  garnish

Grease a 4-cup loaf pan. Place wax paper in pan, leaving a small overhang. Grease sides and bottom of paper lining. Set aside.

Melt chocolate with cream and butter in the top of a double boiler over simmering water. Beat with a wire whisk until mixture is smooth and glossy. Remove from heat and add yolks, one at a time, beating well after each addition. Whisk in powdered sugar until smooth. Mix in rum. Pour mixture into prepared pan and cover with plastic wrap. Freeze overnight.

When ready to serve, remove Pâte by gently loosening wax paper from pan. If it sticks, set pan in hot water for a few seconds. Invert Pâte onto a serving plate and remove wax paper. Using a hot knife, cut Pâte into ⅓- to ½-inch slices.

RASPBERRY SAUCE:

2 (10-ounce) packages frozen
  raspberries in syrup, thawed
¼ cup sugar

2–3 tablespoons Grand Marnier
  liqueur

Drain 1 package raspberries, discarding juice. Reserve juice when draining second package of berries. Purée all berries, reserved juice, sugar, and liqueur in a food processor or blender. Strain purée to remove seeds. Chill until ready to use.

To serve, place a slice of Pâte in a pool of Raspberry Sauce on each plate. Top with a generous dollop of whipped cream. Yields 8–10 servings.

Causing a Stir

Four-Stack Chocolate Pudding Dessert

FIRST STACK:

1 stick margarine, melted
1 cup all-purpose flour

1 tablespoon sugar
½ cup finely chopped nuts

In a bowl, combine margarine, flour, sugar, and nuts. Spread mixture evenly in a 9x13-inch baking pan. Bake at 350° for 15 minutes; remove and allow to cool.

SECOND STACK:

1 (8-ounce) package cream
cheese, softened

1 cup powdered sugar
2 cups Cool Whip

In a bowl, combine cream cheese and powdered sugar and blend well; fold in Cool Whip. Spread over crust.

THIRD STACK:

2 (3-ounce) packages chocolate
instant pudding mix

3 cups cold milk

In a bowl, combine pudding mixes with milk, and stir until smooth. Spread over cream cheese mixture.

FOURTH STACK:

1 (16-ounce) container Cool
Whip

Top with Cool Whip. Chill and serve.

Ohio Cook Book

Harriet Beecher Stowe was living in Cincinnati when she heard the stories of escaped slaves that inspired her landmark novel, *Uncle Tom's Cabin.* The book became a catalyst in the anti-slavery movement.

White Chocolate Mousse

This super thick mousse is a hit every time. My family loves it!

1 cup cold water
2 (1-ounce) boxes sugar-free, fat-free white chocolate instant pudding, dry
½ gallon no-sugar-added, reduced-fat vanilla ice cream, softened

18 sprigs mint for garnish (optional)
18 strawberries, sliced for garnish (optional)

In a large mixing bowl, beat water and pudding with an electric mixer until super thick. Continue beating and add softened ice cream. Beat until well blended, thick, smooth, and creamy. Put ½ cup of the dessert into each dessert cup. Serve as is or keep refrigerated until ready to serve. Garnish with a sprig of fresh mint or a strawberry separated like a fan, if desired. Yields 18 (½-cup) servings.

Nutritional analysis: Cal 85 (0% fat); Fat 0gm; Choles 0mg; Carbo 19gm; Dietary Fiber 0gm; Prot 3gm; Sod 175mg; Diabetic Exchanges 1½ other carbo.

Busy People's Diabetic Cookbook

Ohio has the only state flag with a pennant shape. Adopted in 1902, its large blue triangle represents Ohio's hills and valleys, and the stripes represent roads and waterways. The white circle with its red center not only represents the first letter of the state name, but also its nickname, "the Buckeye State." The seventeen stars grouped about the circle symbolize that Ohio was the seventeenth state admitted to the Union.

Bread Pudding with Whiskey Sauce

1 loaf stale bread
1 quart milk
4 eggs
2 cups sugar

2 tablespoons vanilla
1 cup raisins
2 apples, peeled, cored, sliced
4 tablespoons butter

Preheat oven to 350°. Crush bread into milk and mix well. Beat eggs and add to bread and milk, together with sugar, vanilla, raisins, and apples. Mix well. Melt butter in pan in which you're going to bake the pudding, then pour in remaining ingredients. Bake about 50 minutes, or until pudding is firm. This can be served as is, or with Whiskey Sauce.

WHISKEY SAUCE:

1 stick butter, melted
1 cup sugar

1 egg, beaten
Whiskey to taste

Cream butter and sugar in a double boiler over medium heat. Add egg and stir rapidly so that the egg doesn't curdle. When well mixed, allow to cool. Add whiskey to taste (a jigger or two). Bon appetit!

Cincinnati Recipe Treasury

Ohio's state flag

Pumpkin and Gingersnap Delight

16 gingersnap cookies, crushed
1 (1-ounce) box sugar-free,
  fat-free butterscotch pudding
  mix, dry
½ cup skim milk

4 cups fat-free, sugar-free frozen
  vanilla ice cream, softened
1 cup canned pumpkin
1 teaspoon pumpkin pie spice

Coat a 9x13-inch glass pan with nonfat cooking spray. Set aside ¼ cup gingersnap cookie crumbs. Sprinkle remaining crumbs on bottom of prepared pan. In a large mixing bowl, mix pudding mix and milk together with an electric mixer until well blended and thick. Add ice cream, pumpkin, and pumpkin pie spice, and continue mixing until well blended. Pour over cookie crumbs and spread evenly. Sprinkle remaining crumbs on top. Keep refrigerated until ready to eat. Do not freeze. If desired, top each serving with a dab of fat-free whipped topping. Yields 15 servings.

Note: To make gingersnap crumbs, put the cookies into a plastic zip-top bag and seal shut while letting all the air out. Gently hit the sealed bag with the side of a 16-ounce can or rolling pin.

Nutritional analysis: Cal 91 (12%fat); Fat 1gm; Choles 0mg; Carbo 18gm; Dietary Fiber 1gm; Prot 2gm; Sod 135mg; Diabetic Exchanges 1 other carbo.

Busy People's Diabetic Cookbook

Kelley's Island is located in the western basin of Lake Erie, about four miles north of Marblehead. It is the largest American island in Lake Erie. Inscription Rock, the most extensive and best preserved prehistoric Native American pictograph ever found in America, and the 30,000-year-old, 400-feet-long Glacial Grooves, are two of the island's unique sites. The entire island is on the National Register of Historic Places.

Cannoli Shells and Filling

PASTRY:

2 cups flour
3 tablespoons shortening,
  melted

3 tablespoons sugar
3 tablespoons vinegar
2 large eggs

Mix ingredients and work together. Let rest for 20 minutes. Next, roll out dough almost paper thin. Cut in 3-inch squares. Start at corner of dough square and wrap around bamboo stick, 4 inches long, or metal cannoli tubes, and press at end to seal. Deep fry quickly, turning. Color is light brown. Cool and remove from stick or tube. They are very delicate. Handle gently. Set aside to fill.

FILLING:

2 pounds ricotta cheese
½ pound powdered sugar
2 almond chocolate bars,
  crushed

1 cup chopped citron (optional)
2 teaspoons cinnamon
1 (4½-ounce) bottle maraschino
  cherries, chopped, drained

In large bowl, place ricotta and powdered sugar, and mix by hand or mixer very well. Add remaining ingredients to batter except cherries; fold in. Fill shells and sprinkle with powdered sugar. You may place a maraschino cherry piece at each end of cannoli. Sprinkle with powdered sugar to serve. Do not put Filling in shells until time to serve; shells will get soft. Makes about 2 dozen.

Favorite Recipes Home-Style

Fruit Pizza

1 package sugar cookie dough
1 (8-ounce) package cream
  cheese, softened
1 cup powdered sugar
½ cup milk
1 (3-ounce) package vanilla
  instant pudding mix

½–⅔ (8-ounce) container Cool
  Whip
Fruit, such as strawberries, kiwi,
  bananas, peaches, Mandarin
  oranges

Grease pizza pan lightly. Press sugar cookie dough into pan. Bake at 350° for 10–12 minutes or until baked through. Cool well. Take out of pan. Clean pan and line with foil. Replace cookie.

Mix cream cheese, powdered sugar, milk, and pudding until well blended. Add Cool Whip as desired. Spread on cookie. Clean and drain fruit well and place on top of filling. Cover fruit with Glaze.

GLAZE:

3 tablespoons strawberry gelatin
3 tablespoons sugar

2 tablespoons cornstarch
1½ cups water or juice

Mix gelatin, sugar, and cornstarch well. Add water or juice a little at a time so it will be smooth. When all is added, cook just until thickened, stirring constantly. Cool. Pour over fruit. Refrigerate. Best made a day ahead.

Sharing Recipes Cookbook

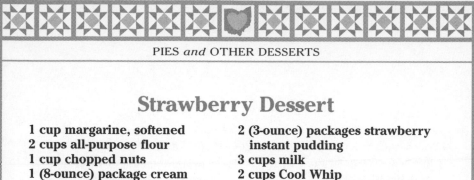

Strawberry Dessert

1 cup margarine, softened
2 cups all-purpose flour
1 cup chopped nuts
1 (8-ounce) package cream
  cheese, softened
1 cup powdered sugar
1 cup Cool Whip

2 (3-ounce) packages strawberry
  instant pudding
3 cups milk
2 cups Cool Whip
1 quart fresh strawberries,
  stemmed, sliced

Mix margarine, flour, and nuts together to make a crust. Pat into lightly buttered 9x13-inch pan. Bake at 325° for 20–25 minutes. Mix cream cheese and powdered sugar. Whip together, then blend in Cool Whip. Spread on cooled crust. Mix pudding and milk. Spread on top of cream cheese mixture. Refrigerate until set. Spread Cool Whip on top. Mix strawberries with Glaze. Spread on top of Cool Whip.

GLAZE:
3 tablespoons strawberry Jell-O
3 tablespoons sugar

2 tablespoons cornstarch
1½ cups water

Cook until just thickened, stirring constantly. Cool.

Sharing Recipes Cookbook

 Troy is proclaimed by locals to be the Strawberry Capital of Ohio. Their annual Strawberry Festival attracts more than 250,000 visitors each year, who consume over 12,000 servings of strawberry shortcake, 60,000 strawberry donuts, and 2500 chocolate-covered strawberries.

Key Lime Dessert

This tangy dessert is an extra special treat if you thought you no longer could enjoy Key lime desserts on a diabetic lifestyle!

4 (0.3-ounce) boxes sugar-free
  lime gelatin, dry
4 cups boiling water
16 individual packets Splenda

2 (12-ounce) packages fat-free
  cream cheese, softened
2 (10.5-ounce) angel food cakes,
  torn into 2-inch pieces

Coat a springform pan or 9x13-inch pan with nonfat cooking spray. Set aside. In a large bowl, stir gelatin into boiling water until completely dissolved. With an electric mixer on low speed, mix Splenda and cream cheese into gelatin until completely dissolved and well mixed. Add angel food cake pieces and continue mixing on low speed until all cake pieces are crumbled and are well mixed in the gelatin. Pour into prepared pan. Cover and refrigerate 3 hours. Serve chilled. Yields 15 servings.

Nutritional analysis: Cal 164 (0% fat); Fat 0gm; Choles 8mg; Carbo 27gm; Dietary Fiber 1gm; Prot 10gm; Sod 578mg; Diabetic Exchanges 2 other carbo, 1 very lean meat.

Busy People's Diabetic Cookbook

Cherry Meringue Christmas Dessert

6 egg whites, beaten stiff
¾ teaspoon cream of tartar
½ teaspoon almond flavoring
2½ cups sugar, divided
2 cups broken soda crackers
¾ cup chopped nuts

1 (3-ounce) package cream
  cheese, softened
1 (8-ounce) carton Cool Whip
1 (21-ounce) can cherry pie
  filling, or your choice fruit pie
  filling

Beat egg whites and cream of tartar until stiff peaks form. Add almond flavoring and gradually add only 2 cups sugar. Fold crackers and nuts into meringue mixture. Pour into a greased 9x13-inch pan and bake at 350° for 25 minutes. Cool completely. Whip together cream cheese and remaining ½ cup sugar. Fold in Cool Whip. Spread over baked meringue, then cover with cherry pie filling. Chill overnight.

Favorite Recipes–First Church of God

Fudgesicle Dessert

This reminds me of a creamy fudgesicle on top of a thin cookie.

13½ squares chocolate graham crackers

1½ cups cold water

2 (1.4-ounce) boxes sugar-free, fat-free chocolate instant pudding mix, dry

4 cups no-sugar-added, reduced-fat vanilla ice cream

2 tablespoons mini chocolate chips

Arrange graham crackers on bottom of a 9x13-inch glass pan. In a large mixing bowl, beat water and pudding mix with an electric mixer on medium speed until well blended and super thick. Continue beating and mix in the ice cream. Beat until well blended. Spread over graham crackers. Sprinkle with chocolate chips. Cover and keep refrigerated until ready to serve. Yields 16 servings.

Nutritional analysis: Cal 92 (13% fat); Fat 1gm; Choles 0mg; Carbo 18gm; Dietary Fiber 0gm; Prot 2gm; Sod 252mg; Diabetic Exchanges 1 other carbo.

Busy People's Diabetic Cookbook

Ice cream on a stick was invented in 1920 by Youngstown candy maker Harry Burt. Harry's new creation was a huge success. The "Good Humor Bar" was so called because it was widely believed that a person's "humor" or temperament was related to the humor of his palate or taste.

Crunchy Ice Cream Dessert

Prepare dessert the day before serving.

DESSERT:

½ gallon vanilla ice cream
¼ cup butter
½ cup firmly packed brown
   sugar

2 cups crisp rice cereal squares
⅔ cup chopped pecans
⅔ cup flaked coconut

Place ice cream in large bowl and soften at room temperature for 2 hours. Melt butter with brown sugar in skillet over medium heat, stirring constantly. Remove from heat. Add cereal, pecans, and coconut to skillet, mixing well. Press ½ of cereal mixture into a 9x13x2-inch baking pan. Spread ice cream on cereal layer and top with remaining cereal mixture. Freeze overnight.

HOT FUDGE SAUCE:

1 (6-ounce) package semisweet
   chocolate chips
1 (14-ounce) can sweetened
   condensed milk

1 (7-ounce) jar marshmallow
   crème

Melt chocolate chips in top of double boiler over simmering water. Stir in condensed milk and marshmallow crème, heating and stirring until well blended. To serve, cut ice cream into squares and top with Hot Fudge Sauce. Serves 15.

I'll Cook When Pigs Fly

The "Y" Bridge in Zanesville was proclaimed by "Ripley's Believe It or Not" as the only bridge in the world that you can cross and still be on the same side of the river. And it's the only bridge in the country with three ends. First built in 1814 to span the confluence of the Licking and Muskingum rivers, the structure has been rebuilt five times.

Watermelon Sorbet

I feel like I am at an expensive restaurant splurging when eating this. Serve soft.

3 teaspoons lime juice
6 firmly packed cups frozen
watermelon*

½ cup Splenda granular
1 cup cold water

In blender put lime juice, frozen watermelon, Splenda, and water. Cover and process on highest speed for 1–2 minutes or until smooth. Serve in dessert cups immediately. Garnish each dessert cup with a sprig of fresh mint, if desired. Yields 5 (½-cup) servings.

*Cut watermelon into chunks (beforehand), and freeze in zipper bags until ready to use. Frozen watermelon in and of itself is also a good healthy frozen novelty instead of popsicles.

Nutritional analysis: Cal 65 (0% fat); Total Fat 0gm; Choles 0gm; Carbo 16gm; Dietary Fiber 1gm; Prot 1gm; Sod 2mg; Diabetic Exchanges 1 fruit.

Busy People's Low-Carb Cookbook

PHOTO @WWW.WIKIPEDIA.COM

The "Y" Bridge

Baklava

The Greeks and Lebanese are known for their Baklava, but the Greek version is slightly different from the Lebanese in that they use honey and cloves, where the Lebanese use rose or orange blossom water. The Greeks roll their dough into diamond shapes, where the Lebanese make cigar or jellyroll shapes.

BAKLAVA:

2 cups medium chopped walnuts
1 cup sugar
1 tablespoon rose water
1 pound filo dough (damp towel to cover)
1 pound drawn butter

Combine nuts, sugar, and rose water. Set aside. Take 2 filo sheets and brush lightly with drawn melted butter. Fill baking pan halfway with filo dough. Place nut mixture on this layer of filo dough until it is about ½–¾-inch thick. Continue layering filo on top. With a sharp knife, cut dough into diamond-shaped pieces. To make the best diamond shapes, let your knife start at the top left corner of the baking pan and cut through layers to the bottom right corner. Then cut through layers from top right corner to bottom left corner; repeat.

Bake at 300° for an hour or until golden brown. Remove from oven and pour cold Rose Water Syrup over all the diamond-shaped pieces. Be sure the dough is well saturated.

BASIC ROSE WATER SYRUP:

2 cups sugar
1 cup water
1 scant teaspoon fresh lemon juice
1 teaspoon rose water or orange blossom water

Combine sugar, water, and lemon juice in a saucepan. Boil on MEDIUM heat for 10 minutes or until slightly thick (or until it reaches 225°). Before removing from heat, add rose water and let come to a boil. Remove quickly from stove and cool. Pour cold syrup on warm baklava for best results. This applies to any dessert using this Basic Rose Water Syrup.

Note: Do NOT mix rose water and orange blossom water. Use only one or the other. Can be purchased in any Mid-Eastern grocery store.

Cooking Along the Lincoln Highway in Ohio

Catalog of
Contributing Cookbooks

Perry's Victory and International Peace Memorial at Put-In-Bay opened in June 1915. Master Commandant Oliver Hazard Perry achieved one of the most significant victories of the War of 1812 in the Battle of Lake Erie. Soon after the victory, Perry wrote his now famous message to General William Henry Harrison: "We have met the enemy and they are ours."

Catalog of Contributing Cookbooks

All recipes in this book have been selected from the cookbooks shown on the following pages. Individuals who wish to obtain a copy of any particular book may do so by sending a check or money order to the address listed by each cookbook. Please note the postage and handling charges that are required. State residents add tax only when requested. Prices and addresses are subject to change, and the books may sell out and become unavailable. Retailers are invited to call or write to same address for discount information.

AMERICA CELEBRATES COLUMBUS

Junior League of Columbus Cookbook   Phone 614-464-2717
583 Franklin Avenue   Fax 614-464-2718
Columbus, OH 43215-4715   jlcolumbus@sbcglobal.net
     www.jlcolumbus.org

America Celebrates Columbus has been created from the excellent recipes contributed by Junior League members, families, and friends. Every recipe was tested, retested, the tested again. Celebrate the rich tradition of the heartland in this culinary tour of Columbus.

$24.95   Retail price   Visa/MC accepted
  $5.00   Postage and handling   ISBN 0-9613621-1-1

Make check payable to Junior League of Columbus, Inc.

ASTHMA WALK COOK BOOK

American Lung Association of Ohio
Kaiser Wells Asthma Walk Team   Phone 800-231-5864
226 State Route 61 East   Fax 419-668-2575
Norwalk, OH 44857   www.ohiolung.org/cookbook.htm

This book is a collection of over 200 local recipes from those that care about asthma education and research. A total of $9.36 from each book is donated to À LA of Ohio. It's a cookbook you will keep coming back to use for the easy recipes it includes.

$10.00   Retail price   Visa/MC/Disc/Amex accepted
  $4.00   Postage and handling

Make check payable to American Lung Assoc. of Ohio

AUNT PAULA'S AMERICAN HUNGARIAN COOKBOOK

by Mathilde Misek (1901–1982)
c/o Albert Misek   misek.albert@juno.com
33250 Ledge Hill Drive
Solon, OH 44139

Originally published in 1948, *Aunt Paula's American Hungarian Cookbook* is a collection of over 500 authentic Hungarian recipes. Republished in 1998 on its 50th anniversary, this book is a tribute to my late mother and author of the original book, Mathilde Misek. Available only on CD.

$15.00   Retail price

Make check payable to Albert Misek

BEGINNINGS

The Junior League of Akron, Inc.
929 West Market Street
Akron, OH 44313

Phone 330-836-4905
Fax 330-836-4906
jrleagueakron@sbcglobal.net
www.juniorleagueakron.org

Beginnings: A Collection of Appetizers Presented by The Junior League of Akron, Ohio is your one-stop cookbook for the best recipes for entertaining friends and family. From easy dips to delicious hors d'oeuvres, every recipes has been triple-taste-tested to ensure your delight.

$22.95	Retail price	Visa/MC accepted
$1.55	Tax for OH residents	ISBN 0-9671721-0-1
$4.00	Postage and handling	

Make check payable to Junior League of Akron

BUSY PEOPLE'S DIABETIC COOKBOOK

by Dawn Hall
Rutledge Hill Press
P. O. Box 141000
Nashville, TN 141000

Phone 800-658-5830
www.thomasnelson.com

Busy People's Diabetic Cookbook is the answer for everyone who wants to eat healthier without sacrificing what is most important to them—delicious flavor! These recipes are not just for those people with diabetes, but everyone in the family can enjoy these healthy and well-balanced recipes.

Visa/MC accepted
ISBN 1-4016-0188-X

BUSY PEOPLE'S DOWN-HOME COOKING WITHOUT THE DOWN-HOME FAT

by Dawn Hall
Rutledge Hill Press
P. O. Box 141000
Nashville, TN 141000

Phone 800-658-5830
www.thomasnelson.com

Give your family nutritious, home-cooked meals, the Busy People's™ way. What is a Busy People's recipe? It's one with seven ingredients or less that can be cooked in thirty minutes or less. A dream-come-true for busy cooks everywhere.

Visa/MC accepted
ISBN 1-4016-0104-9

BUSY PEOPLE'S FUN, FAST, FESTIVE CHRISTMAS COOKBOOK

by Dawn Hall
Rutledge Hill Press
P. O. Box 141000
Nashville, TN 141000

Phone 800-658-5830
www.thomasnelson.com

Dawn Hall's seven-ingredients or less, thirty-minutes or less formula is adapted for the Christmas season. As a working mom, she knows how hard it can be for busy moms. Here are the best recipes and plans to get you through this busy season.

Visa/MC accepted
ISBN 1-4016-0226-6

BUSY PEOPLE'S LOW-CARB COOKBOOK
by Dawn Hall
Rutledge Hill Press
P. O. Box 141000
Nashville, TN 141000

Phone 800-658-5830
www.thomasnelson.com

Here's the answer for everyone who wants to embrace the low-carb lifestyle but still wants enough variety to stay on the program and keep everyone happy! Using her signature seven ingredients or less and thirty minutes or less preparation plan, Hall also meets the needs of time-stressed cooks.

Visa/MC accepted
ISBN 1-4016-0215-0

BUSY PEOPLE'S LOW-FAT COOKBOOK
by Dawn Hall
Rutledge Hill Press
P. O. Box 141000
Nashville, TN 141000

Phone 800-658-5830
www.thomasnelson.com

Over 300,000 copies of *Busy People's Low-Fat Cookbook* have already been sold! Here's a cookbook with more than 240 fast and easy, homestyle, heart-healthy recipes. Each recipe in *Busy People's Low-Fat Cookbook* has nutritional information, preparation time, and cooking time as well as menu ideas.

Visa/MC accepted
ISBN 1-4016-0105-7

BUSY PEOPLE'S SLOW COOKER COOKBOOK
by Dawn Hall
Rutledge Hill Press
P. O. Box 141000
Nashville, TN 141000

Phone 800-658-5830
www.thomasnelson.com

Slow cookers are convenient and save time. And *Busy People's Slow Cooker Cookbook* makes even the preparation quick and easy. Each of the more than two hundred recipes in this book is made with seven or fewer easy-to-find, grocery store ingredients.

Visa/MC accepted
ISBN 1-4016-0226-6

CAMP WHITEWOOD CAMP COOKBOOK
Camp Alumni and Staff
7983 Wiswell Road
Windsor, OH 44099

Phone 440-272-5275
Fax 440-272-5276
king.800@osu.edu
www.ag.ohio-state.edu/~wwood4h/

Enjoy this tasty collection of recipes from Lena's Kitchen, alumni, and friends of Camp Whitewood.

$10.00   Retail price
$5.00   Postage and handling

Make check payable to Camp Whitewood

CARROLL COUNTY HUMANE SOCIETY MEMBERS & FRIENDS COOKBOOK VOLUME I

Carroll County Humane Society
Malvern, OH

Our committee asked for real recipes of dishes you actually make and feed to your family and they liked it. We received a great collection of down-home, delicious recipes using common ingredients. This book is currently out of print.

CARROLL COUNTY HUMANE SOCIETY MEMBERS & FRIENDS COOKBOOK VOLUME II

Carroll County Humane Society   Phone 330-627-0344 or 330-863-1878
P. O. Box 234
Malvern, OH 44644

Our committee wanted to publish "real" recipes. Our plea was "send us the recipes of dishes you actually make and feed to your family and they liked it." These recipes are down-home, different, and use common ingredients.

  $7.00   Retail price
  $.42   Tax for OH residents
  $2.00   Postage and handling

Make check payable to Carroll County Humane Society

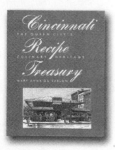

CAUSING A STIR

Junior League of Dayton   Phone 937-222-5541
601 W. Riverview Avenue, 4th Floor   Fax 937-222-8646
Dayton, OH 45406   office@jldayton.org
                          www.jldayton.org

This unique cookbook's highlights include: menus and ideas for entertaining; wine and side dish suggestions with each entrée recipe; stories celebrating Dayton's history; a section full of recipes and party ideas especially for kids; a generous helping of indispensable cooking tips.

  $22.95   Retail price   Visa/MC accepted
  $1.61   Tax for OH residents   ISBN 0-9603082-2-9
  $4.50   Postage and handling

Make check payable to Junior League of Dayton

CINCINNATI RECIPE TREASURY
The Queen City's Culinary Heritage

Ohio University Press   Phone 740-593-1154 • Fax 740-593-4536
19 Circle Drive, The Ridges   jwilson1@ohio.edu
Athens, OH 45701   www.ohioswallow.com

The finest old and new "secret formulas" have been collected from many sources. Every page speaks of the book's authenticity, containing historical anecdotes, celebrity comments, and collectible line drawings of Cincinnati. Mary Anna DuSablon was a freelance writer and editor. She passed away in 2005.

  $24.95   Retail price   Visa/MC/Disc/Amex accepted
  $2.25   Tax for IL residents   ISBN 0-8214-0933-6
  $5.00   Postage and handling

Make check payable to Ohio University Press

COLUMBUS COLONY CREATIONS

Columbus Colony Elderly Care
1150 Colony Drive
Westerville, OH 43081

Phone 614-891-5055
Fax 614-794-7461
josborn@columbuscolony.org

Columbus Colony Creations was compiled with lots of care, help, and love from all our friends and family to benefit the residents of Columbus Colony Elderly Care with outings and parties. These delicious recipes will surely tempt your taste buds!

$10.00   Retail price
$.68   Tax for OH residents
$4.00   Postage and handling
Make check payable to Columbus Colony Elderly Care

COOKIES & TEA

College Women's Club of Dayton, Ohio
Attn: Joan Hardy
401 East Drive
Dayton, OH 45419

Phone 937-299-1376

The ritual of *Cookies & Tea* follows every College Women's Club meeting. Members wanted to share their cookie recipes and raise funds for scholarships and the YWCA Domestic Violence programs. This cookbook accomplishes both with the added delight of learning the origin of the recipes.

$10.00   Retail price (Postage and handling included)
Make check payable to College Women's Club of Dayton

COOKING ALONG THE LINCOLN HIGHWAY IN OHIO

Bucyrus Tourism and Visitors Bureau
301 South Sandusky Avenue
Bucyrus, OH 44820

Phone 419-562-0727
tourism@cybrtown.com
www.bucyrus.org

This cookbook is full of history, pictures, maps, and memories of the Lincoln Highway. Included are pictures, stories, and recipes of many of the former and present restaurants in Bucyrus. Closing pages are recipes of local media personnel and friends of the bureau.

$15.00   Retail price
$4.00   Postage and handling
Make check payable to Bucyrus Tourism and Visitors Bureau

COOKING UP A CURE

Always Friends (Light the Night Team)
15 N. Main Street
West Milton, OH 45383

Phone 937-698-3076
walway@woh.rr.com

This cookbook has recipes collected from our Light the Night team members and supporters. All proceeds go to the Leukemia and Lymphoma Society. It has a wide variety of family-friendly recipes in all categories.

$10.00   Retail price
$3.00   Postage and handling
Make check payable to Laura Alway

COUNTRY COLLECTIONS COOKBOOK II

Fry's Valley Moravian Church
594 Fry's Valley Road SW   Phone 740-254-9373
New Philadelphia, OH 44663

Our cookbook is comprised of recipes from congregation members and friends. Some recipes are traditionally made in the Moravian church. Our cookbook contains historical information about the founding of the Moravian Church in 1457 and its customs.

$12.00   Retail price
$3.50   Postage and handling

Make check payable to Fry's Valley Moravian Church

CROWD PLEASERS

The Junior League of Canton   Phone 330-491-4552
4450 Belden Village Street NW, Suite 106   Fax 330-491-5562
Canton, OH 44718   jlcanton@aol.com • www.jlcanton.org

The Junior League of Canton, Ohio, Inc. proudly presents *Crowd Pleasers,* a cookbook full of our favorite places and favorite flavors. With over 300 specially selected and tested recipes, we are sure to tempt many taste buds.

$21.25   Retail price   Visa/MC accepted
$5.00   Postage and handling   ISBN 0-971023-0-X

Make check payable to The Junior League of Canton–Cookbook

DAWN TO DUSK

Jonna Sigrist Cranebaugh
Olde World Bed & Breakfast   Phone 330-343-1333
2982 SR 516 NW   info@oldeworldbb.com
Dover, OH 44622   www.oldeworldbb.com

Dawn to Dusk features 260 recipes for delicious menus anytime of the day. Breakfast and afternoon tea recipes are our specialty! The book also features a history of our 1881 Victorian Italianate home, as well as photos.

$12.00   Retail price   Visa/MC/Disc/Amex accepted
$.78   Tax for OH residents
$2.50   Postage and handling

Make check payable to Olde World B&B

DISCOVER DAYTON

Junior League of Dayton   Phone 937-222-5541
601 W. Riverview Avenue, 4th Floor   Fax 937-222-8646
Dayton, OH 45406   office@jldayton.org • www.jldayton.org

This book will help you enhance your family meals, impress your friends, and rejuvenate your culinary talents. *Discover Dayton* includes gourmet tidbits, including microwave and food processor tips, celebrity recipes, favorite restaurant recipes, and a wine guide to educate about cooking with and serving wine.

$19.95   Retail price   Visa/MC accepted
$1.40   Tax for OH residents   ISBN 0-9603082-3-7
$4.50   Postage and handling

Make check payable to Junior League of Dayton

DON'T FORGET THE INNGREDIENTS!

Jan Westfall Rogers
Spitzer House Bed and Breakfast
504 West Liberty Street
Medina, OH 44256

Phone 330-725-7289
cmspitzer@verizon.net
www.spitzerhouse.com

A collection of favorite recipes from our kitchen as well as from friends and family. This cookbook is dedicated to the memory of our loving sister Sherry Annette Westfall.

$17.95   Retail price
$1.08   Tax for OH residents
$3.50   Postage and handling

Visa/MC/Disc accepted

Make check payable to Jan Westfall Rogers

ENTERTAINING MADE EASY

Barbara Smith
1460 E. Choctaw Drive
London, OH 43140

Phone 740-852-9924
barbarajsmith@aol.com

Author Barbara Smith has attended and hosted many parties and was encouraged by family, friends, and co-workers to put some menus, recipes, decorations, tips, and party ideas into an easy-to-follow book. This is a must-have for all who love to entertain!

$13.00   Retail price
$3.00   Postage and handling

ISBN 1-59571-033-7

Make check payable to Barbara Smith

FAVORITE RECIPES

Women of the First Church of God
1723 State Route 141
Gallipolis, OH 45631

Phone 740-446-4404 (Church)
or 740-441-0428 (Sara Cheney)
critters785141@sbcglobal.net

This cookbook is a history of the First Church of God, Gallipolis, with 700 recipes in 14 categories. Many recipes are those of loved ones who have gone to be with the Lord. Some are more than 50 years old.

$20.00   Retail price
$3.50   Postage and handling

Make check payable to Women of the First Church of God

FAVORITE RECIPES FROM THE DELAWARE POLICE DEPARTMENT

Delaware Police Department
70 N. Union Street
Delaware, OH 43015

Phone 740-203-1141
Fax 740-203-1198
lthompson@delawareohio.net

This cookbook contains recipes from employees of the Delaware Police Department. All proceeds from the sales benefit the American Cancer Society Relay for Life. This soft-cover cookbook is perfect for the kitchen "cop" in any family.

$8.00   Retail price
$2.25   Postage and handling

Make check payable to American Cancer Society

FAVORITE RECIPES HOME-STYLE

by Carmela Pesa
1835 Coronado Avenue   Phone 330-747-8510
Youngstown, OH 44504   ampesa@msn.com

This book is dedicated in memory of my mother, Lena Feriozzano. Chapters cover everything from appetizers to desserts. An index and calorie counter are included.

$10.00   Retail price
$3.00   Postage and handling

Make check payable to Carmela Pesa

FEEDING THE FLOCK

The First Church of God   Phone 419-457-3971
P. O. Box 7   Fax 419-457-3971
Risingsun, OH 43457   ferniesgirl2@aol.com

Our cookbook is compiled of favorite and treasured recipes we've shared through the years. Some recipes are from elder ladies who are no longer able to cook them, making the recipe a gift to prepare and share. Praise the Lord!

$12.50   Retail price
$2.00   Postage and handling

Make check payable to The First Church of God

FEEDING THE FLOCK

Trinity United Methodist Church
United Methodist Women   Phone 740-773-6640
24 S. Mulberry Street   tumc@trinityumchurch.net
Chillicothe, OH 45601   www.trinityumchurch.net

There are many good cooks at Trinity. Many good meals are served from the church kitchen. This book is a treasury of prized recipes of past and current members. (This is the cookbook published in 2003 with two additional supplements added later.)

$15.00   Retail price
$2.00   Postage and handling

Make check payable to Trinity United Methodist Women

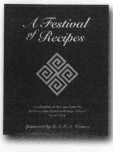

A FESTIVAL OF RECIPES

Annunciation Greek Orthodox Church
500 Belmonte Park, North   Phone 937-224-0601
Dayton, OH 45405   dfricioni@aol.com

A Festival of Recipes is a collection of favorites from the Annunciation Greek Orthodox Church in Dayton. The title is in recognition of our annual Greek Festival, which, for the past 49 years, has allowed us to share our culture, traditions, and food with thousands of visitors.

$25.00   Retail price
$3.00   Postage and handling

Make check payable to Annunciation Greek Orthodox Church

50 YEARS AND STILL COOKIN'!

Christ Child Society of Akron
P. O. Box 5855
Akron, OH 44372

Phone 330-836-5217
dlucia9089@aol.com

50 Years and Still Cookin'! celebrates our chapter's golden anniversary. It is a tribute to the creativity of our membership, featuring new recipes from current members and friends along with favorites from previous cookbooks published by the Akron chapter.

$15.00   Retail price
 $3.00   Postage and handling

Make check payable to Christ Child Society of Akron

FOOD, GLORIOUS FOOD

First Unitarian Universalist Church of Columbus
93 W. Weisheimer Road
Columbus, OH 43214

Phone 614-267-4946
Fax 614-267-4924
office@firstuucolumbus.org
www.firstuucolumbus.org

In keeping with the rich and varied experiences of members and friends of First UU, we celebrate our favorite food tastes in this 415-recipe cookbook. It is uniquely presented and beautifully illustrated.

$20.00   Retail price
 $1.35   Tax for OH residents
 $5.00   Postage and handling

Visa/MC accepted

Make check payable to First Unitarian Universalist Church of Columbus

FOOD FOR THOUGHT

Alzheimer's Association
Northwest Ohio Chapter
2500 N. Reynolds Road
Toledo, OH 43615

Phone 419-537-1999
Fax 419-536-5591
bob.mackowiak@alz.org
www.alz.org/nwohio

Recipes are from great cooks throughout northwest Ohio, including appetizers, breads, cakes and cookies, desserts, main dishes, soups and salads, vegetables, and more. This cookbook is a fundraiser for Alzheimer's Association, NW Ohio Chapter. (Note: Recipes do not necessarily promote brain health.)

$10.00   Retail price
 $4.00   Postage and handling

Visa/MC accepted

Make check payable to Alzheimer's Association

FRANKLIN COUNTY 4-H FAVORITES

Franklin County 4-H Teen Council
1850 Holton Road
Grove City, OH 43123

Phone 614-875-9650
cookbook4h@aol.com

This cookbook was created by the Franklin County 4-H Teen Council. It includes almost 300 recipes from 4-H participants, supporters, and alumni. It includes 4-H history and is dedicated to all past and present 4-H'ers and supporters.

$10.00   Retail price
 $2.00   Postage and handling

Make check payable to Elizabeth Hirth

THE "FRIENDS" COOKBOOK

Friends of Darke County Parks
P. O. Box 175
Pitsburg, OH 45358

Phone 937-548-0165
Fax 937-548-2935
info@darkecountyparks.org
www.darkecountyparks.org

This cookbook is compiled of favorite recipes from members of the Friends of Darke County Parks, a nonprofit organization who assists in promoting nature and the parks in Darke County, Ohio.

$10.00   Retail price
$3.95   Postage and handling

Make check payable to Friends of Darke County Parks

I'LL COOK WHEN PIGS FLY

Junior League of Cincinnati
3500 Columbia Parkway
Cincinnati, OH 45226

Phone 513-871-9339
Fax 513-871-3632
www.jlcincinnati.org

Pigs do fly . . . in Cincinnati! Allow us to put you in "hog heaven" with almost 400 scrumptious recipes along with photographs by famous local photographers. This is your meal ticket to the best of Queen City cuisine.

$21.95   Retail price
$1.43   Tax for OH residents
$4.00   Postage and handling

Visa/MC accepted
ISBN 0-9607078-2-4

Make check payable to Junior League of Cincinnati

LOVE, MOM: Stories and Recipes from Kingston, Ohio

by Brenda McGuire
7036 Fieldstone Place
Columbus, OH 43235

Phone 614-846-2348
bmcguire@gmail.com
www.bampublishing.com

This cookbook is a tribute to stay-at-home moms, with stories about growing up in a small, midwest town in the 1960s. The book showcases all of Mom's best recipes. Profits donated to the hospice that cared for her before her death.

$13.50   Retail price
$.91   Tax for OH residents
$4.00   Postage and handling

Make check payable to BAM Publishing

MORE NUTRITIOUS STILL DELICIOUS

Nutrition Council of Greater Cincinnati
2400 Reading Road, Suite 201-B
Cincinnati, OH 45202

Phone 513-621-3262
Fax 513-621-9355
info@nutritioncouncil.org
www.nutritioncouncil.org

Discover the pleasure of eating foods that are nutritious and delicious with this collection of over 175 recipes. Each recipe was tested in home kitchens. Step-by-step instructions make it easy to bring healthy, flavorful foods to your table.

$20.00   Retail price
$1.30   Tax for OH residents
$5.00   Postage and handling

Visa/MC accepted
ISBN 978-1-932250-55-8

Make check payable to Nutrition Council

MT. ZION LUTHERAN CHURCH COOKBOOK

Mt. Zion Ladies Aid
55300 Shriver Road   Phone 740-685-8486
Pleasant City, OH 43772   dakack@clover.net

The third edition of *Mt. Zion Lutheran Church Cookbook* is a collection of fine recipes compiled by the women of the Mt. Zion community. The book includes recipes from the previous editions published in 1943 and 1953, as well as new entries.

$12.00   Retail price
$2.00   Postage and handling

Make check payable to Mt. Zion Ladies Aid

OHIO COOK BOOK

by Donna Goodrich
Golden West Publishers   Phone 800-658-5830
4113 N. Longview Avenue   Fax 602-279-6901
Phoenix, AZ 85014   www.goldenwestpublishers.com

Ohio Cook Book brings you more than 125 Buckeye State favorites! From tasty appetizers to delightful desserts, and from hearty breakfasts to delicious entrées, this book has it all, including Amish dishes and heritage specialties. Also includes fascinating Ohio trivia.

$9.95   Retail price   Visa/MC accepted
$4.00   Postage and handling   ISBN 1-885590-47-4

Make check payable to Golden West Publishers

OHIO STATE GRANGE COOKBOOK (GOLD)

Ohio State Grange   Phone 740-694-1669
P .O. Box 121   Fax 740-694-1679
Fredericktown, OH 43019-0121   osg@ohiostategrange.org

The recipes in the *Ohio State Grange Cookbook* (Gold) have been contributed by Grange women from all over Ohio. Though not all original, they are all delicious, and have been made over and over again. 216 pages. Spiral-bound.

$5.00   Retail price
$.35   Tax for OH residents
$2.50   Postage and handling

Make check payable to Ohio State Grange

OHIO STATE GRANGE COOKBOOK (BLUE)

Ohio State Grange   Phone 740-694-1669
P. O. Box 121   Fax 740-694-1679
Fredericktown, OH 43019-0121   osg@ohiostategrange.org

These delicious recipes were submitted by Grangers from Ohio, who have always had their roots in quality cooking and baking. All recipes are tried-and-true favorites. 433 pages. Spiral-bound.

$8.00   Retail price
$.56   Tax for OH residents
$2.50   Postage and handling

Make check payable to Ohio State Grange

OHIO TRADITIONS WITH P. BUCKLEY MOSS

Trees of Life–P. Buckley Moss Society
Defiance, OH

This cookbook was published in 2003 to commemorate Ohio's Bicentennial. The cover and divider pages feature artwork of artist Pat Buckley Moss. The P. Buckley Moss Society is a philanthropic group. Funds from this cookbook were donated to Hospice of Northwest Ohio. This book is currently out of print.

RECIPES AND REMEMBRANCES:
Around St. George's Tables

St. George's Episcopal Church
5520 Far Hills Avenue
Dayton, OH 45429

Phone 937-434-1781
Fax 937-434-2148
business@stgeorgeohio.org
www.stgeorgeohio.org

A celebration of St. George's first 50 years of ministry, this cookbook contains nearly 200 recipes, an overview of food trends, and a bit of parish history. Sections are arranged by decade and contain popular recipes from each era. Indexed.

$7.50   Retail price
$2.50   Postage and handling

Make check payable to St. George's Episcopal Church

ROSE HILL RECIPES

Bay Village Historical Society
P. O. Box 40187
Bay Village, OH 44140

A collection of favorites from Bay Village Historical Society as we approach our small town's 200th anniversary. Includes a history of our town's founding, amusing recipes from the early 1900s, and 180 delicious treats for you to try.

$8.50   Retail price
$3.50   Postage and handling

Make check payable to Bay Village Historical Society

SHARING OUR BEST

Lockland Christian Church
231 Mill Street
Cincinnati, OH 45215

Phone 513-821-4159
locklandcc@aol.com
www.locklandchristian.org

Lockland Christian Church members and friends (ages 30-something to 90-plus) shared favorite family recipes. May of them came north with families arriving from southern Kentucky. Proceeds from the cookbook purchased new tables and chairs for our fellowship hall.

$10.00   Retail price
$.65   Tax for OH residents
$2.00   Postage and handling

Make check payable to Lockland Christian Church

SHARING RECIPES COOKBOOK

by Betty Chumney
16496 Leatherwood Road   Phone 740-685-5297
Lore City, OH 43755-9761

Contains over 500 recipes like Grandma used to make using common ingredients from your cupboard and easy-to-follow steps. Features simple, down-
home, family cooking passed through several generations. Includes an extensive appendix of helpful hints, tips, and charts.

$5.00   Retail price
$3.00   Postage and handling

Make check payable to Betty Chumney

SHARING THE BEST FROM OUR KITCHEN

Colonel Taylor Inn B&B
Attn: Patricia Irvin   Phone 740-432-7802
633 Upland Road   coltaylor@coltaylorinnbb.com
Cambridge, OH 43725   www.coltaylorinnbb.com

This 482-page hardcover cookbook includes over 900 family-favorite recipes!
Some new and some old, some from my husband's family restaurant menu, and
many from my family's collection. Also, thanks to our many friends for sharing
their recipes along the way!

$22.95   Retail price   Visa/MC/Disc/Amex accepted
 $3.95   Postage and handling

Make check payable to Colonel Taylor Inn

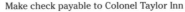

A TASTE OF FAITH

Faith United Methodist Women   Phone 419-526-0240
3775 Franklin Church Road   Fax 419-526-0580
Mansfield, OH 44903   umcfaith@aol.com
                                                          www.umcfaith.com

This cookbook is a compilation of recipes from rural mid-Ohio representing several generations. *A Taste of Faith* includes recipes for large quantities, as well as
favorites from ice cream socials and church suppers.

$8.00   Retail price
$3.00   Postage and handling

Make check payable to Faith United Methodist Women

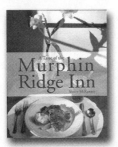

A TASTE OF THE MURPHIN RIDGE INN

by Sherry McKenney   Phone 937-544-2263
Murphin Ridge Inn   Fax 937-544-8151
750 Murphin Ridge Road   murphinn@bright.net
West Union, OH 45693   www.murphinridgeinn.com

A Taste of the Murphin Ridge Inn captures the magic of owning a country inn
through food and the Inn's gardens as well as those of her Amish neighbors.
Over 130 of our visitors' most requested recipes.

$20.00   Retail price   Visa/MC/Disc accepted
 $1.40   Tax for OH residents   ISBN 1-57860-155-X
 $1.50   Postage and handling

Make check payable to Murphin Ridge Inn

TASTEFUL TREASURES COOKBOOK:
Celebrating Our Roots

Arcadia Ohio Sesquicentennial   Phone 419-894-6315
P. O. Box 235   Fax 419-894-6316
Arcadia, OH 44804   arcadiaclerk@tds.net

This cookbook was compiled and printed to celebrate our community's sesqui-centennial. This cookbook is a blend of 650 recipes featuring the past and the present.

$10.00   Retail price
$2.00   Postage and handling

Make check payable to Village of Arcadia

A TREASURY OF RECIPES FOR MIND, BODY & SOUL

by Laurie Hostetler   Phone 419-832-1733
17777 Beaver Street, Box 363   Fax 419-832-4303
Grand Rapids, OH 43522   tkerrhouse@aol.com
                                              www.thekerrhouse.com

This book features recipes for leading a healthy, happy life as well as over 350 easy-to-prepare recipes using unprocessed, natural ingredients. The hard cover has an inner spiral binding for easy use. Naturally low in calories, cholesterol, and fat, these recipes will nourish your mind, body, and soul.

$29.95   Retail price   Visa/MC/Disc/Amex accepted
$1.95   Tax for OH residents   ISBN 0-9662077-9-3
$5.00   Postage and handling

Make check payable to The Kerr House

WITH GREAT GUSTO

Junior League of Youngstown   Phone 330-743-3200
201 E. Commerce Street, Suite 320   Fax 330-743-3284
Youngstown, OH 44503   info@jlyoungstown.org

This cookbook is a collection of favorite recipes from the members of the Junior League of Youngstown, their families, and friends. All proceeds made from the sale of this cookbook are used to fund programs and projects sponsored by the Junior League of Youngstown.

$20.00   Retail price   ISBN 0-9619415-0-2

Make check payable to JLY

Ohio Timeline

Presented below is a brief chronology of historical Ohio events.

1670: René-Robert Cavelier explores and claims the Ohio region for France.

1750: The Ohio Company of Virginia claims the Ohio region for England.

1763: French surrender's claim to Ohio to Britain.

1795: Treaty of Greenville ends the Indian Wars in Ohio.

1802: Congress authorizes formation of a state government in Ohio.

1803: Ohio is admitted to the Union as the 17th state; Chillicothe is named state capital.

1804: Ohio University is founded in Athens.

1810: Zanesville is named state capital.

1811: Tecumseh is defeated at the Battle of Tippecanoe.

1813: British suffer defeat in the Battle of Lake Erie.

1816: Columbus is named state capital.

1833: The nation's first interracial coed college, Oberlin College, is founded.

1842: The Wyandottes, Ohio's last Indian tribe, leave Ohio.

1851: Current Ohio constitution is adopted.

1861: Ohio statehouse is completed.

1863: The Battle of Buffington Island becomes the only Civil War battle in Ohio.

1869: Cincinnati Red Stockings become the first fully professional baseball team.

1870: Ohio State University is founded; Benjamin Goodrich opens a rubber plant in Akron.

1902: Ohio flag is adopted by Ohio Legislature.

1903: Ohio celebrates centennial.

1934: The first state sales tax is imposed at three percent.

1953: Congress discovers it neglected to officially recognize Ohio's statehood and passes a formal resolution declaring Ohio's entry into the Union as March 1, 1803.

1958: "With God All Things Are Possible" becomes the state motto.

1967: Great Seal of Ohio is standardized.

1971: State income tax is adopted.

2000: Federal Census: state population = 11,353,140; white population = 9,645,453; African-American population = 1,301,307; Hispanic population = 217,123; all others = 189,257.

Index

The National Underground Railroad Freedom Center stands as a monument to freedom, bringing to life the importance of struggles for freedom throughout history. Its location recognizes the significant role of Cincinnati, where thousands of slaves escaped to freedom before the Civil War by crossing the Ohio River.

Special Discount Offers!

Best of the Month Club

Capture the taste of America, one state at a time!

Individuals may collect the BEST OF THE BEST STATE COOKBOOKS on a monthly (or bi-monthly) basis by joining the **Best of the Month Club**. Best of the Month Club members receive a 25% discount off the list price of each book ($16.95 – 25% = $12.70. Individuals who already own certain Best cookbooks may specify which new states they wish to receive. No minimum purchase is required; individuals may cancel at any time. For more information on this purchasing option, call **1-800-343-1583.**

NOTE: The entire BEST OF THE BEST STATE COOKBOOK SERIES can be purchased at a 40% discount off the total list price. Some titles may be out-of-print, please call **1-800-343-1583** for an exact price.

Visit our website at **www. quailridge.com** for special discounts on selected titles.

Recipe Hall of Fame Collection
The BEST of the Best of the Best

From the approximately 20,000 suberb recipes in the entire BEST OF THE BEST STATE COOKBOOK SERIES, over 1,600 of the most outstanding have been selected for the four volumes of the RECIPE HALL OF FAME COLLECTION. These recipes have been given elite status for consistently creating exceptionally tasteful dishes.

All books: Paperbound • 7x10 • Illustrations • Index
The Recipe Hall of Fame Cookbook • 304 pages • $19.95
Recipe Hall of Fame Dessert Cookbook • 240 pages • $16.95
Recipe Hall of Fame Quick & Easy Cookbook • 304 pages • $19.95
The Recipe Hall of Fame Cookbook II • 304 pages • $19.95

NOTE: The four HALL OF FAME cookbooks can be ordered individually at the price noted above or can be purchased as a **four-cookbook set for $40.00**, almost a 50% discount off the total list price of $76.80. Over 1,600 incredible HALL OF FAME recipes for about 2½¢ each–an amazing value!

Quail Ridge Press cookbooks make treasured corporate gifts. Your employees and/or customers will cherish this thoughtful expression of your appreciation. The cookbooks can be personalized with your company logo and message. Call 1-800-343-1583 for more information and a discount schedule showing the great savings on bulk purchases (20 copy minimum only).

BEST OF THE BEST STATE COOKBOOK SERIES

ALABAMA
(all-new edition)
(original edition)*

ALASKA

ARIZONA

ARKANSAS

BIG SKY
Includes Montana and
Wyoming

CALIFORNIA

COLORADO

FLORIDA
(all-new edition)
(original edition)*

GEORGIA
(all-new edition)
(original edition)*

GREAT PLAINS
Includes North and South
Dakota, Nebraska, and
Kansas

HAWAII

IDAHO

ILLINOIS

INDIANA

IOWA

KENTUCKY
(all-new edition)
(original edition)*

LOUISIANA

LOUISIANA II

MICHIGAN

MID-ATLANTIC
Includes Maryland,
Delaware, New Jersey, and
Washington, D.C.

MINNESOTA

MISSISSIPPI
(all-new edition)
(original edition)*

MISSOURI

NEVADA

NEW ENGLAND
Includes Rhode Island,
Connecticut, Massachusetts,
Vermont, New Hampshire,
and Maine

NEW MEXICO

NEW YORK

NO. CAROLINA
(all-new edition)
(original edition)*

OHIO
(all-new edition)
(original edition is out-of-
print)

OKLAHOMA

OREGON

PENNSYLVANIA
(revised edition)

SO. CAROLINA
(all-new edition)
(original edition)*

TENNESSEE
(all-new edition)
(original edition)*

TEXAS

TEXAS II

UTAH

VIRGINIA

VIRGINIA II

WASHINGTON

WEST VIRGINIA

WISCONSIN

*Original editions only available while current
supplies last.

All BEST OF THE BEST STATE COOKBOOKS are 6x9 inches
and comb-bound with illustrations, photographs, and
an index. They range in size from 288 to 352 pages
and each contains over 300 recipes.

Retail price per copy $16.95.

To order by credit card, call toll-free
1-800-343-1583, visit **www.quailridge.com**,
or use the order form shown below.

- -

Order Form

Send check, money order, or credit card info to:
QUAIL RIDGE PRESS • P. O. Box 123 • Brandon, MS 39043

Name _____

Address _____

City _____

State/Zip _____

Phone # _____

Email Address _____

❏ Check enclosed
Charge to: ❏ Visa ❏ MC ❏ AmEx ❏ Disc

Card # _____

Expiration Date _____

Signature _____

Qty.	Title of Book (State) or HOF set	Total

Subtotal _____

Mississippi residents add 7% sales tax _____

Postage ($4.00 any number of books) + $4.00

TOTAL _____